THE ILLUSTRATED DICTIONARY OF

SPACE

First published 1995 in this format by
Bloomsbury Books
42 Bloomsbury Street
London WC1B 3QJ

Design: Jane Brett, Steven Hulbert
Illustrations: Paul Doherty; Jeremy Gower (B.L. Kearley Ltd); Ray Hutchins and Craig Warwick (Linden Artists Ltd); Oxford Illustrators; Jeremy Pyke
Consultant: Dr P.A.H. Saymour, MSc, FRAS, CPhys, MInst Phys, MIN, Principal Lecturer in Astronomy, University of Plymouth

Printed in Great Britain.

ISBN 1 85471 624 7

THE ILLUSTRATED DICTIONARY OF

SPACE

Contributors
Michael Pollard
Felicity Trotman

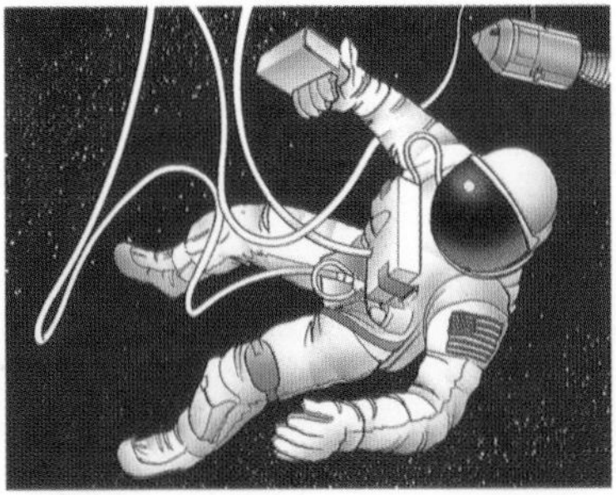

BLOOMSBURY

Reader's notes

The entries in this dictionary have several features to help you understand more about the word you are looking up.

- Each entry is introduced by its headword. All the headwords in the dictionary are arranged in alphabetical order.
- Each headword is followed by a part of speech to show whether the word is used as a noun, adjective, verb or prefix.
- Each entry begins with a sentence that uses the headword as its subject.
- Words that are bold in an entry are cross references. You can look them up in this dictionary to find out more information about the topic.
- The sentence in italics at the end of an entry helps you to see how the headword can be used.
- Many of the entries are illustrated. The labels on the illustrations highlight all the key points of information.
- Many of the labels on the illustrations have their own entries in the dictionary and can therefore be used as cross references.

A

A-1, A-2 *noun*
A-1 and A-2 are the names for two types of **rocket** made by the Soviet Union. Both types burn liquid oxygen and kerosene fuel. The A-1 could lift five tonnes into low Earth **orbit**. The A-2 rocket was more powerful than the A-1, and was important for the Soviet space programme. It has been used to launch the Voskhod, Soyuz, Soyuz T, Soyuz TM and Progress spacecraft and many Cosmos satellites.
The A-2 rocket can lift a load of 7.5 tonnes into low Earth orbit.

aberration *noun*
Aberration is the way the **stars** appear to shift their positions in the sky. This shift is due to the movement of the Earth as it **orbits** around the Sun, and also the fact that light travels at a particular speed.
The aberration of starlight was discovered by the English astronomer James Bradley in 1729.

ablation *noun*
Ablation is the melting or evaporation of the surface layers of an object, such as a **spacecraft** or a **meteorite**. This happens when the object enters the Earth's atmosphere at very high **velocity**. The process of ablation takes away part of the intense heat produced by air friction. Ablation of a spacecraft's heat shield prevents it from burning up as it re-enters the Earth's atmosphere.
The outer layer of Vostok I was designed as a heat shield to protect the spacecraft against ablation on re-entry.

absolute magnitude *noun*
Absolute magnitude is the **magnitude** that a **star** would seem to have if it could be observed from a distance of 10 **parsecs** or 32.6 **light years**. It is related to the brightness of a star as seen by the human eye. A star of the first magnitude is 100 times brighter than a star of the sixth magnitude.
The absolute magnitude of Deneb differs from that of the Sun by a factor of 11, which means it is 70,000 times brighter.

absolute zero *noun*
Absolute zero is the lowest possible temperature. It is the zero of the absolute temperature scale, which uses the **kelvin** unit for measurement. Zero kelvin is written as OK by scientists. Absolute zero is the temperature at which the movement of atoms and molecules ceases.
On the Celsius scale, absolute zero is 273.16 degrees below the temperature of pure melting ice, or –273.16°C.

absorption spectrum *noun*
An absorption spectrum is a **spectrum** that is produced when **electromagnetic radiation** has been absorbed by matter. An absorption spectrum is produced when radiation from a very hot source, which has a **continuous spectrum**, passes through cooler material. Radiation is absorbed at certain wavelengths so that a pattern of absorption lines is shown on the continuous spectrum.
The pattern of lines produced by an absorption spectrum can tell an astronomer what a star's atmosphere is made of.

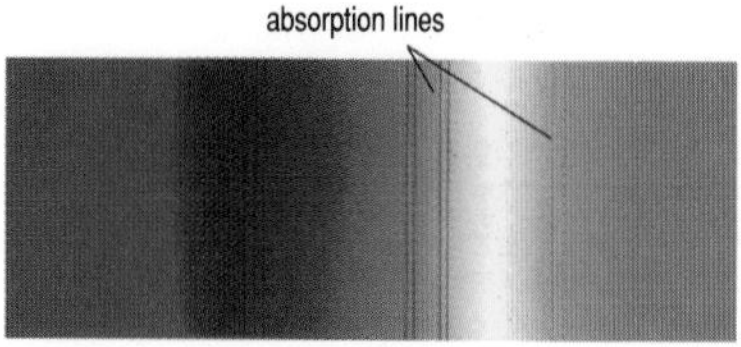

acceleration *noun*
Acceleration is the increase in **velocity** of a moving object in a given length of time. Acceleration is measured in metres per second per second. The opposite of acceleration is deceleration, or **retardation**.
The scientists measured the acceleration of the rocket.

Achernar *noun*
Achernar is a **star** in the **constellation** Eridanus, the River. It is the ninth brightest star in the sky and has a bluish-white colour, which can be seen with the **naked eye**. Achernar is in the **southern hemisphere**. It lies too far south in the sky to be seen from Europe or North America. Achernar is 780 times more luminous than our Sun.
Achernar lies at a distance of 85 light years from the Sun.

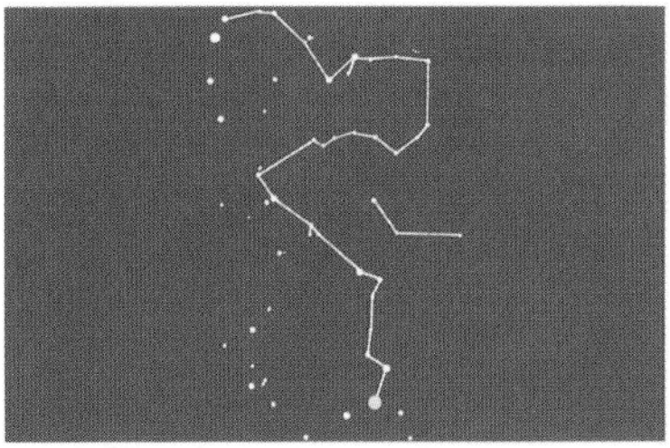

Active Magnetospheric Particle Explorer (AMPTE) *noun*
The Active Magnetospheric Particle Explorer (AMPTE) is a series of three **satellites** built by the United States of America, Germany and the United Kingdom. They were launched in August 1984. The Active Magnetospheric Particle Explorer satellites helped scientists to understand Earth's **magnetosphere** and how it is affected by the **solar wind**.
The Active Magnetospheric Particle Explorer is a good example of international co-operation in astronomy.

Advanced X-ray Astrophysics Facility (AXAF) *noun*
The Advanced X-ray Astrophysics Facility (AXAF) is an X-ray observatory. It will be built by **NASA** and launched aboard the **space shuttle** in 1996. AXAF will study the X-rays given out by such objects as **black holes** and **neutron stars**. It will also study the X-rays coming from galaxies. Its information will help astronomers learn more about the **universe**.
AXAF will orbit about 600 kilometres above the Earth.

aerial ► **antenna**

aerodynamics *noun*
Aerodynamics is the study of how solid objects behave when moving through gases like air. It is also the study of how gases move against or around solid objects. Aerodynamics explains how aircraft fly and how a **spacecraft** will behave when it is moving through Earth's atmosphere.
They studied the aerodynamics of rockets to find ways of making them fly faster.
aerodynamic *adjective*

Agena *noun*
Agena is a **rocket** built by the United States of America. It has been used on more space missions than any other rocket. Agena can carry many different kinds of **spacecraft**. The engine can be re-started, so Agena can be left attached to spacecraft and used to boost them to different orbits.
Astronauts from a Gemini flight re-started an Agena rocket motor in space in 1966.

air *noun*
Air is the mixture of gases that makes up the **atmosphere** of the Earth. Air is made up of 78 per cent nitrogen, 21 per cent oxygen, and argon. Carbon dioxide, other gases and water vapour are also present in small quantities in air.
There is no air on the Moon.

airglow *noun*
Airglow is a faint glow in the Earth's upper atmosphere which can be most clearly seen at night. The airglow is caused when intense **radiation** from the Sun falls upon gases, particularly oxygen and nitrogen. This causes reactions that turn neutral atoms and molecules into **ions**. When these ionized atoms and molecules join together again, light is given off.
Airglow continues into the night, long after the Sun has set.

airlock *noun*
An airlock is a small room in a **spacecraft**. It allows crew members and their equipment to move between two places that have different air pressures. Air can be removed from the airlock, or replaced, without affecting supplies of air in the rest of the spacecraft. Astronauts have to pass through an airlock if they want to leave the spacecraft to go on a **spacewalk**.
An airlock is a very important part of a spacecraft.

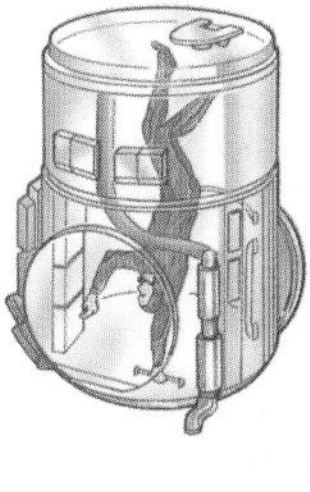

air pressure ► atmospheric pressure

Algol ► Demon star

alien *noun*
An alien is a being from another planet found somewhere else in the **universe**. Scientists do not know for certain whether aliens exist, but many people think that it is likely. The problem is that there are countless billions of stars. Many probably have planets going around them, but it is not known whether alien life forms have developed on any of these planets.
The Pioneer and Voyager probes carry messages about Earth in case they are found by aliens.

almanac *noun*
An almanac is a book, issued every year, that gives information about the **calendar**. It also gives all kinds of useful information for astronomers and navigators. An almanac may give the positions of the **Sun**, **Moon**, **planets** and the brighter **stars** for every day of the year. It may include twilight and details of **eclipses** of the Sun and Moon. It may also give the times of high **tide** and low tide.
They looked at the almanac to find out what time the Sun set.

Alpha Centauri *noun*
Alpha Centauri is a **star** in the **constellation** of Centaurus, the Centaur. It is the third brightest star in the night sky. Alpha Centauri is in the **southern hemisphere**. It lies too far south to be seen from North America or Europe. Alpha Centauri is a triple star, formed by three stars close together in the sky. Two of the three are yellow-orange stars similar in size to the Sun. The third is a very dim, red dwarf star.
Alpha Centauri may be called Rigel Kent.

alpha particle *noun*
An alpha particle is the **nucleus** of an atom of **helium**. It is made up of two **protons** and two **neutrons**.
Alpha particles have a positive electric charge.

altitude *noun*
Altitude is a word used to describe the distance of an object in the sky above or below the **horizon**, measured as an angle. A **star** which is overhead has an altitude of 90 degrees.
Altitude is also used to describe the height of an artificial satellite in kilometres above the Earth's surface.

Andromeda galaxy *noun*
The Andromeda galaxy is a large, spiral **galaxy** in the constellation of Andromeda. It is just visible to the **naked eye** as a faint, misty patch. The Andromeda galaxy is the largest galaxy in the Local Group of galaxies and contains roughly twice as many stars as the **Milky Way**. The Andromeda spiral lies about 2.2 million **light years** from our galaxy.
The Andromeda galaxy is the most distant object visible to the naked eye.

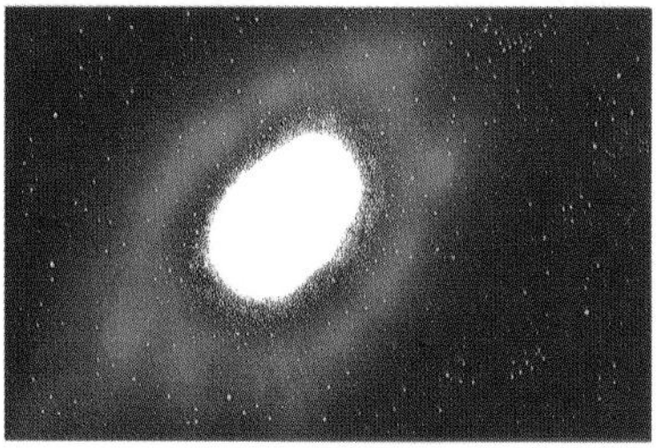

angstrom *noun*
The angstrom is a unit of length equal to one ten-thousand millionth of a metre, or one tenth of a **nanometre**. It is mainly used to measure the **wavelength** of light and ultraviolet radiation. The human eye is most sensitive to yellow-green light that has a wavelength of 5,500 angstroms.
The angstrom is named after the Swedish physicist A.J. Angstrom (1814–1874).

Anik *noun*
Anik is the name given to a family of Canadian communications **satellites**. The name Anik was chosen in a nationwide competition in Canada. The first Anik satellite, Anik A-1, was launched on 17 November 1972. The latest are the Anik-E series. Canada was the first country to have its own network of communications satellites.
Anik is the Eskimo word for 'brother'.

annular eclipse ► eclipse

antenna (plural **antennae**) *noun*
An antenna is a wire, rod or disc used for transmitting or receiving radio signals. If an antenna is connected to a **transmitter**, electric currents are produced in the antenna. These send out radio waves into space. When connected to a receiver, radio waves coming from space produce electric currents in the antenna. These are picked up by the receiver.
An antenna can also be called an aerial.

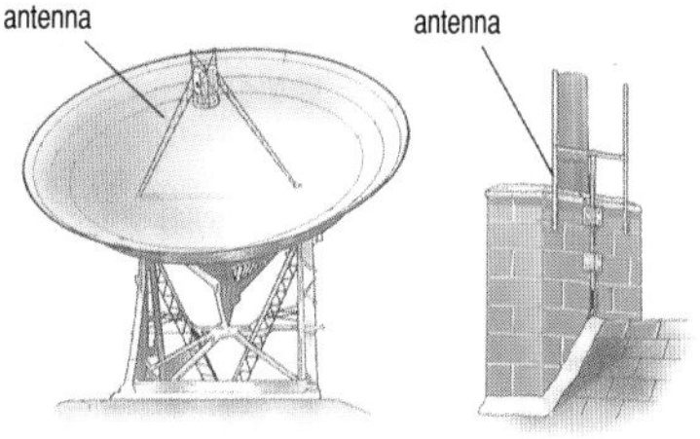

anti-matter *noun*
Anti-matter is a kind of matter. It is made up of particles which are the exact opposites of ordinary particles. Ordinary matter is made up of **electrons**, **protons** and **neutrons**. Anti-matter is made up of positrons, anti-protons and anti-neutrons. Particles and anti-particles have an equal but opposite electric charge.
If ordinary matter and anti-matter met, they would destroy each other and be changed totally into energy.

aperture *noun*
The aperture is the diameter of the main **lens** in a **refracting telescope**, or the main mirror in a **reflecting telescope**. If the aperture is increased, the telescope will collect more light and will detect fainter objects. The word aperture also describes the opening in the front of a camera through which the light passes.
The Yerkes Observatory has a refracting telescope with an aperture of 102 centimetres.

aperture synthesis *noun*
Aperture synthesis is a method used in **radio astronomy** to make a **radio telescope** with a large **aperture**. It uses a number of small radio telescopes that can be moved and placed different distances apart. The information from all the dishes is put together to give a size equal to the spacing between each telescope.
Aperture synthesis was used to build the Very Large Array telescope in New Mexico.

Aphrodite Terra *noun*
Aphrodite Terra is the largest highland region on the surface of the planet **Venus**. It lies close to the planet's equator and is about the size of Africa on Earth. The central and eastern parts are divided by a huge trench.
Aphrodite Terra's mountains rise to about l,800 metres high.

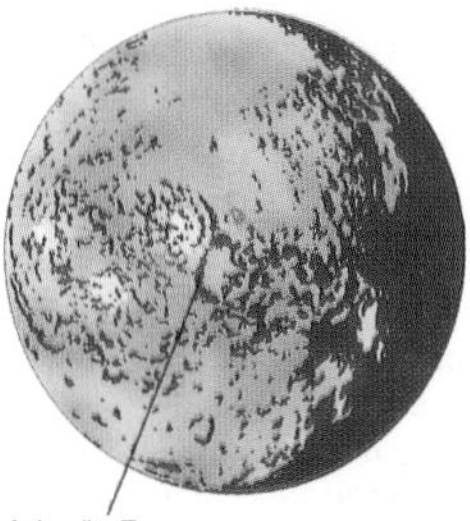

Apollo asteroids *noun*
The Apollo asteroids are a family of **asteroids**. Their **orbits** cross Earth's orbit. One or two of them get even closer to the Sun than Mercury.
All the Apollo asteroids are less than two kilometres across, and highly irregular in shape.

Apollo Lunar Science Experiment Package (ALSEP) *noun*
The Apollo Lunar Science Experiment Package, or ALSEP, was the name given to the experimental packages carried to the Moon during the **Apollo Project** between 1969 and 1972. They were set up on the Moon's surface by the astronauts, and left there to send information automatically back to Earth.
ALSEP has allowed scientists to find out a great deal about the surface of the Moon.

Apollo Project ► page 10

Apollo-Soyuz Test Project (ASTP) *noun*
The Apollo-Soyuz Test Project was the first joint **spaceflight** between the United States of America and the Soviet Union. It took place in July 1985. Three US astronauts in Apollo 18 took part in experiments with two Soviet cosmonauts in Soyuz 19, while the two craft were docked together.
Many ceremonial events took place during the Apollo-Soyuz Test Project.

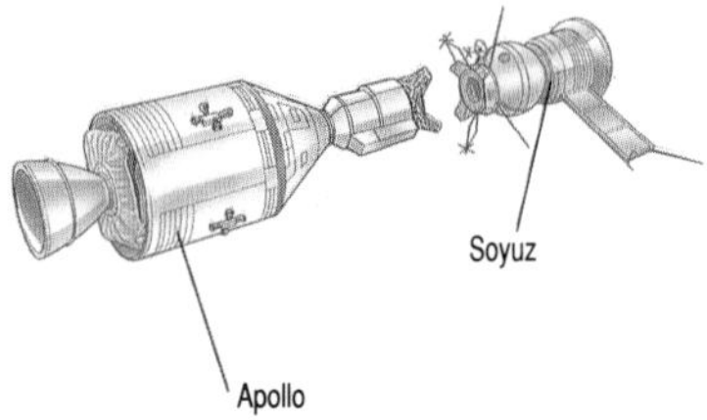

Apollo project *noun*

The Apollo project was a project in which the United States of America planned to land men on the **Moon**. There were 17 Apollo missions. The first six were unmanned test flights. Between 1969 and 1972, there were six successful Apollo missions to the Moon. Saturn rockets were used to launch the Apollo **spacecraft**. The **astronauts** who flew to the Moon on the Apollo project carried out many experiments.

Astronauts on the Apollo project brought rocks from the Moon back to Earth.

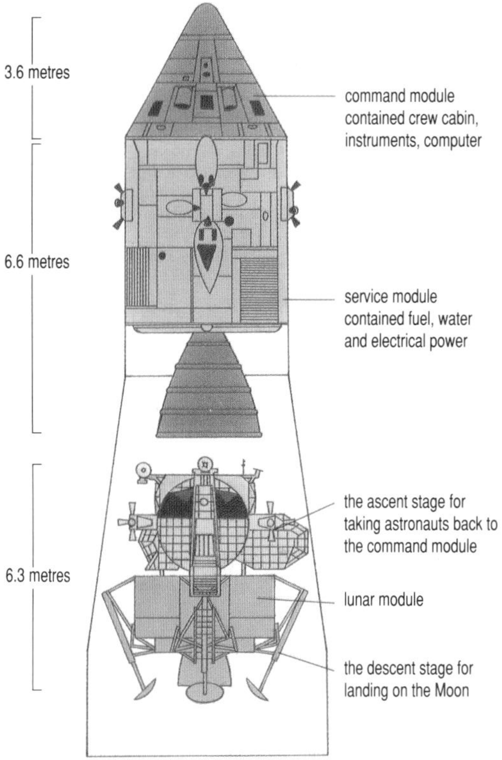

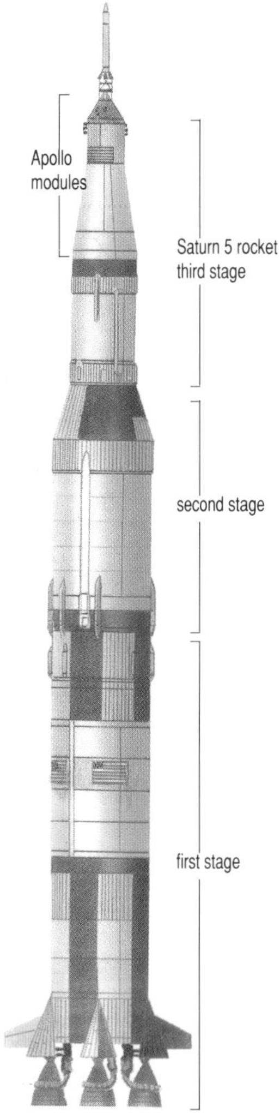

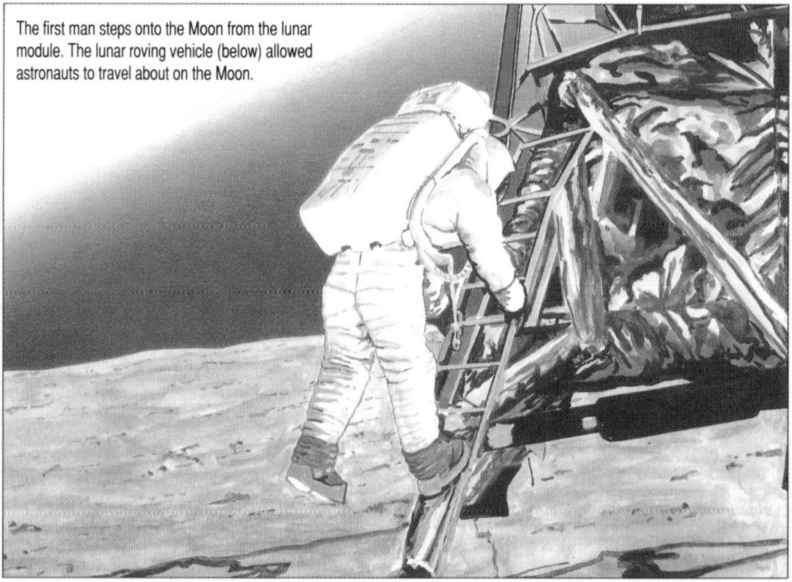

The first man steps onto the Moon from the lunar module. The lunar roving vehicle (below) allowed astronauts to travel about on the Moon.

apparent magnitude *noun*
Apparent magnitude is related to the **brightness** of a **star** as it appears from the Earth. The apparent magnitude depends on the true brightness of the star, its distance from the Earth, and the amount of light absorbed by matter lying between the star and the Earth. The only way to judge the true brightness of stars is by their **absolute magnitude**.
The faintest stars that can be seen with the naked eye under good conditions are magnitude 6.

Aquarids *noun*
The Aquarids are two meteor showers. The Eta Aquarids are seen in the first week of May. They are believed to be dust debris from Halley's comet. The Delta Aquarids are seen in the last week of July. Their origin is still uncertain.
The Aquarids appear to begin in the constellation Aquarius.

Aquarius *noun*
Aquarius, or the Water-Bearer, is one of the **constellations** of the **Zodiac**. Aquarius contains no really bright stars, but there are a bright globular cluster, and two interesting planetary nebulae. These are called the Saturn nebula and the Helix nebula.
Aquarius covers a fairly large area of sky just south of the celestial equator between Capricornus and Pisces.

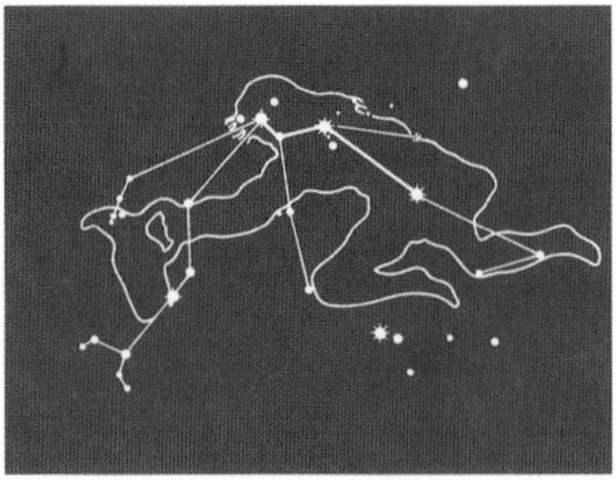

Archer ► Sagittarius

Arcturus *noun*
Arcturus is a **star** in the **constellation** Bootes, the Herdsman. It is the fourth brightest star in the sky, and has an orange colour. Arcturus lies near the celestial **equator** and can be seen from every continent. It is a giant star, nearly 30 times the diameter and 105 times more **luminous** than our own Sun.
Arcturus lies at a distance of 36 light years from the Sun.

Arecibo Observatory *noun*
The Arecibo Observatory is an **observatory**. It is the home of the world's largest **radio telescope** dish. The observatory is built in a natural hollow in the ground at Arecibo, on the island of Puerto Rico. The telescope is 304 metres across.
The radio telescope at Arecibo Observatory can pick up fainter signals than any other dish.

Ariane *noun*
Ariane is a **rocket** built by the **European Space Agency**. It is mainly used to launch communications **satellites**. Ariane 44L, which weighs 483 tonnes at lift-off, can carry between 4.2 and 7 tonnes into **orbit**. A new version, Ariane 5, is planned to be built after 1995.
Ariane is launched from French Guiana in South America.

Ariel *noun*
Ariel is one of the **moons** of the planet **Uranus**. The spacecraft **Voyager** 2 flew by Ariel in January 1986. The surface has many **craters**. There are also long, straight grooves in the surface and some smooth patches. It is made up mostly of ordinary ice, mixed with rock. Ariel **orbits** at an average distance of 190,930 kilometres from the centre of Uranus.
Ariel has a diameter of about 1,158 kilometres.

Ariel *noun*
Ariel is the name of a series of six United Kingdom scientific **satellites**. They were launched by **NASA** between 1962 and 1979. Ariel satellites were used mainly for the study of the Earth's **ionosphere**, **ultra-violet astronomy**, **X-ray astronomy**, **radio astronomy** and the study of **cosmic rays**.
Ariel 5 discovered many new X-ray sources and spent five years in orbit.

Aries *noun*
Aries, or the Ram, is one of the **constellations** of the **Zodiac**. It can be seen north of the celestial equator between Pisces and Taurus. Aries contains no really bright stars but it is quite easy to recognize. The brightest star is of the second **magnitude**.
Aries is always given first place in the list of the constellations of the Zodiac.

artificial satellite *noun*
An artificial satellite is any **spacecraft** launched into **orbit** around the Earth or other planet. Sputnik 1 became the world's first artificial satellite when it went into orbit on 4 October 1957. Many thousands of satellites have been launched since then. Satellites have a wide range of uses, including astronomy, communications, remote sensing and weather forecasting.
Most artificial satellites are unmanned.

ascending node ► **node**

Asp *noun*
The Asps were a series of **rockets** built in the 1950s, in the United States of America. They were a type of rocket known as sounding rockets, which are still in use today. Asp rockets were used to carry scientific equipment and experiments into the upper **atmosphere** of Earth. They were developed from the **V-2** rockets of the Second World War.
Asp rockets could probe the atmosphere at heights of 80 to 160 kilometres above Earth.

association *noun*
An association is a loose group of mainly young **stars**. The group may extend over a distance of up to several hundred **light years**. The stars in each association are the result of multiple star births that happened at about the same time from the same cloud of dust and gas.
About 70 star associations are known.

asteroid ► page 14

asteroid belt *noun*
The asteroid belt is the region between the **orbits** of **Mars** and **Jupiter** that contains most of the **asteroids**. These asteroids are often called the main belt asteroids. They orbit within the belt at distances between 322 million kilometres and 494 million kilometres from the Sun. These asteroids orbit the Sun in periods ranging from three to six years.
Some scientists think the asteroid belt is made up of material that failed to form a planet.

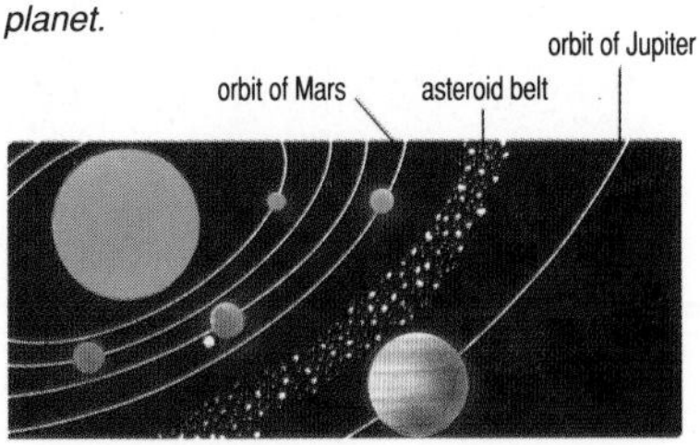

asteroid *noun*
An asteroid is a rocky body. Asteroids range in size from objects several hundred kilometres in diameter to dust particles. Thousands of asteroids have been found. Most orbit the Sun in a belt between Mars and Jupiter. There are also two groups of asteroids which take the same orbital path as Jupiter. Scientists think that asteroids are pieces of the material that formed the solar system, or planetesimals. The pieces failed to stick together to form a planet.
The largest asteroid is called Ceres.

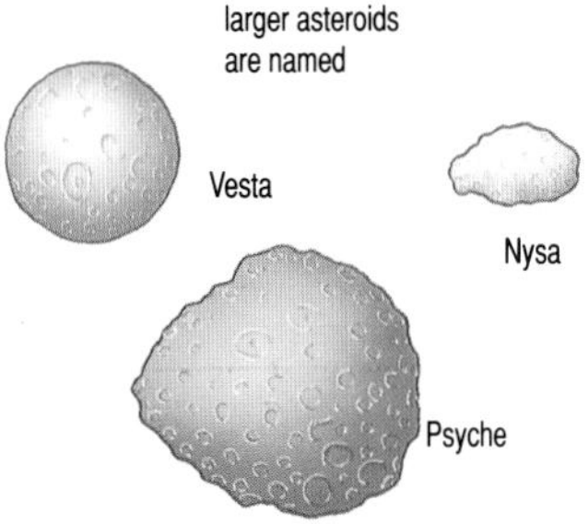

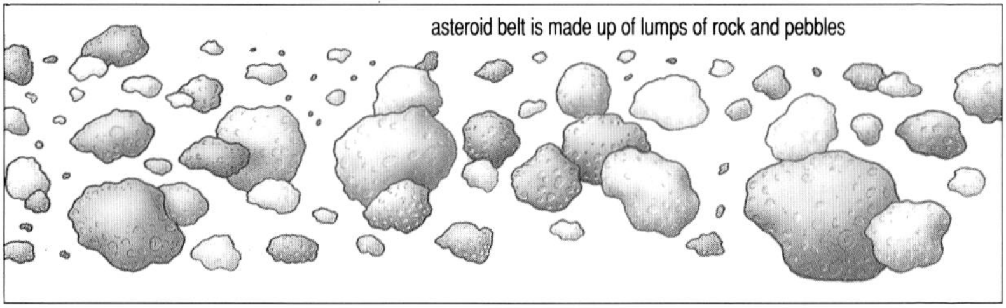

asteroid belt is made up of lumps of rock and pebbles

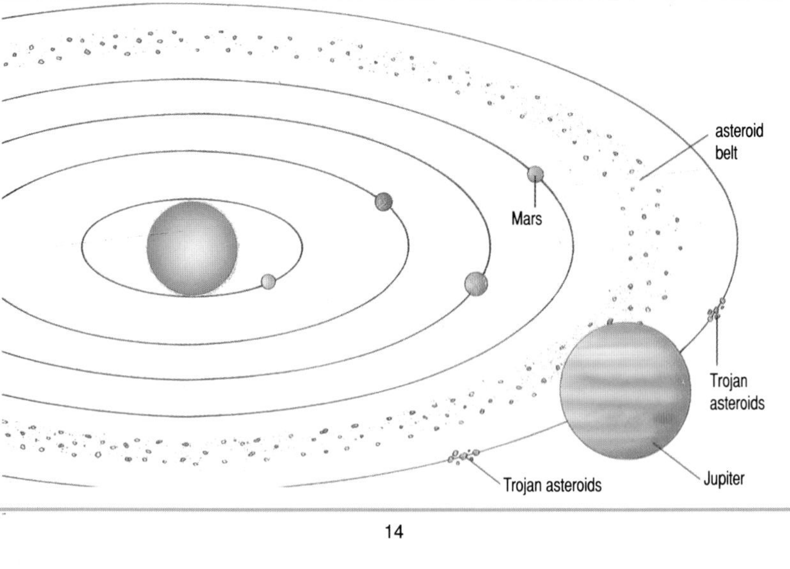

Astro-1, -2 observatories *plural noun*
The Astro-1 and Astro-2 observatories were built by the **European Space Agency**. They are part of **Spacelab payloads** launched by the US **space shuttle**. Astro-1 carried four separate telescopes, three for ultraviolet astronomy and one for X-ray astronomy. It studied hot **stars**, **supernova** remnants, **galaxies** and distant **quasars**.
The Astro-2 observatory will probably fly without the X-ray telescope.

astrolabe *noun*
An astrolabe was an instrument used by **astronomers** and navigators many years ago to measure the **altitudes** of astronomical bodies. It was made up of a circular disc with a scale marked off in degrees around its rim. There was a moveable arm at the centre of the disc. This was used to focus on the object. The altitude could then be read off the scale.
An astrolabe could be used to discover the latitude of a place.

astrology *noun*
Astrology is a subject that studies the positions of the Sun, Moon and planets against the background of the **Zodiac** at the time of a person's birth. It claims that this can predict the person's personality and behaviour.
There is no apparent scientific basis for astrology.

astrometry *noun*
Astrometry is a branch of **astronomy**. It deals with the measurement of the movements of astronomical objects and their exact positions in the sky on the **celestial sphere**. Astrometry also studies the reasons why these positions change with time.
The instruments and methods used for making the measurements are an important part of astrometry.

astronaut ► page 16

astronautics *noun*
Astronautics is the science of travelling in **space**. It uses space vehicles, which are either manned or unmanned. Astronautics also includes the building of the powerful **rockets** or **launch vehicles** that are needed to overcome the pull of Earth's gravity. Astronautics covers the many different types of **spacecraft** and their **missions**.
The science of astronautics uses the most up-to-date technology.

astronomer ► page 18

astronomical unit *noun*
An astronomical unit is a unit of measurement. It is used for measuring distances in **astronomy**, mainly within the **solar system**. It is the average distance between the centre of the **Earth** and the centre of the **Sun**.
One astronomical unit is equal to 149,597,870 kilometres.

astronomy *noun*
Astronomy is the scientific study of everything in the **universe** beyond the **atmosphere** of the Earth. Astronomy covers such an enormous field that today it is divided into areas of study. These are the study of **stars** and interplanetary **dust**, the study of **galaxies**, and the study of the **solar system** and everything in it.
Astronomy includes ideas, such as cosmology, and the Big Bang theory.

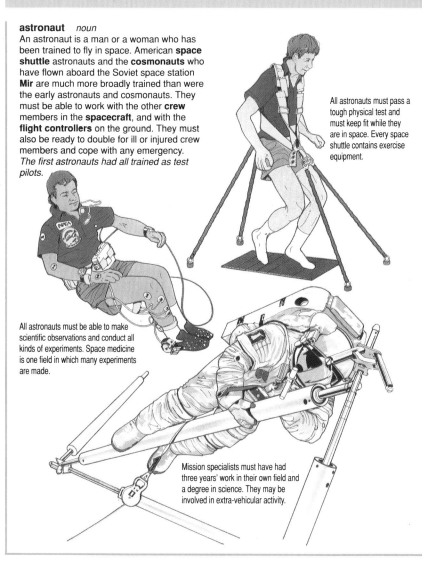

astronaut *noun*
An astronaut is a man or a woman who has been trained to fly in space. American **space shuttle** astronauts and the **cosmonauts** who have flown aboard the Soviet space station **Mir** are much more broadly trained than were the early astronauts and cosmonauts. They must be able to work with the other **crew** members in the **spacecraft**, and with the **flight controllers** on the ground. They must also be ready to double for ill or injured crew members and cope with any emergency.
The first astronauts had all trained as test pilots.

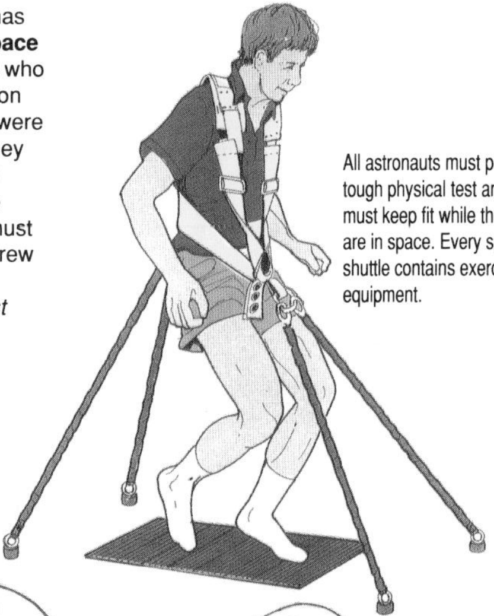

All astronauts must pass a tough physical test and must keep fit while they are in space. Every space shuttle contains exercise equipment.

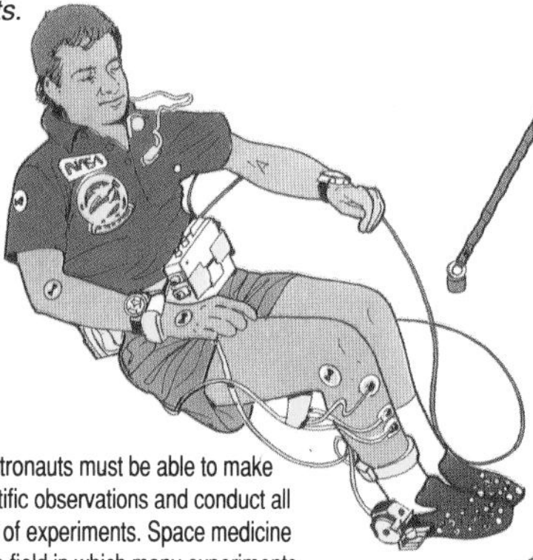

All astronauts must be able to make scientific observations and conduct all kinds of experiments. Space medicine is one field in which many experiments are made.

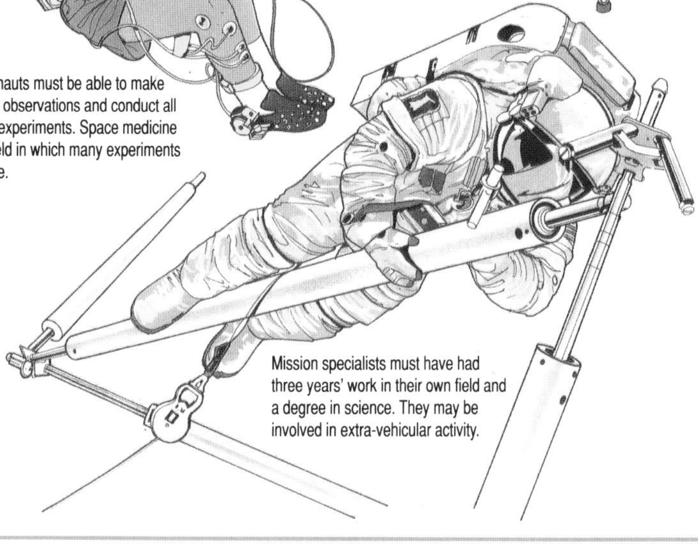

Mission specialists must have had three years' work in their own field and a degree in science. They may be involved in extra-vehicular activity.

Pilots and commanders must have at least a university degree in a science subject such as engineering.

One of the most ambitious projects that involved astronauts was the Apollo programme which sent men to the Moon.

Eating in space — food and drink are served in special containers to stop them floating about.

Sleeping in space — in free fall, an astronaut will usually sleep attached to a surface by special bands.

astronomer *noun*
An astronomer is a scientist who studies the **stars** and other heavenly bodies. Astronomers use **telescopes** and other instruments to collect information. They have used **satellites** and **space probes** to explore the solar system. Astronomers would like to know how the universe began, and what will happen to it in millions of years' time. Astronomers have studied the heavens for many thousands of years, and in many countries.
Astronomers have made many exciting discoveries about the universe.

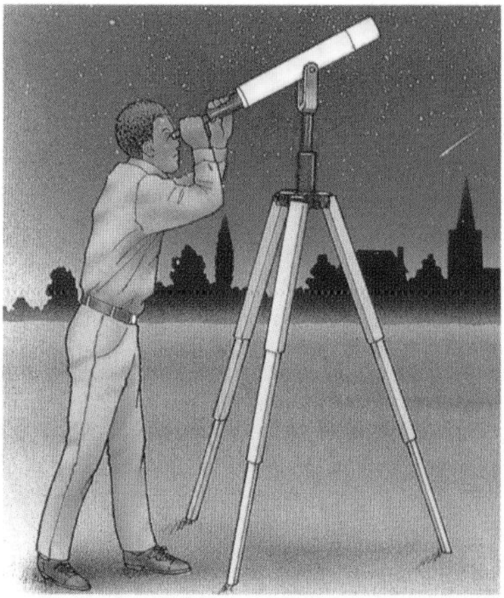

An astronomer may make observations at night with a small, portable telescope.

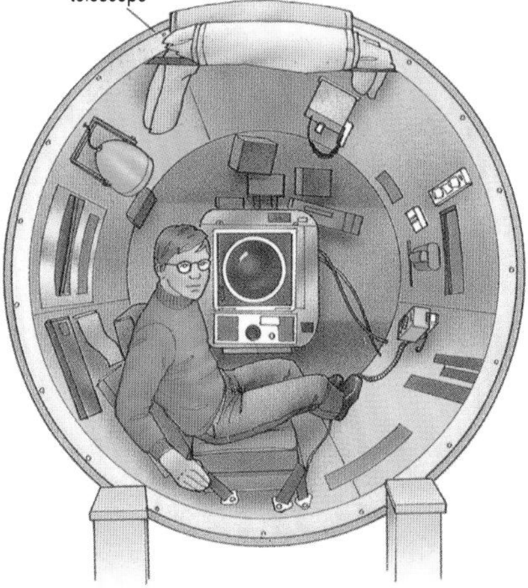

When using a radio telescope, the astronomer sits in front of the main mirror.

The computer control console can move the telescope and receive signals.

astrophotography *noun*
Astrophotography describes the photography of the night sky or of astronomical objects. Most astronomical objects are faint, and hard to photograph. Film may be exposed to the light of a faint object for a long time, perhaps over an hour. As the Earth rotates, the camera must be guided to follow objects as they change position in the sky.
For many studies, astrophotography is still the best way to get information.

astrophysics *noun*
Astrophysics is an important branch of **astronomy**. It uses the very latest methods to study the physics and chemistry of astronomical objects and the regions of space between them. Astrophysics deals with the production and use of energy in the **universe**. It also looks at how objects change as time passes.
Astrophysics began in the 1800s with the invention of spectroscopy.

Atlas *noun*
Atlas is the name of a family of **rockets**. It was used to launch the first Americans into space during the Mercury Project. Atlas was also used to launch the Ranger, **Surveyor** and **Lunar Orbiter** spacecraft to the Moon. It was later used to launch satellites, such as **Intelsat** 5, into **orbit**.
A new series of Atlas rockets, the Atlas 1 and Atlas 2, has been developed.

atmosphere *noun*
An atmosphere is a blanket of gases that surrounds a **planet**, a **moon** or a **star**. Small bodies, such as the Moon and Mercury, have little or no atmosphere. Venus, Earth and Mars all have atmospheres. The giant planets, Jupiter, Saturn, Uranus and Neptune, have huge, deep atmospheres. Stars are made up entirely of gases.
Surface temperature and escape velocity help to decide if a body has an atmosphere.
atmospheric *adjective*

atmospheric pressure *noun*
Atmospheric pressure is a measurement. It measures the force pushing downwards at any point in an **atmosphere**. The pressure is caused by the weight of the gases in the atmosphere above that point. Atmospheric pressure can be measured in units of newtons per square metre, millibars or atmospheres. The standard atmospheric pressure at the surface of the Earth is 325 newtons per square metre.
The atmospheric pressure at the surface of Venus is about 90,000 millibars.

A-type star *noun*
An A-type star is a hot, bluish-white or white **star**. It has a surface **temperature** of between 8,000 degrees kelvin and 10,000 degrees kelvin. In the **absorption spectrum** of an A-type star, dark lines of hydrogen are very obvious, and also lines of ionized calcium metal.
The bright stars Sirius, Vega, Altair and Deneb are all A-type stars.

aurora *noun*
The aurora is the name given to bands of coloured lights in the night sky. In the **northern hemisphere**, they are called the aurora borealis, or northern lights. In the **southern hemisphere**, they are called the aurora australis, or southern lights. The aurora is caused when electrified particles from space collide with atoms and molecules of **air** in the Earth's upper atmosphere. This causes the atoms to glow.
An aurora forms from 80 to 600 kilometres above the Earth's surface.

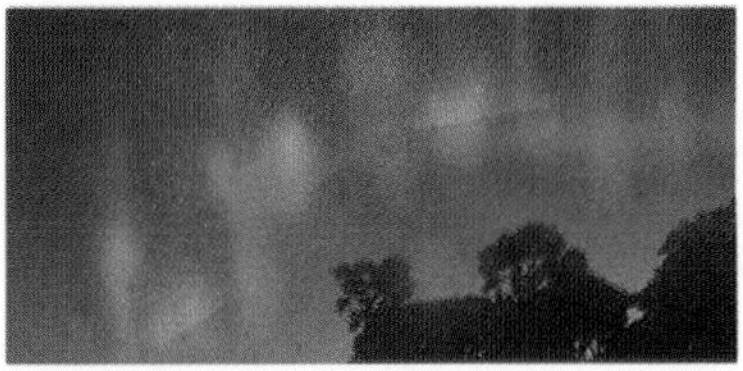

axis *noun*
An axis is an imaginary straight line passing through the centre of an object. If the object rotates, it turns on its axis. The time taken for the object to complete one **rotation** on its axis is called its axial period.
The Earth rotates on its axis once every 24 hours.

B

background radiation *noun*
Background radiation is a kind of **electromagnetic radiation**. It is found all over the **universe**. Scientists think it is the heat left over from the formation of the universe in the **Big Bang**. The background radiation found now has a **temperature** of only three degrees **kelvin**. This temperature is just three degrees above **absolute zero**, or –270 degrees Celsius.
Background radiation can also be called the 3K background or cosmic microwave background radiation.

backup crew *noun*
The backup crew is a **crew** of **astronauts**. It is trained to replace the main crew of a **spacecraft** on a manned **spaceflight**. This may be necessary if one or more members of the main crew became ill or had an accident.
The backup crew has exactly the same training as the main crew and at the same time.

Baikonur Cosmodrome *noun*
The Baikonur Cosmodrome is the name of an important space centre in Kazakhstan, in the Commonwealth of Independent States. Work at Baikonur began in 1955. Most of the important launches of the Soviet space programme have taken place from there. These include the launch of the first **satellite**, Sputnik 1, in October 1957. They also include the launch of the first man in space, Yuri Gagarin, in April 1961.
Many space probes and artificial satellites have been launched from the Baikonur Cosmodrome.

Baily's Beads *noun*
Baily's Beads are brilliant points of light, seen during a total **eclipse** of the **Sun**. They look like a string of glowing, white beads. They can be seen at the edge of the dark disc of the **Moon**, for a few moments just before or after the Sun is darkened. They are caused by the Sun's light shining down valleys on the extreme edge of the Moon.
Baily's Beads are named after the English astronomer Francis Baily, who saw them in May 1836.

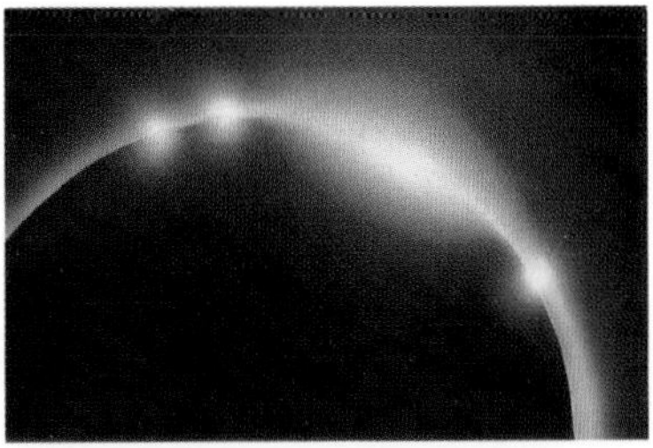

balloon astronomy *noun*
Balloon astronomy is a type of astronomy in which studies are made using scientific instruments sent up in balloons. These instruments can make observations of astronomical objects from heights of over 27,400 metres, where they are above most of the air. Here, they can observe **radiation** coming from objects in the universe that is blocked by the Earth's **atmosphere**.
Balloon astronomy has been largely replaced by the use of satellites and space probes.

Barnard's Star *noun*
Barnard's Star is a small red **dwarf star** in the **constellation** of Ophiuchus, the Serpent Bearer. It is not visible to the **naked eye**. Barnard's Star is only six light years from us. It is the fourth nearest star to the Sun, and the nearest beyond **Alpha Centauri**.
Many scientists think that Barnard's Star has two planets.

barred spiral galaxy ► galaxy

basin *noun*
A basin is a huge crater. Basins are found on the surface of a **planet** or planet's **moon**. They are surrounded by many roughly circular rings of mountains and valleys. Most scientists believe that such basins were produced during the first 700 million years of the planets' life, when very large **asteroids** crashed into them.
The youngest basins on the Moon were formed around 3,900 million years ago.

beam *noun*
A beam is a narrow stream of particles or **waves**. Beams can be made up of particles, such as **electrons**, or of **electromagnetic radiation**, such as radio waves, down which energy passes.
The beam of radio waves was received by the antenna.

Becklin-Neugebauer Object *noun*
The Becklin-Neugebauer Object is a very massive, luminous and young **B-type star**. It is hidden in the dust clouds of the **Orion nebula**. The Becklin-Neugebauer Object has a surface temperature of 20,000 degrees kelvin. It can only be seen by using **infra-red astronomy**.
The Becklin-Neugebauer Object formed just a few tens of thousands of years ago.

Betelgeuse *noun*
Betelgeuse is a **star** in the **constellation** Orion, or the Hunter. It is the second brightest star in Orion. Betelgeuse is a bright red **supergiant**. It has a diameter of 402 million kilometres, nearly 290 times larger than our own Sun. The star slowly swells and shrinks. This causes variations in its brightness. Betelgeuse lies at a distance of 590 light years from our Sun.
The orbit of the Earth around the Sun would fit inside Betelgeuse.

Big Bang theory ► page 22

Big Bang theory *noun*
The Big Bang theory is the theory that all the matter and **radiation** in the **universe** came into being at one moment of time, about 15 thousand million years ago, in a huge explosion. After the Big Bang, all the matter was thrown outwards at immense speed. The expansion of the universe began.
About 10 thousand million years after the Big Bang, the Sun and its solar system were formed.

20 billion years ago

	0	Big Bang
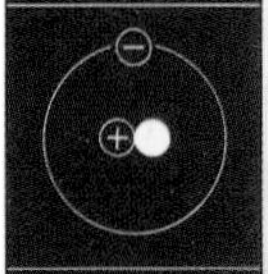	100 seconds	the first atoms, deuterium, formed
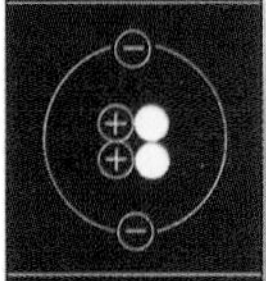	3 minutes	formation of helium atoms
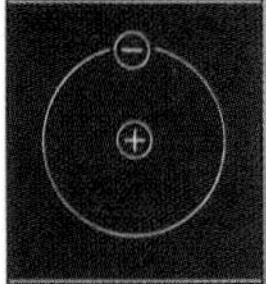	1 million years	formation of hydrogen atoms
	1 billion years	galaxies start to form
	4.5 billion years	stars start to develop in galaxies

Big Crunch *noun*
The Big Crunch is an idea. Some scientists think it is what could happen in a **closed universe**. The universe would stop growing and start to become smaller. Eventually all the matter and **radiation** in the universe would come together at one point in an enormous collision, called the Big Crunch. It would be the opposite to the **Big Bang**.
Some scientists even think that after the Big Crunch there might be another Big Bang.

Big Dipper ► Ursa Major

binary star *noun*
A binary star is a pair of stars that move round a common centre. The stars are held together because they are attracted to each other in paths which are not circles but **ellipses**. Binary and multiple stars are very common in our **Galaxy**.
Sirius is a well-known binary star.

black hole *noun*
A black hole is an object which has collapsed. It has collapsed so much and become so dense that its **escape velocity** is greater than the **speed of light**. No light can escape from it, and to an observer it appears totally dark. No black hole has yet been found, but scientists have very strong evidence that they exist. Black holes may form when huge **stars** explode.
Huge black holes containing as much material as a thousand million Suns may lie at the centre of some very active galaxies.

blazar *noun*
Blazar is a word that describes a **galaxy**. Enormously **energetic** processes are going on in the central regions of blazars. They are also sources of radio waves. Jets of gas often shoot out from the centre of active galaxies at speeds close to the speed of light. Blazars might be an end-on view of these jets.
The scientist studied the way the light from the blazar changed.

blue shift ► Doppler effect

bolide ► fireball

booster rocket *noun*
A booster rocket is a type of **rocket**. It can use either solid or liquid fuel. A booster is attached to the main **launch vehicle** to give extra **thrust** at take-off and for a short time afterwards.
The space shuttle uses two large, solid booster rockets to provide added thrust during the first 120 seconds of flight.

bright star ► page 25

B-type star *noun*
A B-type star is a rather massive, bluish **star**. It is extremely hot, with a surface temperature of between 12,000 and 25,000 degrees kelvin. The hottest B-type stars are 20,000 times more luminous than our Sun. Compared to the Sun, they use up their nuclear fuel quickly. The B-type stars that we see today must be quite young — between 5 million and 500 million years old.
The bright star Rigel is a B-type star.

Buran *noun*
Buran is the name given to the Soviet space shuttle orbiter. Buran does not carry re-useable rocket engines. It blasts off, sitting 'piggy-back' on the giant Energia carrier rocket. At a height of about 160 kilometres, Buran separates from Energia. Its own engine takes it into Earth orbit at a height of 250 kilometres.
Buran has a crew of four and can carry up to six passengers.

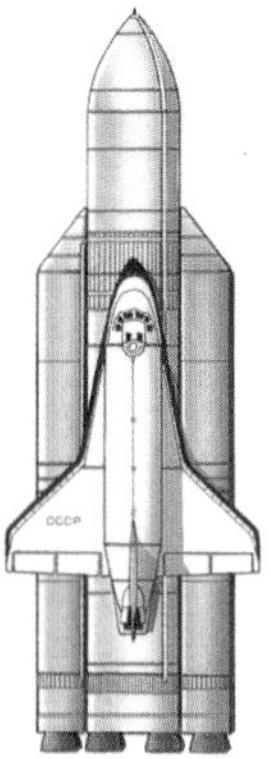

brightest stars *noun*
The brightest stars are the **stars** which look brightest to the **naked eye**. Their brightness, or **magnitude**, is measured on a scale from –1.5, very bright, to 2.00. A very large, dim star may seem bright when seen from Earth because it is close. A star which is further away from Earth may not look as bright, although it may be much hotter and more luminous.
The Sun is not very big or hot, but it is the brightest star that can be seen from Earth because it is closest.

Diagram showing brightest stars

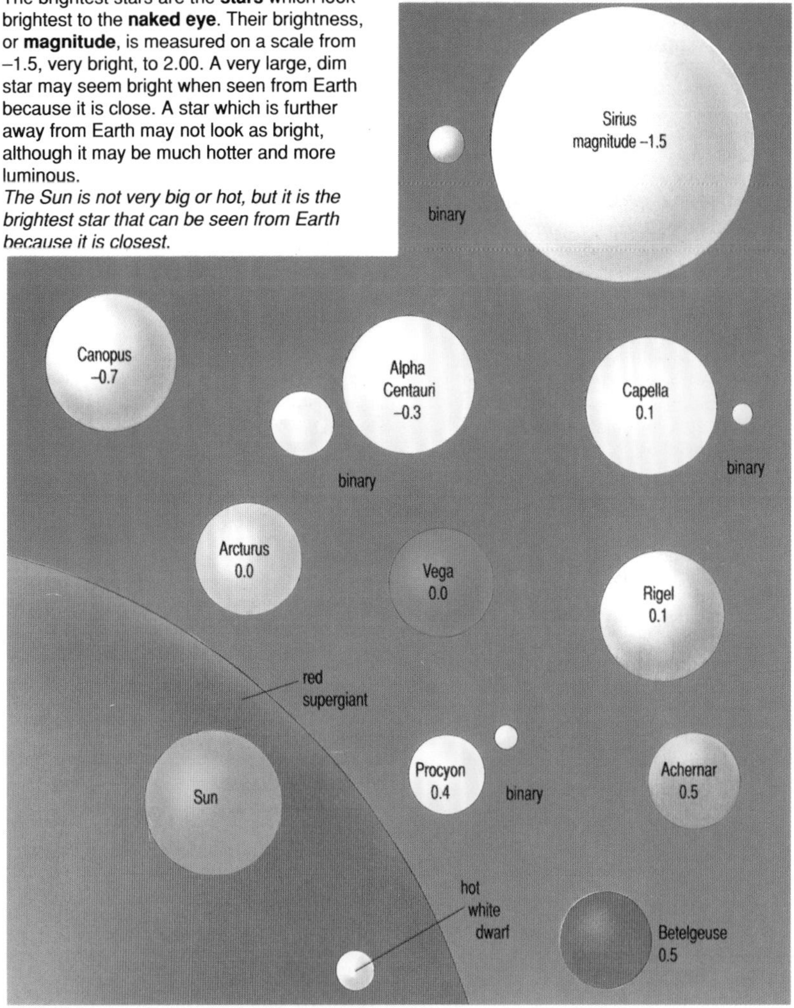

burn *noun*
A burn describes the firing of a rocket engine. For example, the second burn of the engines of the **space shuttle** would mean the second time during the flight that these engines had been fired.
The scientists ordered a burn to put the rocket on the right course.

burster *noun*
A burster is an object which gives out intense bursts of **X-rays**. The bursts begin suddenly, rise to a peak in less than a second, then die slowly away in about a minute. The intervals between bursts can range from hours to days. It is thought that the bursts happen when material falls onto a **star**, such as a **white dwarf** or **black hole**. This causes a brief but intense thermonuclear explosion.
More than 30 X-ray bursters have been found in our Galaxy.

C

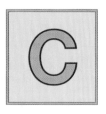

calendar *noun*
A calendar is a way of dividing **time** into convenient periods, such as days, weeks and months. Most calendars are based on the year, or the time taken for the Earth to **orbit** the Sun. The 'true' year is not an exact number of days. When the Earth goes once around the Sun, it spins on its **axis** 365.25 times. The year is taken to be 365 days long. An extra day every fourth year is added on to make up the difference. This is called a Leap Year.
Various calendars have been used throughout history.

Callisto *noun*
Callisto is a **moon**. It is one of the 16 moons of **Jupiter**. It is the fourth and faintest of the four **Galilean satellites**. But it is in fact the second largest, with a diameter of 4,806 kilometres. The two **Voyager** spacecraft flew by Callisto. They found it had many craters. Callisto **orbits** at an average distance of 1,880,000 kilometres from the centre of Jupiter.
Callisto was discovered by the Italian astronomer Galileo in 1610.

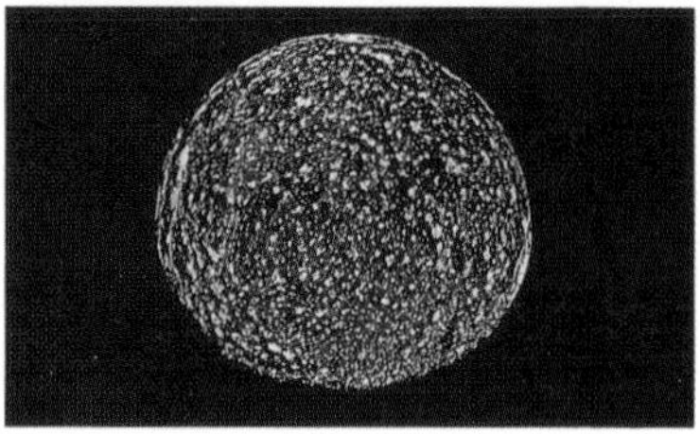

Cancer *noun*
Cancer, or the Crab, is one of the **constellations** of the **Zodiac**. It can be seen in the **northern hemisphere**, between Gemini and Leo. Cancer is a faint pattern of stars, but it is fairly easy to find. Its most interesting feature is an **open cluster** of over 100 stars called Praesepe. This is best seen with binoculars.
Two of the stars in Cancer have been nicknamed 'the asses'.

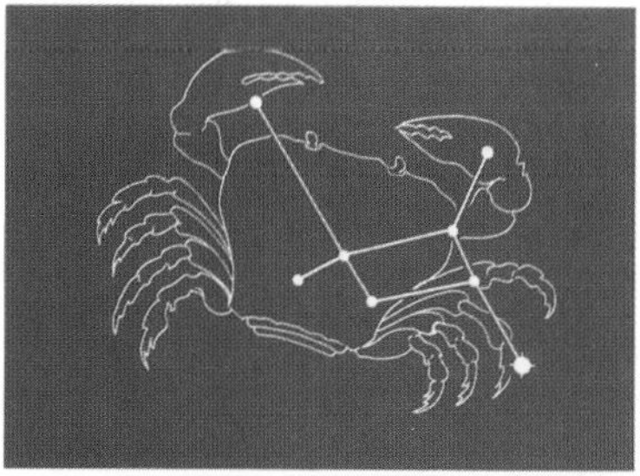

Canopus *noun*
Canopus is a **star** in the **constellation** Carina, or the Keel. It is the second brightest star in the sky. Canopus cannot be seen from Europe or Canada. From the **southern hemisphere** it can be seen high up on winter evenings. Canopus is almost 1,200 light years away from Earth.
Scientists believe that Canopus is 200,000 times brighter than our Sun.

Cape Canaveral *noun*
Cape Canaveral is the major **rocket** launching site in the United States of America. The first American **satellite**, Explorer 1, was launched from here in 1958. This was the beginning of the American programme of space exploration. All the major American manned **spaceflights** have been launched at Cape Canaveral.
The launch pads and other equipment at Cape Canaveral are known as the Kennedy Space Centre.

Capella *noun*
Capella is a **star** in the **constellation** Auriga, or the Charioteer. It is the sixth brightest star in the night sky. Capella has a bright yellow colour and can be seen in the **northern hemisphere**. It is a multiple star and is made up of three stars close together. Capella lies at a distance of about 45 light years from Earth.
The name Capella means 'little she-goat'.

Capricornus *noun*
Capricornus, or the Sea Goat, is one of the **constellations** of the **Zodiac**. It covers a large area of the sky to the south of the **celestial equator**. It lies between Sagittarius and Aquarius. Capricornus contains no really bright stars and it is not very easy to find. The brightest star is a double star that can be seen with the **naked eye**.
There is a globular cluster of stars near Capricornus.

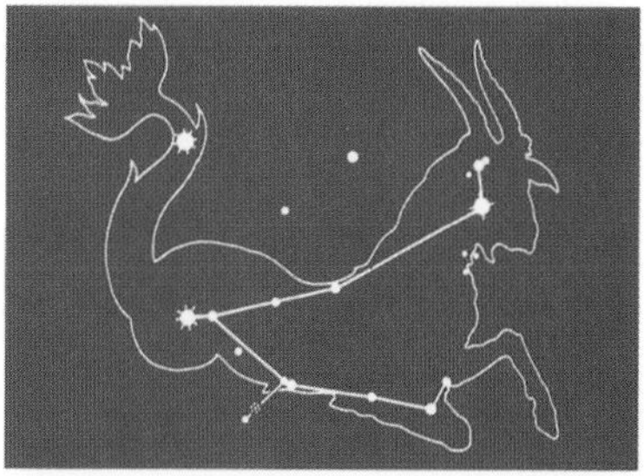

capsule *noun*
A capsule was the small, pressurized cabin found in early American **spacecraft**. An example is the Mercury capsule, in which the first **astronauts** flew into space. There was almost no room to move inside these capsules.
Capsules were designed to splash down in the sea, where they could easily be found.

captured rotation ► **synchronous rotation**

carbon-nitrogen cycle *noun*
The carbon-nitrogen cycle is part of a nuclear reaction. It is a chain of six **nuclear fusion** reactions by which **stars** generate **energy**. The elements carbon, nitrogen and oxygen are all involved at different stages of the chain of reactions.
The carbon-nitrogen cycle is the major source of energy production in hot, massive, bluish-white and white stars.

carbon star *noun*
A carbon star is one of a rare group of **red giant** stars that have a low surface **temperature** of around 2,500 degrees kelvin. They contain unusually high amounts of the elements carbon and lithium and less oxygen. Carbon stars are also known as C-type stars.
Carbon stars are rare in the Milky Way Galaxy.

cargo ► payload

cargo bay ► payload bay

Cassini division *noun*
The Cassini division is a dark gap. It can be found between the first two bright **rings** that circle **Saturn**. The Cassini division is not empty. Photographs taken by the **Voyager** spacecraft show that it contains several very narrow ringlets. These cannot be seen from Earth.
The Italian astronomer Giovanni Cassini first saw the Cassini division in 1675.

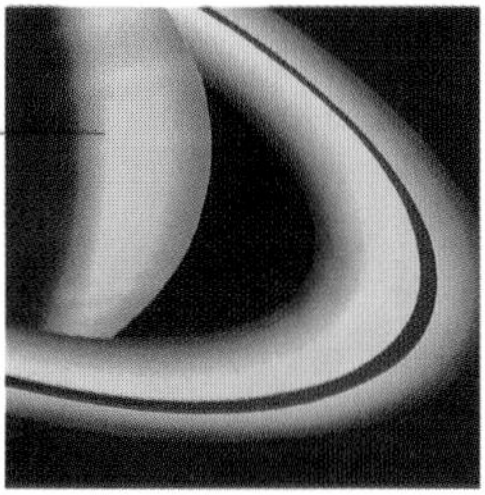

Cassini spacecraft *noun*
The Cassini spacecraft is an interplanetary **spacecraft**. It is due to be launched in April 1996. After making **flybys** of the Earth and Jupiter, the Cassini spacecraft will go into orbit around the planet **Saturn** in October 2002.
Cassini will make a far more detailed study of Saturn than has ever been made before.

celestial equator ► celestial sphere

celestial mechanics *noun*
Celestial mechanics is the study of the movements of astronomical bodies. It includes the study of the **gravitational** forces acting on the bodies. Celestial mechanics uses **Newton's theory of gravitation** and **Newton's laws of motion** to explain and predict the **orbits** of the planets, moons, asteroids and comets.
Gravity is an important part of celestial mechanics.

celestial pole ► celestial sphere

celestial sphere *noun*
The celestial sphere is a huge, imaginary ball. Scientists have imagined that it surrounds the Earth. Stars and other astronomical bodies can be thought of as points on the surface of the celestial sphere. The Earth's **axis** points north to the north celestial pole, and south to the south celestial pole. As the Earth spins round, these poles seem to stay fixed.
The celestial sphere is divided into two equal hemispheres by the celestial equator.

Centaur *noun*
The Centaur rocket is used as part of heavy **launch vehicles** in the United States of America. It was combined with the **Atlas** and **Titan** rockets to make the Atlas-Centaur and Titan-Centaur rockets. Titan-Centaur is used for long-range **missions**.
Centaur was used to launch the Viking probes to Mars and the Voyager spacecraft.

Centaurus A *noun*
Centaurus A is the nearest major radio **galaxy**. It is the third most powerful **radio source** in the sky. In photographs, it looks like a round, or spherical, galaxy cut in half by a dark band of dust. Centaurus A is also a powerful source of **X-rays**, showing that there is violent activity going on inside it.
Centaurus A lies 13 million light years from our own Galaxy.

centrifuge *noun*
A centrifuge is a machine that can copy the effects of high **gravity**. It is a motorized machine with a long arm. At the end of the arm is a small compartment in which humans, animals or equipment can be spun round at various speeds. Riding in a centrifuge is an essential part of an **astronaut's** training. It gives them the experience of the rapid **accelerations** and high **G-forces** they will come across during **space flight**.
The astronauts trained for many hours in the centrifuge.

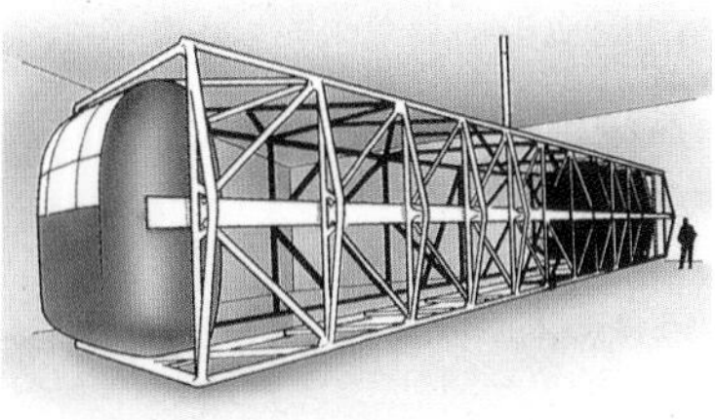

Cepheid variable star *noun*
A Cepheid variable star is a **star** that varies in brightness in a regular way. The brightness varies over periods ranging from a few days to a few weeks. It changes because the Cepheids are expanding and contracting in a very regular way. Cepheids are yellow or orange **supergiants**, far more **luminous** than our Sun.
The first Cepheid variable star to be found was in the constellation Cepheus.

Ceres *noun*
Ceres is an **asteroid**. It was the first and largest asteroid to be discovered. Ceres has a diameter of 933 kilometres. It is never bright enough to be seen with the **naked eye**. It reflects only about six per cent of the sunlight that falls upon it.
Ceres is nearly spherical in shape, and turns on its axis once every 9.075 hours.

Cerro Tololo Observatory *noun*
The Cerro Tololo Observatory is a major astronomical **observatory**. It is located on a mountain peak in Chile, 2,200 metres above sea level. There are eight **telescopes** at the observatory. The two largest of the telescopes are the 4-metre and 1.5-metre reflecting telescopes.
Cerro Tololo Observatory is run by a group of Americans.

Challenger *noun*
Challenger was the name given to an American **space shuttle**. Challenger made its first flight in April 1983, and had completed nine flights by the end of December 1985. Seventy-three seconds after lift-off on its tenth flight, on 28 January 1986, Challenger was completely destroyed in an explosion. All seven crew members were killed.
The space shuttles did not fly for two years after the Challenger accident.

charge-coupled device (CCD) *noun*
A charge-coupled device is a piece of equipment that takes pictures using electronics. It can be used with a camera or **telescope** for recording pictures of astronomical objects. A charge-coupled device is made of a group of small cells, called pixels, on a silicon chip. Light falling on to each cell is changed into small amounts of electric charge. These can be transferred from the charge-coupled device into a computer memory.
A charge-coupled device is often far more effective than photographic film.

Charon *noun*
Charon is a **moon**. It is the only known moon of **Pluto**. Charon has a diameter of 1,190 kilometres and is about half the size of Pluto. Charon orbits Pluto every 6.387 days, at a distance of only 19,640 kilometres from the centre of Pluto. Charon orbits around Pluto in exactly the same time as Pluto spins on its **axis**. This is unique in the solar system.
Charon is almost certainly made of ice.

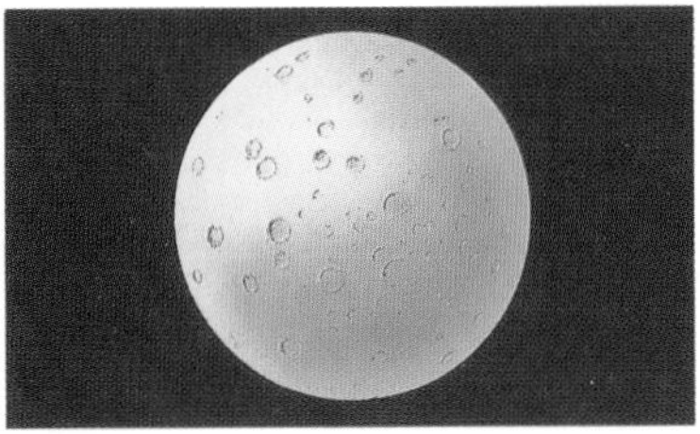

Chiron *noun*
Chiron is thought to be an **asteroid**. It is an unusual object, discovered in 1977. Chiron moves mainly between the **orbits** of **Saturn** and **Uranus**. It takes 49 years to go once round its orbit. Some scientists think that Chiron is one of the brightest members of a distant swarm of asteroids. The rest of the asteroids have yet to be discovered.
Chiron is probably somewhere between 100 and 320 kilometres in diameter.

chromosphere *noun*
The chromosphere is part of the **atmosphere** of the Sun. It lies immediately above the Sun's **photosphere**. The chromosphere can be seen easily only during a total **eclipse** of the Sun. Using a **spectrohelioscope**, the chromosphere can be studied at any time. It is red in colour.
The chromosphere is made up chiefly of hydrogen gas.

circumpolar stars *noun*
Circumpolar stars are **stars** which never set below the **horizon**. They seem to circle the pole. From Great Britain and North America, the Great Bear is circumpolar. It never goes out of view. From New Zealand, the Southern Cross is circumpolar.
At the Equator, there are no circumpolar stars as they all rise and set.

Clarke orbit ► geosynchronous orbit

closed universe *noun*
The closed universe is an idea. In a closed universe, the **expanding universe** that can be observed would stop growing. Then it would start to become smaller. This would end with a **big crunch**, as the matter comes together. It would be the opposite of the **Big Bang**. Some scientists think that the big crunch could be followed by another big bang, and a new universe would be born.
In a closed universe, big bangs and big crunches could go on for ever.

cluster *noun*
A cluster is a group of **stars**. In a cluster the stars are close enough together to form an **association**. Most stars form in clusters rather than on their own. Open clusters are loose groups of between a few score and a few hundred stars, found within the **Galaxy**. Globular clusters are thickly-packed, ball-shaped clusters containing from tens of thousands up to maybe a million stars.
Globular clusters form a giant halo around our Galaxy.

Cluster mission *noun*
The Cluster mission is a series of four identical **satellites** to be launched by the **European Space Agency**. The satellites will be placed in **orbit** around the Earth by an Ariane rocket in 1995. They will draw a three-dimensional map of the Earth's **magnetic field**, and study the **solar wind**.
The four Cluster mission satellites will be positioned in space one at each corner of a huge, imaginary pyramid.

clusters of galaxies *noun*
Clusters of galaxies are groups of **galaxies**. There may be a few thousand members in a cluster. Most galaxies seem to occur in clusters. Our Galaxy belongs to a small, irregular cluster called the **Local Group**. The nearest large cluster of galaxies is the **Virgo cluster**. Clusters of galaxies may in turn be grouped into **superclusters**.
Clusters of galaxies are held together by their gravitational pull.

Coal Sack nebula *noun*
The Coal Sack nebula is a famous dark **nebula**. It lies in the **constellation** of Crux Australia, the Southern Cross. The Coal Sack is in the **southern hemisphere**. It is too far south to be seen from Europe or North America. The Coal Sack is 555 light years away from Earth. Like all such clouds of dust-laden gas, the Coal Sack is seen only in silhouette.
The Coal Sack nebula can be seen as a dark patch against the bright background of the Milky Way.

Columbus *noun*
Columbus is a major project of the **European Space Agency**. It has several different parts. The first is a fully automatic, unmanned orbital laboratory called the European Retrievable Carrier, or Eureca. A manned laboratory, the attached pressurized module or APM, will be joined to the international **space station**, **Freedom**.
In the Columbus project, one or two orbiting polar platforms will carry instruments for observing the Earth.

coma *noun*
The coma is the thin cloud of gas and dust surrounding the **nucleus** of a **comet**. This cloud is roughly the shape of a ball, or spherical. The coma may stretch from 10,000 kilometres to as far as 1 million kilometres from the comet's nucleus. Many comets are also surrounded by a vast coma of **hydrogen**. This may be up to 10 million kilometres in diameter.
The coma is usually largest just after the comet has passed closest to the Sun.

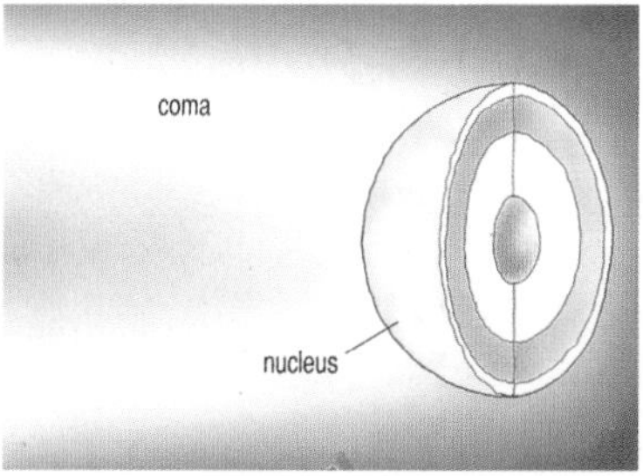

combustion chamber *noun*
A combustion chamber is part of a **rocket**. It is the part of the engine in which the burning of the **fuel** takes place. The combustion chamber and the cone-shaped nozzle of the rocket engine are together called the rocket's **thrust** chamber.
The combustion chamber was designed to withstand very high pressure.

comet ► page 33

command *noun*
A command is a signal or an instruction. It triggers some action to be taken either by a human, or by a machine which receives the signal. For example, the command might be a signal sent, or **transmitted**, to a spacecraft's cameras, telling them to switch on at a certain time. It might be an instruction to a computer program, telling the computer what to do.
The command instructed the spacecraft to change course.
command *verb*

command module ► page 34

commander *noun*
The commander of a **spacecraft** is the senior **crew** member. He is responsible for the safety of the other crew members. The commander can change flight plans and the jobs of the other crew members, if the safety of the crew or spacecraft is at risk. The commander must also carry out the orders of flight controllers on the ground. He makes sure that all the aims of the **mission** are achieved.
The commander made sure the crew kept themselves in good condition by exercising every day.

communications satellite ► **satellite**

constellation ► page 36

continuous spectrum *noun*
A continuous spectrum is a **spectrum** that is produced by gas which can be hot, glowing solid, liquid or high-density. A continuous spectrum appears as a rainbow of colours. The brilliant surface, or **photosphere** of the Sun produces a continuous spectrum of **ultraviolet radiation**, **visible light** and **infra-red radiation**.
The filament of an ordinary light bulb produces a continuous spectrum.

Copernican theory *noun*
The Copernican theory is an idea held by the Polish monk Nicolaus Copernicus. Copernicus thought that the planets, including the Earth, moved around the Sun. This was also called the **heliocentric** theory. The Copernican theory was correct. Before the Copernican theory, people thought the Earth was the centre of the universe. This was the **Ptolemaic theory**.
The Copernican theory was published by Copernicus in 1543.

Copernicus ► **Orbiting Astronomical Observatory**

core *noun*
The core is the central part of a **star**, such as the **Sun**. It is where all the star's **energy** is produced by **thermonuclear reactions**. The core is also the central region of a **planet**, such as the **Earth**.
Giant planets such as Jupiter, have a small core of rock or metal.

corona *noun*
The corona is the very outer part of the **atmosphere** of the **Sun**. It is divided into the inner corona and outer corona. The solar corona can be seen normally only during a total **eclipse**. The inner corona is made of gas, with a very high temperature of about two million degrees kelvin. The outer corona is made up mainly of **ions**.
The shape of the solar corona changes with the activity of the Sun.

comet *noun*

A comet is a minor member of the **solar system**. It travels around the **Sun** in an **elliptical orbit** that is often very drawn out, or elongated. Most comets have three parts, the **nucleus**, **coma** and tails. The gas and dust tails point away from the Sun. Comets are called short-period or long-period, depending on how long they take to go once round the Sun.

Comets have often been found by amateur astronomers.

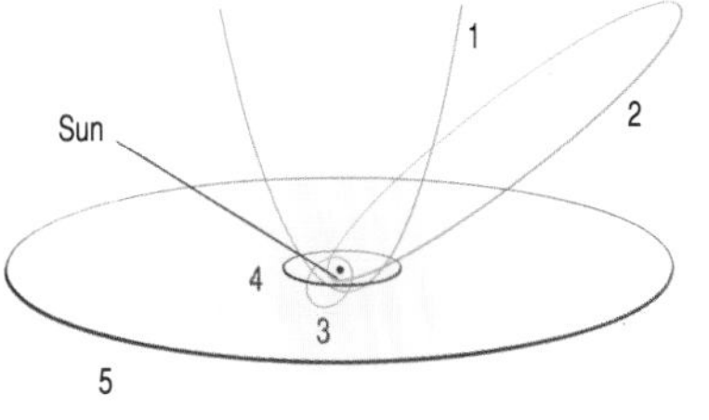

1. orbit of Halley's comet 2. orbit of Schwassmann-Wachmann's comet 3. orbit of Encke's comet 4. orbit of Mercury 5. orbit of Earth

▲ nucleus of ice and rock, coma of gas and dust, tail of very thin gas and dust

▼ orbit of comet around Sun - the tail always points away from the Sun

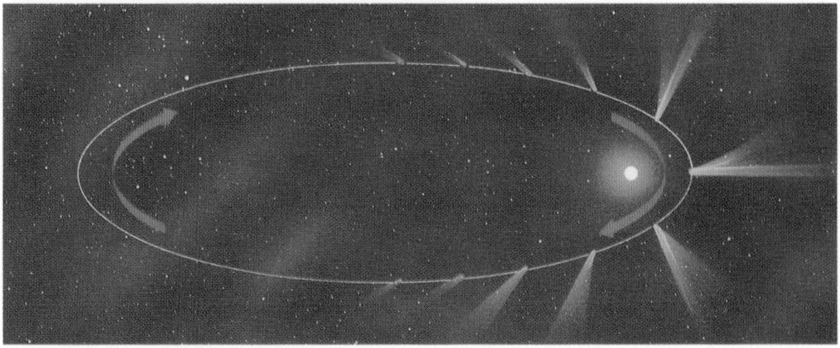

command module *noun*
The command module was a small, cone-shaped part of the **Apollo spacecraft**. The three astronauts travelled to and from the **Moon** in the command module. It was the crew's control centre and living quarters. On returning to Earth, the command module was protected by its **heat shield** from the fiery heat of **re-entry**. Then parachutes opened and it splashed down gently in the sea.
The command module of Apollo 17 was called America.

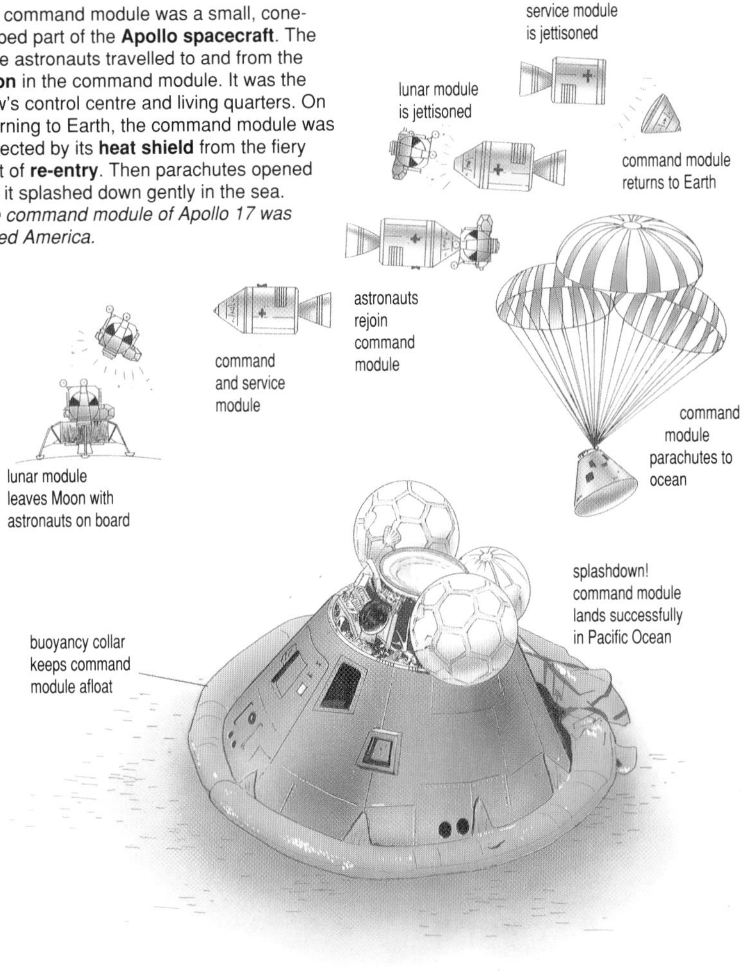

Cosmic Background Explorer (COBE) *noun*
The Cosmic Background Explorer, or COBE for short, was a space **mission** launched by the United States of America. The COBE spacecraft was launched on 18 November 1989 into a circular **orbit,** 900 kilometres above the Earth. The spacecraft carried three instruments, designed to search for **radiation** from the earliest **galaxies**.
The COBE mission answered some of the most basic questions about the Big Bang.

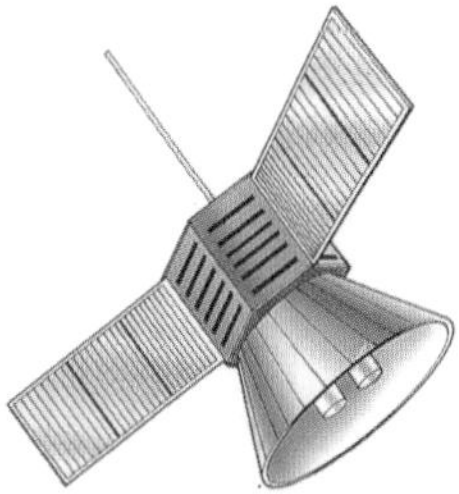

cosmic dust *noun*
Cosmic dust describes the particles of dust found everywhere in space. These particles range in size from dust specks far smaller than a grain of sand to large boulders. The dust is found in **craters** on the surfaces of the Moon and planets, in the region between the planets, and in the space between the stars. Cosmic dust particles also clump together to form **dark nebulae**.
Cosmic dust is also called interplanetary dust or interstellar dust.

cosmic rays *noun*
Cosmic rays are particles with very high **energy**. They move through space almost at the **speed of light**. They hit the Earth's **atmosphere** all the time and from all directions. Some low-energy cosmic rays come from the Sun or from **supernova** explosions.
A very high-energy cosmic ray may have a million million times the energy of a low-energy cosmic ray.

cosmic year *noun*
The cosmic year is the name given to the **time** taken for the **Sun** to make one turn around the centre of the **Galaxy**.
The cosmic year is equal to about 225 million years.

cosmo- *prefix*
Cosmo- is a prefix meaning of the universe, or of space.
The word cosmonaut means 'space sailor'.

cosmology *noun*
Cosmology is the study of how the **universe** began, and of how it changes as time passes. Theories about the universe have been put forward by scientists for many centuries. They try to explain the present structure of the universe, describe how it was in the past, and predict what might happen to it in the distant future.
The most popular cosmology theory today is the Big Bang theory.

cosmonaut *noun*
A cosmonaut is a person who has been trained to fly in space. Most cosmonauts have come from Russia. Many flew in **spacecraft** launched by the Soviet Union. Cosmonauts are trained in the same way as the American **astronauts**. In recent years, several non-Russians have flown as cosmonauts on Soviet space **missions**, as part of the Interkosmos programme.
The first man to fly in space was a Russian cosmonaut.

Cosmos *noun*
Cosmos is the name given to a series of over 2,000 unmanned **satellites** launched by the Soviet Union. The first was launched on 16 March 1962, and the 1,000th in March 1978. The satellites have had many uses, including surveys of the land and oceans, studying the Earth's upper **atmosphere**, and testing new designs of spacecraft.
When Cosmos 954 broke up, some pieces fell through the atmosphere onto Canada.

constellations of the northern hemisphere *noun*

The constellations of the northern hemisphere are the constellations that can be seen from any point north of the Equator on **Earth**. A constellation is a group of **stars**. The groups make up patterns in the night sky. There are 37 constellations in the northern hemisphere, and a total of 88 constellations altogether.

The Greek astronomer Ptolemy listed 48 constellations in the northern hemisphere.

1. Aquila
2. Andromeda
3. Aries
4. Auriga
5. Boôtes
6. Camelopardalis
7. Cancer
8. Canes Venatici
9. Cassiopeia
10. Cephus
11. Cetus
12. Coma Berenices
13. Corona Borealis
14. Cygnus
15. Delphinus
16. Draco
17. Equuleus
18. Gemini
19. Hercules
20. Hydra
21. Lacerta
22. Leo
23. Leo Minor
24. Lynx
25. Lyra
26. Ophiuchus
27. Orion
28. Pegasus
29. Perseus
30. Pisces
31. Sagitta
32. Serpens
33. Taurus
34. Triangulum
35. Ursa Major
36. Ursa Minor
37. Virgo

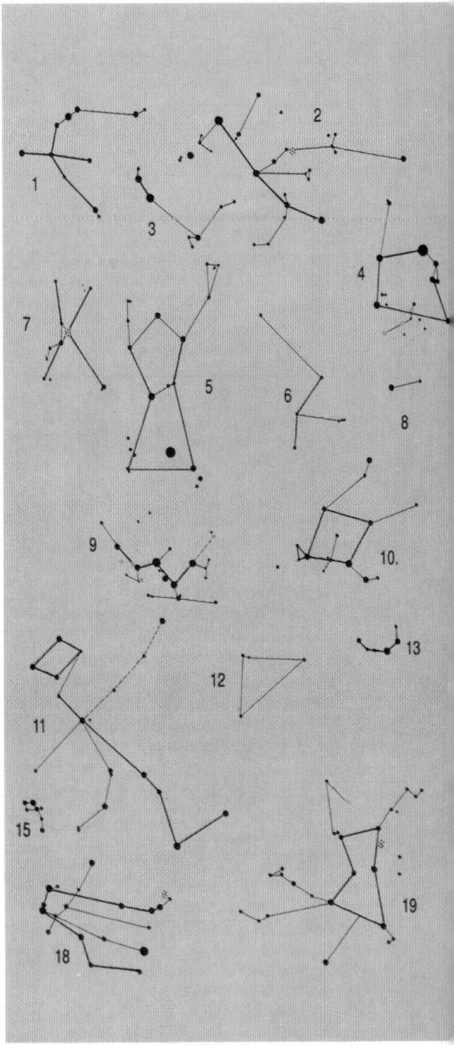

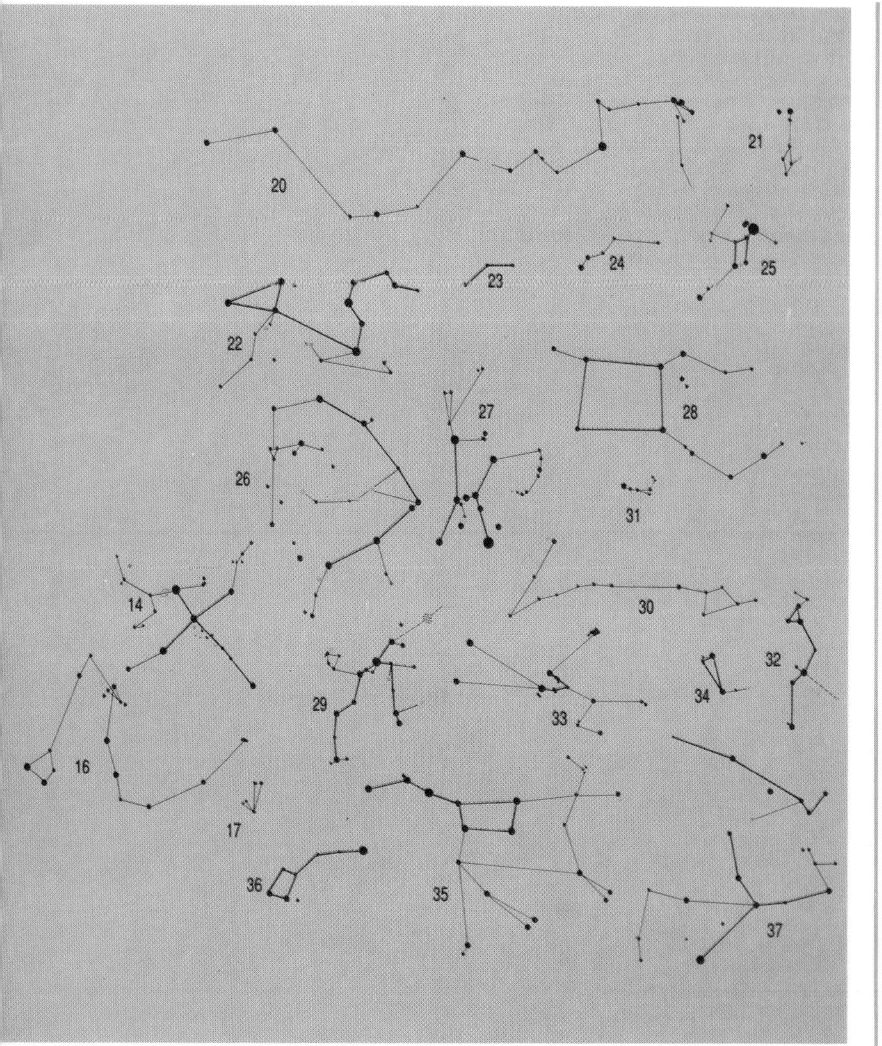
20
21
25
24
23
22
28
27
26
31
14
30
32
29
33
34
16
17
36
35
37

constellations of the southern hemisphere *noun*
The constellations of the southern hemisphere are the constellations that can be seen from any point south of the Equator on **Earth**. A constellation is a group of **stars**. The groups make up patterns in the night sky. There are 51 constellations in the southern hemisphere.
The constellations of the southern hemisphere include Crux Australis and Hydra, the smallest and largest constellations.

1. Antlia
2. Apus
3. Aquarius
4. Ara
5. Caelum
6. Canis Major
7. Canis Minor
8. Capricornus
9. Carina
10. Centaurus
11. Chamaeleon
12. Circinus
13. Columba
14. Corona Australis
15. Corvus
16. Crater
17. Crux Australis
18. Dorado
19. Eridanus
20. Fornax
21. Grus
22. Horologium
23. Hydrus
24. Indus
25. Lepus
26. Libra
27. Lupus
28. Mensa
29. Microscopium
30. Monoceros
31. Musca Australis
32. Norma
33. Octans
34. Pavo

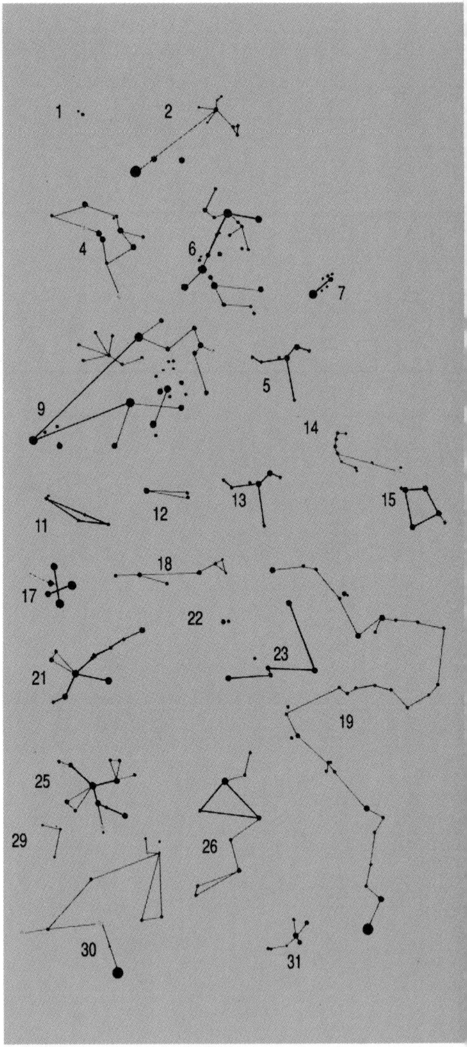

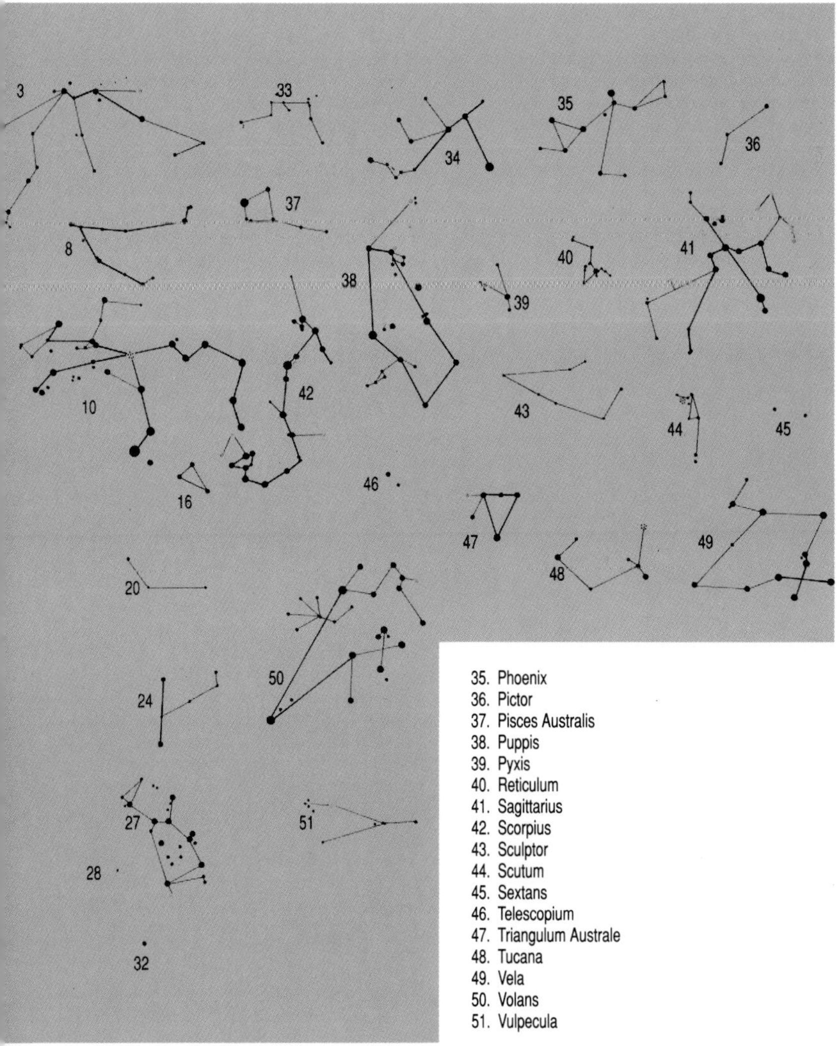

35. Phoenix
36. Pictor
37. Pisces Australis
38. Puppis
39. Pyxis
40. Reticulum
41. Sagittarius
42. Scorpius
43. Sculptor
44. Scutum
45. Sextans
46. Telescopium
47. Triangulum Australe
48. Tucana
49. Vela
50. Volans
51. Vulpecula

countdown *noun*
The countdown is the step-by-step process leading up to the **lift-off** of a **rocket** or other **spacecraft**. It also describes the continuous counting backwards to zero of the time remaining before the launch. The time of the launch is known as T. The countdown 'T-2 minutes' means two minutes to go before lift-off.
When the countdown reached zero, the rocket lifted off the launch pad.

course correction *noun*
A course correction is a small change made to the speed of a **spacecraft**. It makes sure that the spacecraft travels along exactly the right path to its destination, and arrives there at exactly the right time. A course correction is also called a trajectory correction manoevre, or TCM.
Scientists use computers to help them make course corrections.

Crab ► Cancer

Crab nebula *noun*
The Crab nebula is a **nebula**. It is a swirling cloud of expanding gas and dust in the **constellation** of Taurus, the Bull. It is too faint to be seen without binoculars or a **telescope**. The Crab nebula is a **supernova** remnant. The supernova was seen as a brilliant star by Chinese astronomers in 1054.
The Crab nebula is a very powerful source of radio waves, X-rays and gamma-rays.

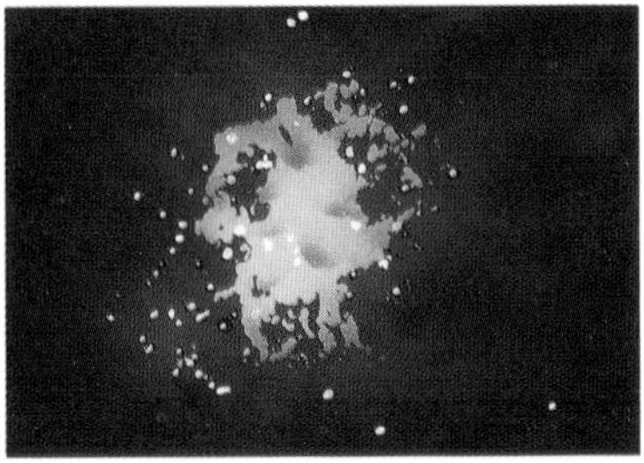

Crab pulsar *noun*
The Crab pulsar is a **star**. It is the energy centre of the **Crab nebula**. In the **supernova** explosion that made the nebula, the **core** of the original star collapsed. This formed a tiny, very dense object called a **neutron star**. As this spins rapidly around, it sends out a pulse of **radiation** like the narrow beam of light from a lighthouse. The spinning neutron star is the Crab pulsar.
Scientists think the Crab pulsar has a diameter of about 19 kilometres.

crater *noun*
A crater is a roughly circular hollow. Craters are found on the surfaces of the **Moon** and many other bodies in the **solar system**. Most craters are formed by rocks from outer space, crashing into the surface. Some are formed from **volcanoes**. Many craters have raised edges or rims. Others have central mountain peaks.
Craters have diameters ranging from less than one metre to over 1,000 kilometres.

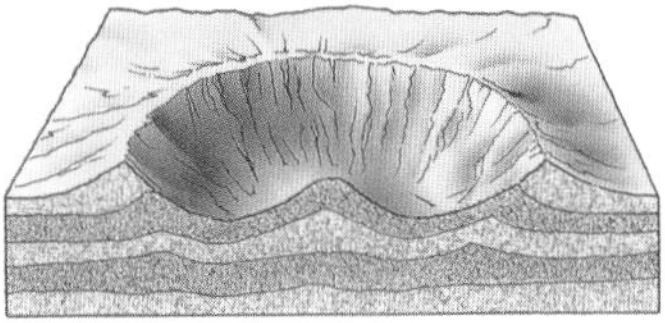

Crepe ring *noun*
The Crepe ring is one of the **rings** of **Saturn**. It is the usual name for Saturn's almost transparent C-ring. The Crepe ring lies inside the B-ring, the brightest ring surrounding the planet. Close-up photographs taken by the **Voyager** spacecraft show that the Crepe ring is made up of countless huge, icy boulders orbiting around Saturn like tiny moonlets.
The Crepe ring was discovered in 1850.

crew *noun*
The crew is the **astronauts** who fly in and operate a **spacecraft**. Normally the crew consists of at least two members. These are the **commander**, who may also be a pilot, and a pilot or flight engineer.
Extra crew members may be needed to carry out experiments while in flight.

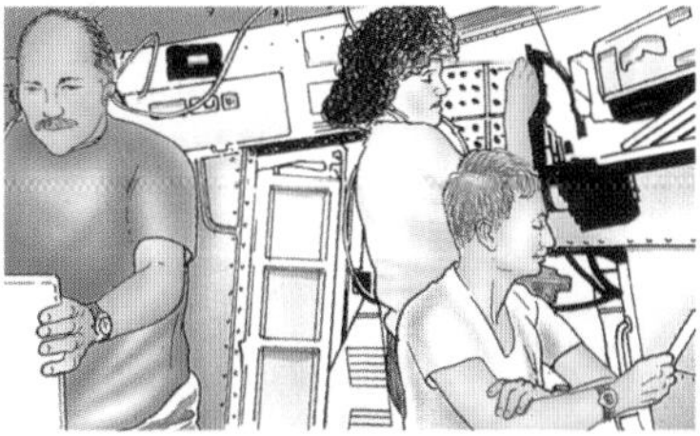

crust *noun*
The crust is the outer part of a solid body, such as a **planet**, a **moon** or a **neutron star**. The Earth has a crust which is about 32 kilometres thick under the continents and 10 kilometres thick under the oceans.
The crust of a solid body is usually made of rock or ice.

Cygnus A *noun*
Cygnus A is a strong **radio source** in the **constellation** of Cygnus, the Swan. It is the third strongest radio source in the sky after the **Sun** and the **supernova** remnant Cassiopeia A. Cygnus A is a radio **galaxy** lying about 555 million light years away.
Cygnus A emits low-energy X-rays.

Cygnus X-1 *noun*
Cygnus X-1 is an intense source of **X-rays**, found in the **constellation** of Cygnus, the Swan. Cygnus X-1 lies in our own Galaxy. It is a **binary star**, a bright **supergiant** orbiting a massive but invisible companion.
Cygnus X-1's dark companion, which is 6 to 15 times as big as our Sun, is probably a black hole.

D

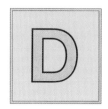

dark matter *noun*
Dark matter is an idea. It describes the material in the **universe** which gives out almost no light at all, or is completely invisible. Even though this dark matter cannot be seen, the effects of its **gravity** show that it is there. Scientists think that we can see only one per cent of the total amount of material that exists in the universe. They think there is a great deal of dark matter in and around the galaxies.
Dark matter may take the form of black holes, particles or small, very dim stars.

dark nebula ► nebula

data rate *noun*
The data rate is the rate at which information, or data, is sent from one place to another. Information from **spacecraft** and **satellites** is received by **ground stations** on the Earth as streams of signals that a computer can read, called bits.
The two Voyager spacecraft had a data rate of 115,200 bits per second as they flew past Jupiter.

day *noun*
A day is the **time** taken for the **Earth** to turn, or rotate, once on its **axis**. A solar day is the time taken for the Earth to rotate once with respect to the **Sun**. The length of the true solar day varies because the Earth's **orbit** around the Sun is not circular. The average length of the solar day during the year is 24 hours.
Most years are 365 days long.

decay *verb*
Decay describes the end of an **orbit** of an **artificial satellite**. It is a slow but steady decrease in height of the orbit. Decay happens to satellites in low Earth orbit. It is caused by the **atmosphere** dragging like a brake at the satellite. At last the satellite plunges into the lower layers of the atmosphere. It breaks into pieces which burn up in the atmosphere.
The orbit of the satellite decayed as it re-entered Earth's atmosphere.

Deep Space Network (DSN) *noun*
The Deep Space Network, or DSN, is a communications and tracking system. It is operated by **NASA** to keep non-stop contact with unmanned **spacecraft** travelling in the **solar system**. The DSN uses three widely-spaced **ground stations**, one in the United States of America, one in Australia and one in Spain. Each ground station has a large 70-metre diameter **dish aerial** and two smaller 34-metre dish aerials.
The Deep Space Network tracked the flights of the Voyager spacecraft.

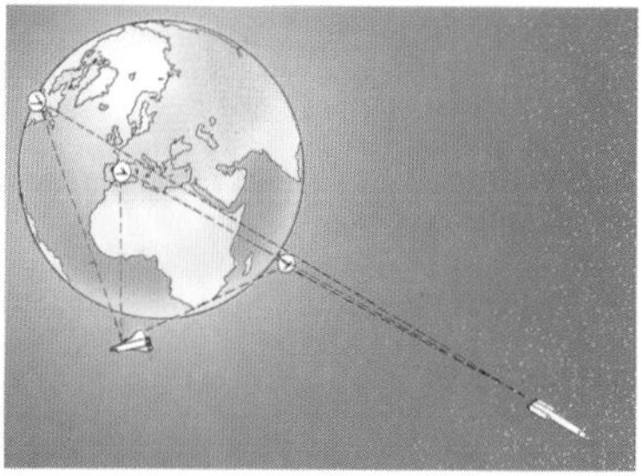

Deimos *noun*
Deimos is the smaller of the two tiny **moons** of **Mars**. Pictures taken by spacecraft show that Deimos is unevenly shaped. It is just 15 kilometres long by 10 kilometres wide. Deimos is rocky and cratered, and covered with a layer of loose rocks and dust.
Deimos orbits Mars once every 30.3 hours.

Delta *noun*
Delta is the name of a highly successful series of **rockets**. The rockets are built in the United States of America and launched by **NASA**. Delta B was first launched in 1962. The Delta is a middleweight launch vehicle. The latest rocket, Delta 2, can launch **payloads** of between 3.175 tonnes and 5.039 tonnes into Earth's **orbit**.
The Delta rocket was developed from the Thor rocket.

Demon star *noun*
The Demon star is a popular name for the whitish **star** Algol. It is the second brightest star in the **constellation** of Perseus, in the **northern hemisphere**. The Demon star is a **multiple star**, made up of at least three and probably four stars. It is also known as the 'Winking Demon'. Every 59 hours, it seems to wink slowly. This happens because its light is cut off when a darker companion passes in front of it.
The correct scientific name for the Demon star is Beta Persei.

Deneb *noun*
Deneb is the main **star** in the **constellation** of Cygnus, the Swan. It is one of the brightest stars in the sky, with a **magnitude** of 1.3. With the two stars Altair and Aquila, Deneb makes up a shape called the Summer Triangle. In 1975, a **nova** in Cygnus flared up and for two days shone more brightly than Deneb.
Deneb is a bright star that lies in the northern hemisphere.

density *noun*
Density is a measurement. It measures the **mass** of one cubic metre of a substance. Substances that are light for their size have a low density because their atoms are far apart. Substances that are heavy for their size have a high density because their atoms are packed more closely together.
The unit of density is kilograms per cubic metre.

de-orbit burn *noun*
A de-orbit burn describes the slowing down of a **spacecraft**. A rocket engine is used in a de-orbit burn. It slows down the spacecraft by reducing the speed, or **velocity**, of its **orbit**. In this way it can re-enter the Earth's atmosphere.
The scientists fired the rocket engines for a de-orbit burn.

descending node ► node

diamond ring effect *noun*
The diamond ring effect is a stage in a total **eclipse** of the **Sun**. It is seen for just a few seconds before and just after the complete covering of the Sun's face. The diamond ring effect takes place when a very small but brilliant part of the Sun shines out through a valley on the edge of the **Moon**. It looks like a flash of light from a diamond ring.
The scientist took photographs of the diamond ring effect.

Dione *noun*
Dione is a medium-sized **moon** of **Saturn**. It is very nearly round, or spherical, with a diameter of 1,120 kilometres. This makes it the fourth largest of Saturn's moons. Dione is made of ice, mixed with a little rock. There are many impact craters, craters made when **meteorites** crashed into the moon.
Voyager 1 flew by Dione and took pictures of the surface.

direct motion *noun*
Direct motion is the direction a **planet** moves in as it **orbits** the Sun. Scientists take a point above a planet's orbit to work out how it moves. All of the planets and asteroids have direct motion. Direct motion is also the apparent movement from west to east of the planets against the stars. It is the opposite of **retrograde motion**.
Direct motion describes the direction of planets orbiting their parent body.

disc *noun*
The disc of a **star** or **planet** is the circular-shaped face that can be seen by someone looking at it.
The Sun's face is a circular disc.

Discovery *noun*
Discovery is the name of a **space shuttle**. It was the third operational space shuttle orbiter. Discovery made its maiden flight in August 1984.
Discovery carried out the first rescue in space of two broken satellites.

dish aerial *noun*
A dish aerial, or dish antenna, is a radio antenna. It is saucer-shaped. A dish aerial collects and focuses radio signals on to a receiving antenna in the centre of the dish. The dish is usually mounted so that it can be steered to point in different directions. In this way it can track a moving object.
Dish aerials are used for communicating with satellites and spacecraft.

distances of the stars *plural noun*
The distances of the stars from the Earth are very great. The **Sun** is only 150 million kilometres from Earth. But the next nearest star is Proxima Centauri, in the **Alpha Centauri** system. It is 4.26 light years, or 40 million million kilometres from Earth. Distances of stars within about 300 light years of Earth are found by **parallax**.
The distances of some of the remote stars are very uncertain.

dock *verb*
Dock is the joining together of two or more **spacecraft** in **orbit**. Docking also means the sealing together of two manned spacecraft so that hatches or doors can be opened between them without losing **atmospheric pressure**. This allows crew members to move from one spacecraft to the other without putting on **spacesuits**.
Very accurate calculations must be made if two spacecraft are to dock successfully.

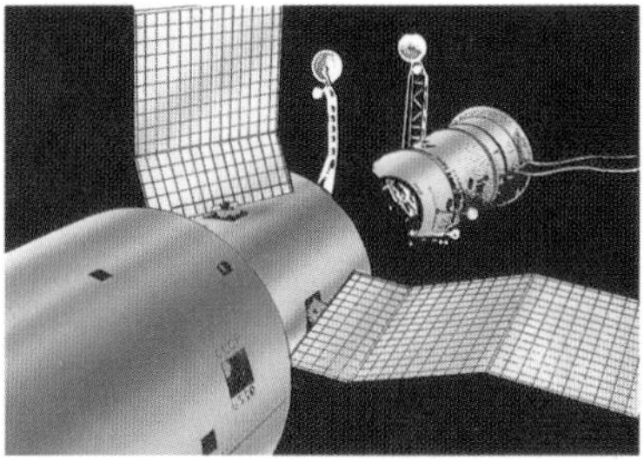

dome *noun*
A dome is a shape. It is a hemisphere, like half a hollow ball. A dome shape is used for the movable roof of an **observatory**. The dome protects the **telescope** and other equipment inside the observatory from bad weather and the heat of the Sun.
The scientists opened the dome so that the telescope pointed at the sky.

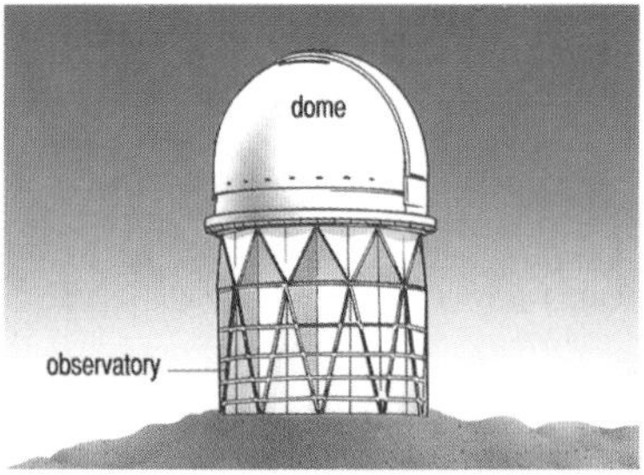

Doppler effect *noun*
The Doppler effect is the apparent change in the **wavelength** of sound **waves** or of **light**. It is caused by the movement of the source of the sound or light. It can also be caused by the movement of the observer. Visible light with long wavelengths is red, light with short wavelengths is blue. When a light source is approaching at high speed, the light waves are pushed together, and it appears too blue. This is called a blue shift. When a light source is going away rapidly, the light waves are stretched out, and it appears too red. This is called a red shift.
Scientists have discovered that the universe is expanding by using the Doppler effect.

Double Cluster *noun*
The Double Cluster is a fine pair of star **clusters**. The stars lie close together in the **constellation** of Perseus. The two clusters are of similar age, only about 10 million years old. The Double Cluster is about 8,000 light years from Earth.
The Double Cluster can be seen with the naked eye.

double star ► binary star

downlink *verb*
Downlink describes the process of **transmitting** information from a **spacecraft** or **communications satellite** to the ground.
The astronauts used the downlink to report on the experiment.

drag *noun*
Drag is the pulling force, or resistance, felt by a body moving quickly through the **atmosphere**. For example, air can act as a drag on an orbiting **spacecraft**. The effect of drag is steadily to lower the **orbit** of a spacecraft. Above a height of 240 kilometres, the **altitude** of the orbit decreases very slowly. Below about 150 kilometres, the orbit **decays** rapidly.
The astronauts felt the drag when their spacecraft re-entered Earth's atmosphere.

drogue parachute *noun*
A drogue parachute is a small parachute. It acts as a brake to slow down a descending space **capsule** or **spacecraft**. A drogue parachute can also be used to pull a larger parachute out of the space in which it has been packed.
Drogue parachutes were used to bring the Apollo command modules back to Earth.

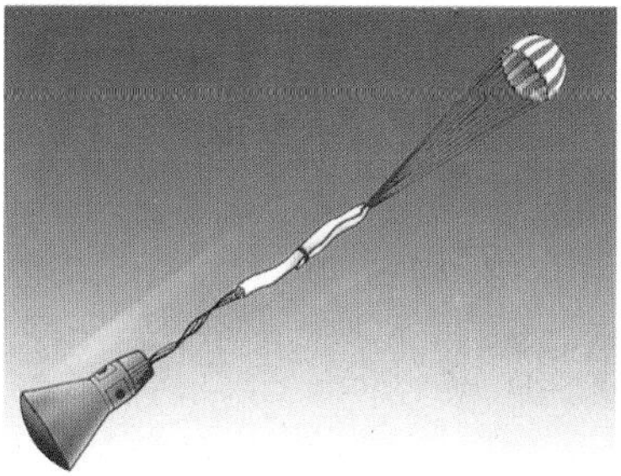

Dumb-bell nebula *noun*
The Dumb-bell nebula is a **nebula**. It is found in the **constellation** of Vulpecula, the Fox. The Dumb-bell nebula is shaped like an hour-glass. It is about one light year across.
The Dumb-bell nebula is about 700 light years from the Sun.

dust ► **cosmic dust**

dust tail *noun*
The dust tail is part of a **comet**. It is a broad, curving tail. The dust tail is made up of millions of tiny grains of dust that reflect and scatter the sunlight. The dust tail usually has a yellow colour. Dust **particles** are carried out from the comet's icy **nucleus** by escaping gases. They are blown away from the **Sun** by the tiny pressure of the sunlight. The dust tail of a comet may be between one million and ten million kilometres in length.
Some comets have more than one dust tail.

dwarf galaxy *noun*
A dwarf galaxy is a **galaxy** that is unusually faint. The faintness can be caused either because the dwarf galaxy is very small or because it is not very luminous, or both. The only dwarf galaxies which can be seen are quite near to Earth. The vast majority of dwarf galaxies are undetected.
Scientists do not know how many dwarf galaxies there are in the universe, or where they are all to be found.

dwarf nova *noun*
A dwarf nova is a type of **variable star**. A dwarf nova experiences sudden increases in brightness of between 6 and 250 times. This can be at intervals ranging from a few weeks to several months. The dwarf nova stays bright for a few days. Most dwarf novae are binary stars made up of a **white dwarf** and a cooler yellow or orange normal star. Gas flowing from the cooler star on to the white dwarf can cause hot spots to form. This can lead to outbursts of brightness from time to time.
The scientist studied the dwarf nova to find out how long it stayed bright.

dwarf star *noun*
A dwarf star is the most common type of **star** in our **Galaxy**. Dwarf stars are normal stars. The most massive blue dwarf stars have a surface **temperature** of 50,000 degrees kelvin and are a million times more luminous than our Sun. The least massive dwarf stars are the very dim red dwarfs, which have a surface temperature of just 2,500 degrees kelvin and are one-thousand times less luminous than the Sun.
The Sun is a typical yellow dwarf star.

Eagle nebula *noun*
The Eagle nebula is a **nebula** found in the **constellation** Serpens, the Serpent. The nebula includes a star **cluster**. These seem to be young stars, perhaps two million years old. The Eagle nebula is an **emission** nebula.
The Eagle nebula is 5,500 light years away from Earth.

Early Bird *noun*
Early Bird was a **satellite**. It was a communications satellite and was the first satellite launched by **Intelsat**. Early Bird was put into orbit over the Atlantic in 1965. It gave the United States of America and Europe a telephone and television link.
The Early Bird communications satellite lasted for four years.

Earth ► page 47

Earth Observing System (EOS) *noun*
The Earth Observing System is a project being developed in the United States of America. **NASA** plan to launch two **satellites**, perhaps in 1995. These will study the whole planet **Earth**. They will look at the **atmosphere**, oceans, regions of ice, and land.
The Earth Observing System will be the biggest plan for studying Earth that has ever existed.

Earth Resources Technology Satellite ► Landsat

eclipse ► page 48

Einstein Observatory *noun*
The Einstein Observatory was a **satellite** launched by the United States of America in 1978. The satellite used an **X-ray telescope** to study **background radiation**, and the gas that gave off X-rays which had been left over from **supernovae**. The Einstein Observatory proved that the **Sun** was a weak source of X-rays.
The Einstein Observatory was the first X-ray observatory that could find faint X-ray sources.

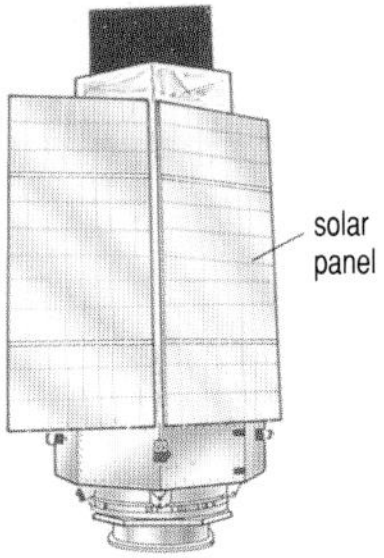

electromagnetic radiation ► page 50

electromagnetic waves ► electromagnetic radiation

electron *noun*
An electron is a particle. It is one of the parts of the atom. Electrons can also be found apart from atoms. Most electrical and magnetic activity is caused by electrons.
Electrons orbit the nucleus of an atom.

element *noun*
An element is a simple substance. It can be a solid, a liquid or a gas. The atoms in an element are all the same. Elements such as **hydrogen** can be found throughout the universe.
There are more than 90 elements which can be found naturally on Earth.

Earth *noun*
Earth is a planet in the **solar system**. It is the third nearest planet to the **Sun**. Seventy per cent of the surface of Earth is covered with water. The presence of water, and of oxygen in the atmosphere, allows life to flourish on Earth. The atmosphere also protects the Earth from harmful radiation from the Sun. The solid surface of the Earth is divided into a number of plates. Along the edges of the plates are regions where volcanoes and earthquakes happen. Earth has one **satellite**, called the **Moon**.
Scientists think that the core of the Earth is made up of iron and nickel.

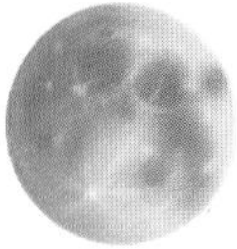

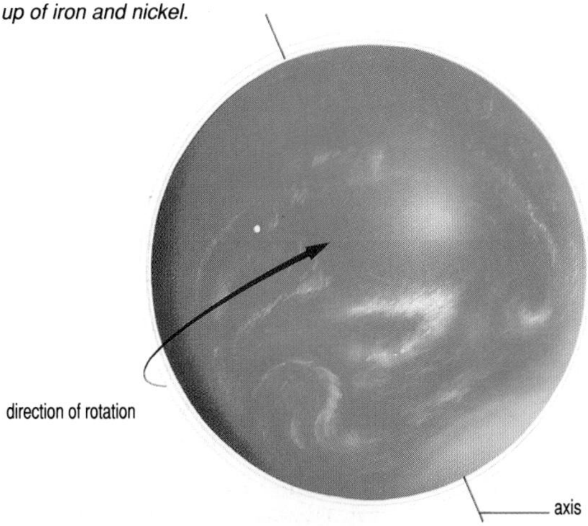

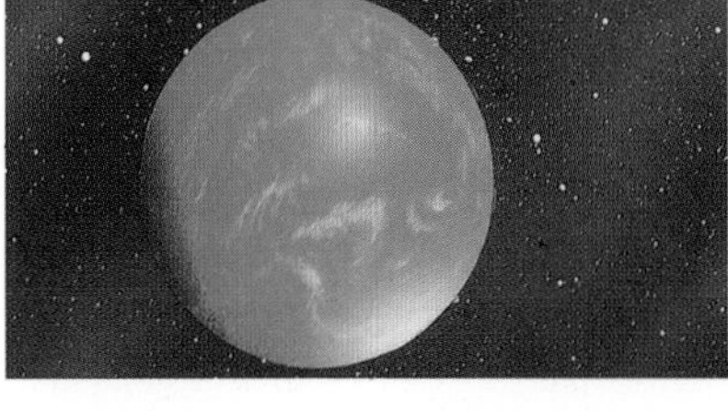

Planetary facts
Diameter: 12,756.32 kilometres at the Equator
Distance from Sun: 150,000,000 kilometres
Orbits the Sun in 365 days, 6 hours, 9 minutes, 9.5 seconds
Rotates on axis once in 23 hours, 56, minutes, 4 seconds
Atmosphere: yes, mostly nitrogen with about 20 per cent oxygen
Magnetic field: yes
Satellites: one, the Moon

eclipse *noun*
An eclipse takes place when the light from one body is cut off by the presence of another. The **Sun** is eclipsed when the **Moon** comes between it and the **Earth**. The Moon is eclipsed when it passes into the shadow cast by the Earth. An eclipse of the Sun can be total, or partial. A third kind of solar eclipse is annular. Eclipses of the Moon can be total, when the Moon passes completely into the shadow cast by the Earth, or partial, when only part of Earth's shadow falls on the Moon.
Eclipses of the Sun are much more common than eclipses of the Moon.

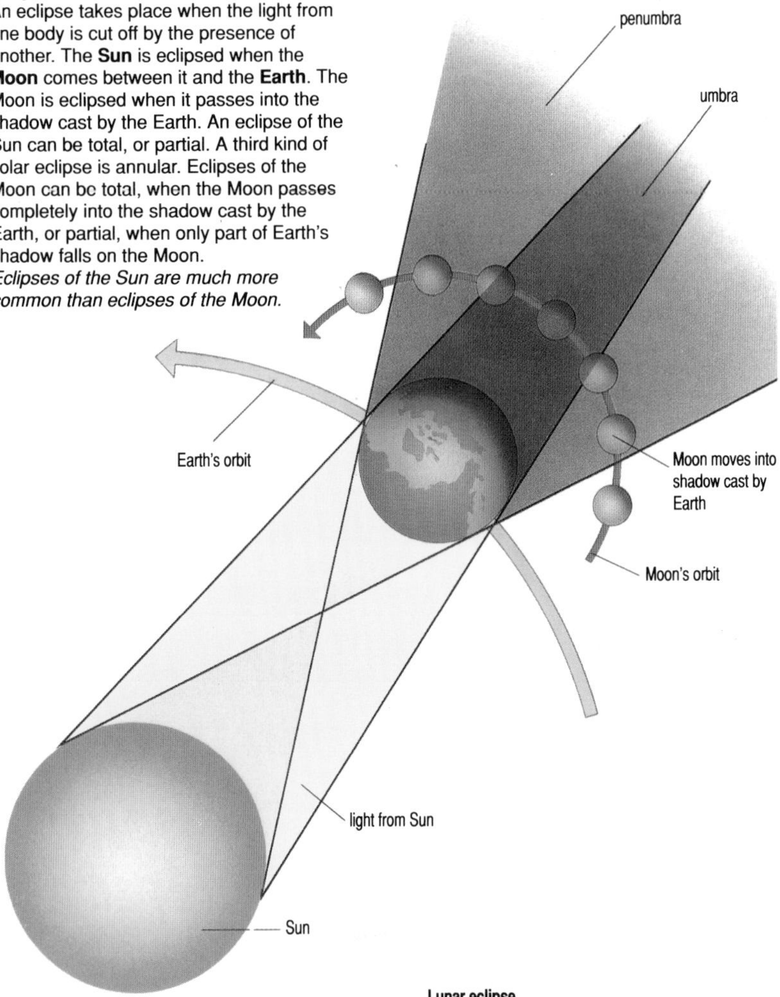

Lunar eclipse

Total eclipse of the Sun

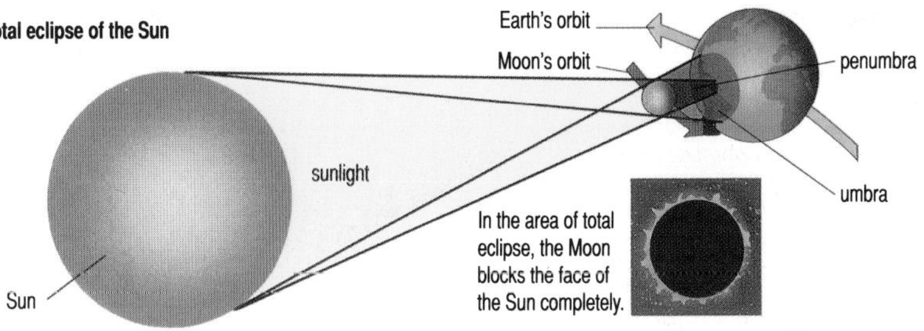

In the area of total eclipse, the Moon blocks the face of the Sun completely.

Annular eclipse of the Sun

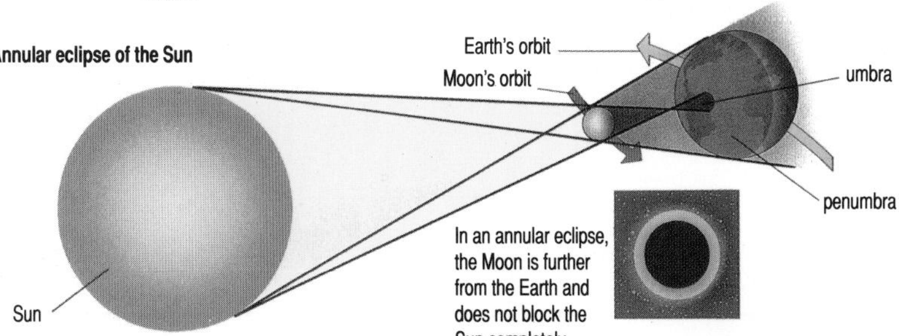

In an annular eclipse, the Moon is further from the Earth and does not block the Sun completely.

Partial eclipse of the Sun

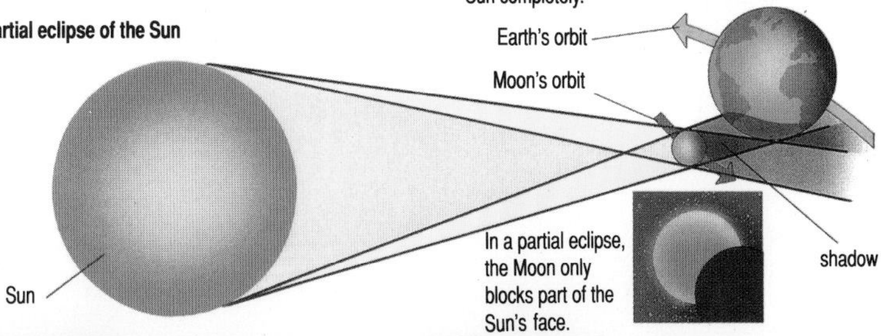

In a partial eclipse, the Moon only blocks part of the Sun's face.

The diamond ring effect is seen at the end of a total eclipse of the Sun.

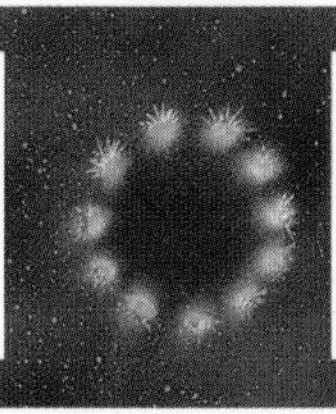

Baily's beads are seen at the beginning of a total eclipse of the Sun.

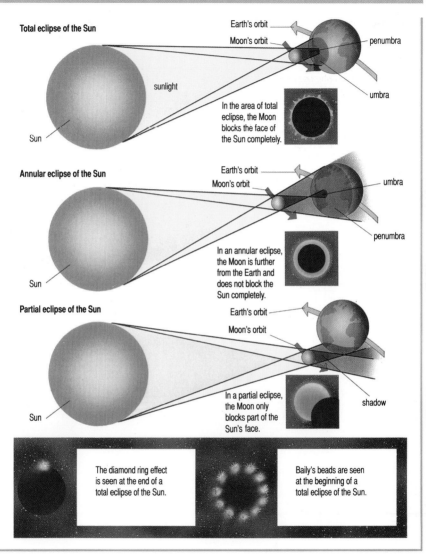

electromagnetic radiation *noun*
Electromagnetic radiation is a form of **energy**. It is found everywhere in the **universe**. Electromagnetic radiation moves in the form of **waves** which have different **wavelengths**. **Radio waves** have the longest wavelength. Other forms of electromagnetic radiation are **microwaves**, **infra-red**, **visible light**, **ultraviolet**, **X-rays**, and **gamma rays**, which have the shortest wavelength.
The electromagnetic spectrum is made up of all the kinds of electromagnetic radiation.

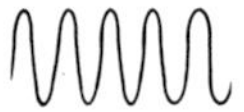
the shortest wavelengths are absorbed by Earth's atmosphere

visible light waves are a very small area of electromagnetic radiation

microwaves and radio waves have long wavelengths

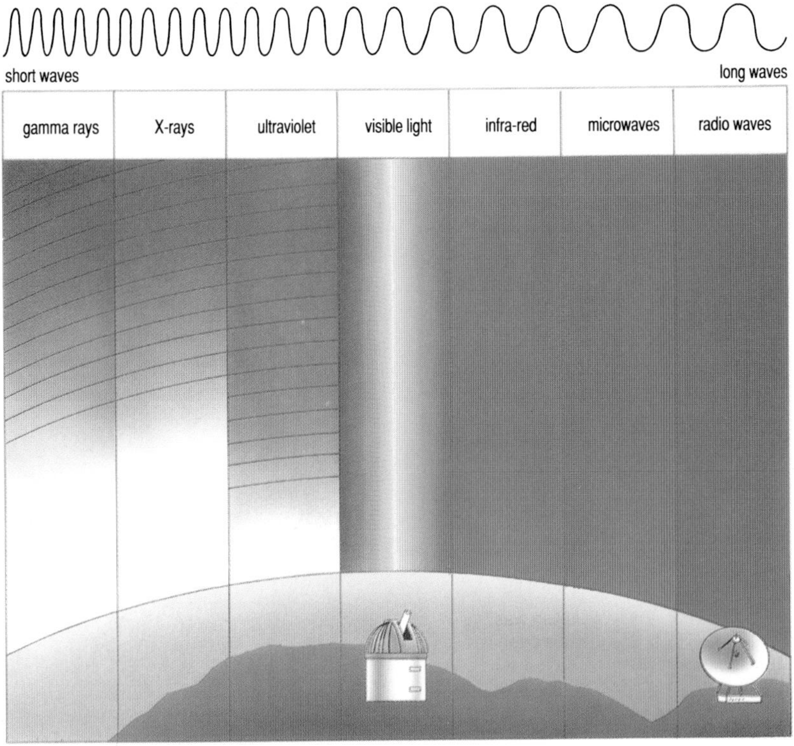

ellipse *noun*
An ellipse is an oval shape. Objects in **orbit** take elliptical paths.
Earth orbits the Sun in an ellipse.
elliptical *adjective*

elliptical galaxy *noun*
An elliptical galaxy is a **galaxy** that has the shape of an oval, or **ellipse**. Elliptical galaxies do not have a spiral form. Most elliptical galaxies are made up of old stars.
There are many red giant stars in elliptical galaxies.

emission *noun*
Emission means giving off, or giving out. A star that is emitting radio waves is giving out radio waves.
An emission nebula gives out energy.
emit *verb*

Enceladus *noun*
Enceladus is a **moon**. It is one of the 18 moons of **Saturn**. **Voyager** 2 flew by Enceladus, and found that it had a surface with few craters. It seems to be coated with ice. Some scientists think that **volcanoes** throwing out water might have caused this.
The surface of Enceladus is very bright.

Encke's comet *noun*
Encke's comet is a **short-period comet**. It **orbits** the **Sun** every 3.3 years. Encke's comet was first seen from Paris, France, in 1786.
The scientist did not have long to wait before she could see Encke's comet again.

Endeavour ► space shuttle

Energia *noun*
Energia is the name of a **rocket**. It was built by the Soviet Union. Energia has been used to put **satellites** of up to 100 tonnes into orbit. Energia has also been used to launch the Buran **space shuttle**.
Energia is about as powerful as the Saturn rocket that took men to the Moon.

energy *noun*
Energy is the ability to do work. There are many kinds of energy, including light, electricity, heat and nuclear energy. One kind of energy can be changed, or converted, to another.
Nuclear fusion makes enormous amounts of energy.
energetic *adjective*

equator *noun*
An equator is an imaginary line that is drawn round a globe, such as Earth. It can also be drawn round a sphere. The celestial equator divides the stars of the **northern hemisphere** from the stars of the **southern hemisphere**.
The star Achernar lies too far south of the celestial equator to be seen in Europe.
equatorial *adjective*

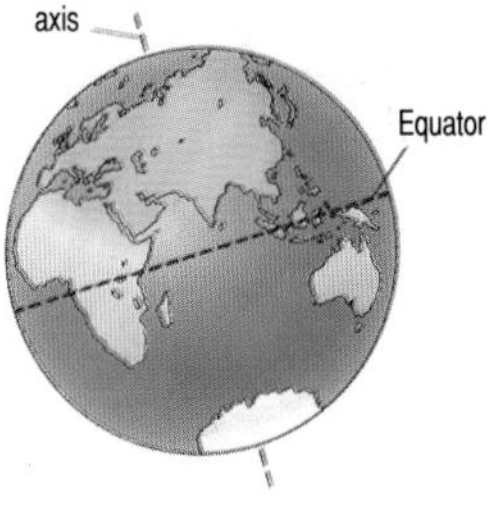

escape velocity *noun*
Escape velocity is the **velocity** needed to escape from the **gravitational** pull of a body. Escape velocity is important for scientists planning to put **spacecraft** into **orbit**, or to launch space probes. The **rockets** that lift the spacecraft must have a **thrust** powerful enough to leave Earth's **gravity**. A rocket must travel at 11.2 kilometres a second to reach the escape velocity of Earth.
The escape velocity of the Moon is much less than that of Earth.

Eta Carinae *noun*
Eta Carinae is a **star** in the **constellation** Carina, the Keel. It lies in the centre of the Eta Carinae **nebula**. About 100 years ago, the star became the second brightest star in the sky, but then it faded. Now it seems to be getting brighter again. Scientists think Eta Carinae might turn into a **supernova**.
Eta Carinae is about 100 times more massive than the Sun.

Europa *noun*
Europa is a **moon**. It is one of the four **Galilean satellites** of **Jupiter**. Jupiter has 16 moons altogether. Europa has a diameter of 3,112 kilometres. The **Voyager** probes have flown by Europa and found that it has a very smooth surface. The surface is covered with light and dark lines which scientists think were cracks in ice. The cracks may have filled with liquid, and frozen again. Europa probably has a rocky **core**.
Five craters have been found on Europa.

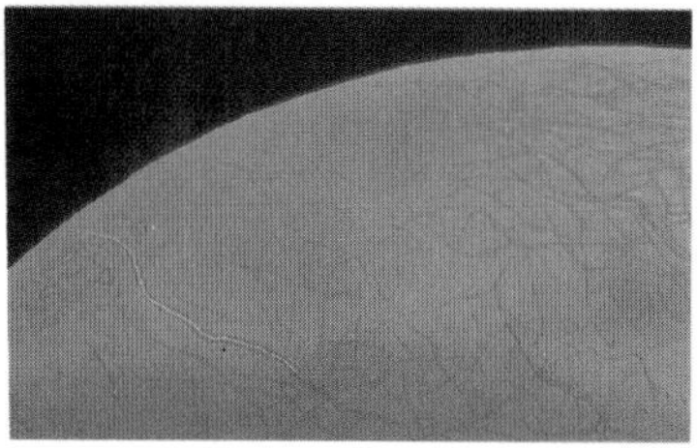

European Southern Observatory *noun*
The European Southern Observatory is an **observatory** set up by eight European countries. They wanted to explore the skies of the **southern hemisphere**. The European Southern Observatory is in Chile, at La Silla, 200 kilometres north of Santiago. The most powerful telescope at the observatory is a 3.6-metre **reflecting telescope**. There is also a 15-metre **radio telescope**.
The European Southern Observatory was built in a desert, where the air is clear.

European Space Agency (ESA) *noun*
The European Space Agency is an organization of 12 European countries. It designs and launches **satellites** for peaceful purposes. The ESA built **Spacelab**, and launched the space probe **Giotto** to study Halley's comet in 1986.
The European Space Agency uses the rocket Ariane as a launch vehicle.

European X-ray Observatory Satellite (EXOSAT) *noun*
The European X-ray Observatory Satellite was a **satellite** launched on 26 May 1983. It was designed to **orbit** Earth very slowly. EXOSAT took four days to complete one orbit. This gave the satellite long periods to study **X-ray** sources. During EXOSAT's life, scientists asked it to make 50 changes to its original programme. This allowed it to study new X-ray sources.
The European X-ray Observatory Satellite worked for three years.

Explorer *noun*
Explorer was the name given to four American **satellites**. Explorer 1 was launched in 1958. It weighed 14 kilograms, and orbited the Earth once every 114 minutes. Explorer 1 found the Van Allen belts of **radiation** around the Earth. Later Explorers continued the work of Explorer 1.
Explorer 1 orbited the Earth for more than 12 years.

extragalactic *adjective*
Extragalactic describes anything that is beyond the **Milky Way Galaxy**.
The Andromeda galaxy is extragalactic.

extraterrestrial *adjective*
Extraterrestrial describes anything that is beyond Earth. The word is also used to describe intelligent life anywhere in the universe.
The Search for Extra-Terrestrial Intelligence programme is interested in finding extraterrestrial life.

extra-vehicular activity (EVA) *noun*
Extra-vehicular activity describes walking in space. The first person to do this was a **cosmonaut** from the Soviet Union. He left his spacecraft, **Voskhod** 2, for 10 minutes. All extra-vehicular activity must be done wearing a **space suit**. The first astronauts and cosmonauts to leave their spacecraft were attached by lines to their vehicles. Recent shuttle astronauts have used a **manned manoeuvring unit**.
Extra-vehicular activity is needed for astronauts to repair their spacecraft.

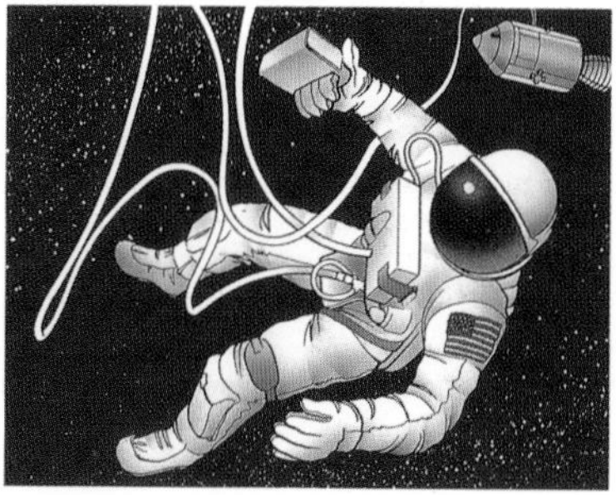

Extreme Ultraviolet Explorer (EUVE) *noun*
The Extreme Ultraviolet Explorer is a **mission** planned by **NASA**. It will gather information about all the sources of **ultraviolet** it can find near the **Sun**. The spacecraft will orbit the Sun and collect information in the shadow of the Earth.
The Extreme Ultraviolet Explorer would use four telescopes.

eyepiece *noun*
An eyepiece is part of a **telescope**. It is a **lens** or lenses at the point of the telescope where the observer looks in. The eyepiece magnifies and **focuses** the image.
In some telescopes, the eyepiece turns the image upside-down.

F

facula (plural **faculae**) *noun*
A facula is a bright spot on the face, or **photosphere**, of the **Sun**. It is a luminous cloud found just above the surface and is mostly made of **hydrogen**. Faculae usually appear in an area where a group of **sunspots** is about to form. They last about 15 days.
Faculae were discovered by Christoph Scheiner in 1611.

false-colour image *noun*
A false-colour image is a kind of picture. It is a picture in colours that would not usually be seen by the **naked eye**. Astronomers use false-colour images to bring out details in a picture that might not be seen in normal colour. False-colour images are also used to make pictures that the eye can see from information collected in **wavelengths** of **electromagnetic radiation**.
The surface of Venus has been mapped as false-colour images.

famous astronomers ► page 54

filter *noun*
A filter is a disc of coloured glass or plastic. It may be used with a **telescope** or a camera. Filters of coloured glass can be used to give better images when observing planets. Filters can be used to narrow the **wavelength** bands when studying **electromagnetic radiation**. This gives clearer information. Filters can also be used to remove **light pollution**.
She used a filter to help her get a good photograph of the planet.

famous astronomers *noun*
There are famous astronomers throughout history. They are people who have made important discoveries about the **universe**. Some famous astronomers, such as Ptolemy and Nicolaus Copernicus, have made their discoveries by observing the **stars** and other heavenly bodies. Others, such as Sir Isaac Newton, have had ideas which have changed the way people think about the universe. We do not know who made the earliest observations of the universe, because they were made so long ago that the names of the astronomers were not written down.
Many famous astronomers found that their discoveries frightened people, and they were not believed during their life.

Ptolemy, ?100-?165, was a Greek astronomer who lived in Alexandria, Egypt. He thought the Earth was the centre of the universe. Ptolemy worked out the movement of the planets and made a catalogue of 1,022 stars, grouped into 48 constellations.

Nicolaus Copernicus, 1473-1543, was a Polish astronomer who believed that the Sun was the centre of the universe and that the planets moved round the Sun.

Johannes Kepler, 1572-1630, was a German astronomer who proved that the Earth travelled round the Sun. He put forward three laws of planetary motion from which a scale model of the solar system could be made.

Tycho Brahe, 1546-1602, was a Danish astronomer who made very detailed and accurate observations of the stars and planets using only a giant quadrant. He discovered and described a supernova in 1572, and proved it was a star.

Galileo Galilei, 1564-1642, was an Italian scientist and astronomer. He was the first astronomer to use a telescope to observe the heavens. He made many important discoveries. He believed the Earth travelled round the Sun, was tried by the Church courts and made to deny his ideas publicly.

Sir Isaac Newton, 1642-1727, was an English scientist who discovered the laws of gravity. These govern the mutual attraction of all masses in the universe.

Albert Einstein, 1879-1955, was a German-born American scientist. He suggested that light might be a stream of tiny particles. He suggested links between space, time and movement in his theory of relativity. A third idea of Einstein's confirmed that matter was made up of atoms.

fireball *noun*
A fireball is a type of **meteor**. It is a very large, luminous meteor. Fireballs may have bright colours. When they fall, they may leave a trail in the sky. Fireballs may not burn up in the Earth's **atmosphere** completely. They can fall to the ground as **meteorites**. Fireballs can also be called bolides.
No one knows just when a fireball will appear.

first contact *noun*
First contact is one of the stages of an **eclipse**. In an eclipse of the **Moon**, first contact is the time when the Moon enters the full shadow, or **umbra**, cast by the Earth. In an eclipse of the **Sun**, first contact is the time when the Moon starts to move across the face, or **photosphere**, of the Sun.
The student timed the eclipse of the Sun from the moment of first contact.

first quarter *noun*
First quarter is one of the **phases of the Moon**. It is a time between new Moon and full Moon, when half the Moon's face can be seen. First quarter is seen when the Moon is **waxing**.
The sky was clear, so they could see the first quarter of the Moon.

Fishes ► Pisces

flare star *noun*
A flare star is a type of **dwarf star**. From time to time, a flare star becomes brighter. This increase in brightness may amount to more than a **magnitude**. Scientists cannot tell when a flare star will become bright. The brightness may only last a few minutes. Scientists think that the energy seen in a flare star may be the same as that in a solar flare.
Proxima Centauri, the star nearest to the Sun, is a flare star.

flight controller ► crew

flight deck *noun*
The flight deck is the part of a **spacecraft** from which it is controlled. The flight deck has seats for the **commander** and a pilot. Either astronaut can fly the spacecraft, as there are two sets of controls. As well as controls for flying, there are displays giving information about the **payload** and about all parts of the spacecraft.
The space shuttle flight deck has more than 2,000 separate controls and displays.

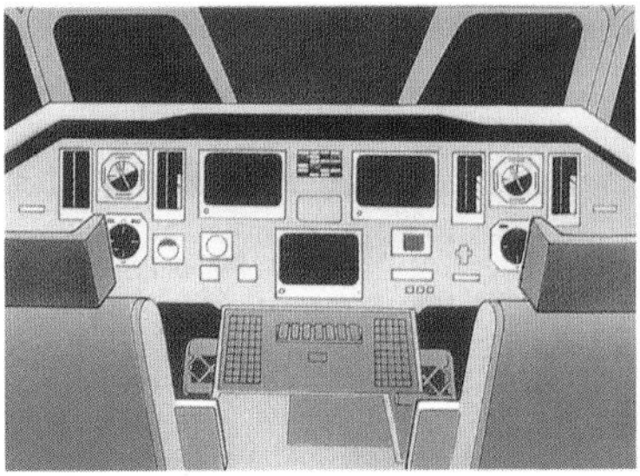

flyby *noun*
A flyby describes a kind of space **mission**. On a flyby, a spacecraft passes close to a target body. It does not land on it, or **orbit** it, or **dock** with it. It takes pictures and records information.
The Voyager spacecraft were on flyby missions to the outer planets.
fly by *verb*

flying saucer ► unidentified flying object

focus *verb*
Focus describes how to make a clear picture, or image. **Lenses** and mirrors in **telescopes** bend light waves so that all the light is collected in one place. This is where the image forms. To focus the image, the position of the lens is changed. This makes the picture sharp and clear.
She focused the telescope to get a clear picture of the Moon.

fourth contact *noun*
Fourth contact is one of the stages of an **eclipse**. In an eclipse of the **Moon**, fourth contact is the time when the Moon leaves the full shadow, or **umbra**, cast by the Earth. In an eclipse of the **Sun**, fourth contact is the time when the Moon moves clear of the **photosphere** of the Sun.
Fourth contact comes at the end of an eclipse.

Freedom *noun*
Freedom is a project for a **space station**. It will be built and run by the United States of America, Canada, Japan and the European Space Agency. Freedom will be built in sections, called **modules**. Each module will be big enough to take a **payload** from a **space shuttle**. The modules will be supplied with air, and energy will be supplied by four very large **solar panels**.
Freedom will orbit at an altitude of 450 kilometres.

free fall *noun*
Free fall is the correct term for **weightlessness**. A **spacecraft** orbiting Earth is still pulled by Earth's **gravity**. The forward movement of the spacecraft cancels out the effect of gravity, so the spacecraft and everything in it are falling endlessly around the Earth. Anything that is falling has no **weight**. Free fall describes this state.
Astronauts have to learn how to work in free fall.

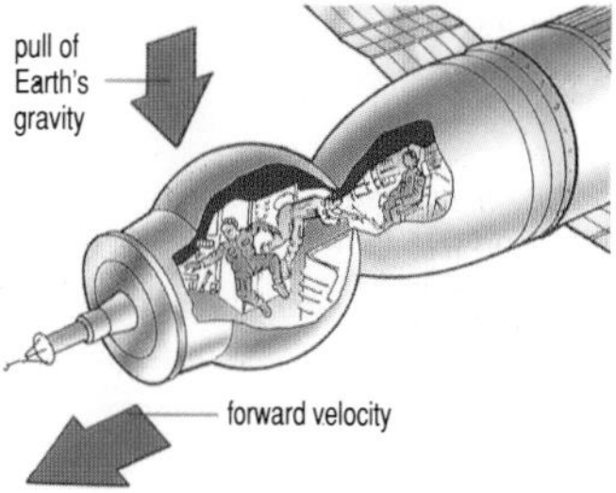

frequency *noun*
Frequency is a measurement. It measures the number of times something happens. **Electromagnetic waves** can be measured by frequency. The number of waves passing a fixed point in one second is measured to find the frequency.
Radio waves have a lower frequency than X-rays.

fuel *noun*
Fuel describes a substance that can be used to make heat **energy**. **Hydrogen** gives the **Sun** fuel for **nuclear fusion**. A **rocket** can use **gas**, liquid or solid fuels.
The first space shuttle used a liquid hydrogen fuel.

fuel cell *noun*
A fuel cell is a source of **energy**. It is a kind of battery. A fuel cell combines oxygen and hydrogen to make electricity. As it does so, the fuel cell also produces water. Fuel cells can be used in regions of space where there is not enough sunlight for **solar panels** to work.
Fuel cells are used to make energy in deep space where sunlight is very weak.

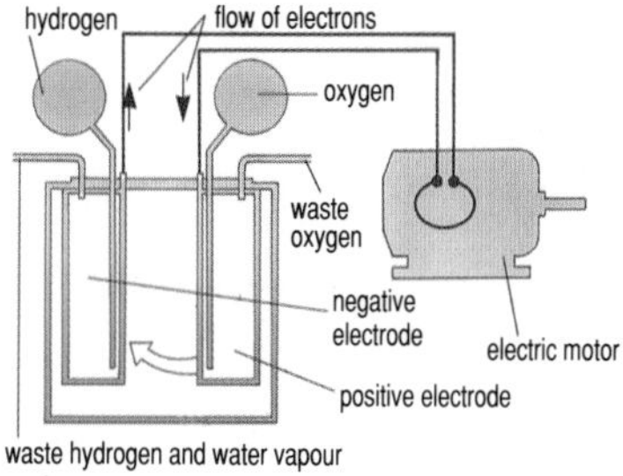

full Moon *noun*
Full Moon is a **phase of the Moon**. It is the time when the Sun's light is reflected from the whole of the Moon's face. There is a full Moon every 29 days.
She could see many craters on the Moon's surface at full Moon.

G

G-force *noun*
G-force describes an effect like a very heavy **gravitational** pull. G-forces are felt by **astronauts** during a **launch**. In early spacecraft, the G-forces measured 7G, or seven gravities. Astronauts could not move their arms and legs. They felt very heavy. Scientists have now reduced the G-force effect. Astronauts in the space shuttle feel a pull three times as great as normal gravity, or 3G. Their bodies are three times as heavy as on Earth.
G-forces last only while the launch rocket is accelerating.

Gagarin, Yuri ► manned space flight

galactic centre *noun*
The galactic centre describes the central region of the **Milky Way Galaxy**. Astronomers cannot see the centre because very large clouds of dust block it from sight. There is a strong source of radio waves coming from the centre of the Galaxy. This is called **Sagittarius A**. There are also many enormous gas clouds near the galactic centre.
Scientists think there is a black hole at the galactic centre.

galactic year *noun*
The galactic year is the time taken for the **Sun** to make a complete **orbit** around the **galactic centre**.
The galactic year is about 220 million years long.

galaxies ► page 60

Galaxy ► page 62

Galilean satellites *noun*
The Galilean satellites are four **moons**. They are the four largest moons of **Jupiter**. The Galilean satellites are called **Europa**, **Io**, **Callisto** and **Ganymede**. Europa is the smallest. It is a little smaller than the **Moon**. Ganymede is larger than **Mercury**. It is probably the largest satellite in the solar system.
The Italian astronomer, Galileo Galilei, discovered the Galilean satellites in 1610.

Galilean telescope *noun*
A Galilean telescope is a simple kind of **telescope**. It is made up of two **lenses**. The main lens, or **object glass**, is a convex lens, with a long focus. A single, concave lens forms the **eyepiece** of the telescope. The two lenses together make an upright picture, or **image**.
The first Galilean telescope was invented by the Italian astronomer, Galileo Galilei.

Galileo *noun*
Galileo is a **space probe**. It was launched by the United States of America in 1989. Galileo will study **Jupiter**, including its **rings** and **moons**. Part of the spacecraft will be released, to drop into Jupiter's **atmosphere** and take the first measurements from inside the clouds.
Galileo will reach Jupiter in 1995.

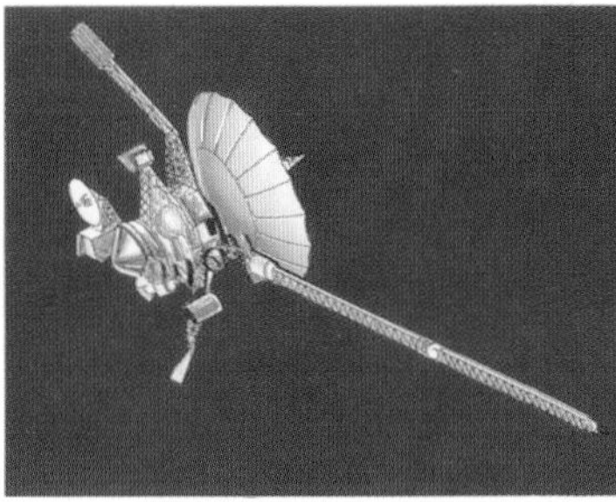

gamma radiation *noun*
Gamma radiation is a form of **electromagnetic radiation**. Gamma rays are very **energetic**. They have a high **frequency**, and are found at one end of the **electromagnetic spectrum**.
Gamma radiation has shorter wavelengths than X-rays.

Gamma-ray Observatory (GRO) *noun*
The Gamma-ray Observatory is a **satellite**, built jointly by the United States of America and Germany. It will study **radiation** from gamma-ray sources. It will also study **bursters**. The Gamma-ray Observatory was due to be launched by NASA in 1990, but has been delayed.
The Gamma-ray Observatory will be launched by the space shuttle.

Ganymede *noun*
Ganymede is a **moon**. It is one of the four **Galilean satellites** of **Jupiter**. Jupiter has 16 moons altogether. Ganymede has a diameter of about 5,300 kilometres. The two **Voyager** probes flew by Ganymede and found dark regions with many **craters**. They also found light regions which seem to be ice crusts. There could be water under these.
Ganymede is bigger than Mercury.

gas *noun*
Gas is a substance which spreads out to fill almost any space. It has a very low **density**. The **gravitational** pull of a large planet keeps the atoms of a gas from flying off into space. **Hydrogen** is the gas most often found in the **universe**. The **atmosphere** of a body such as Earth is made up of gases.
The air in Earth's atmosphere is a mixture of gases.

gaseous nebula *noun*
A gaseous nebula is a glowing cloud of **gas** found in **space**. It can be an **emission** nebula or a reflection nebula.
Any nebula can be described as a gaseous nebula.

Gemini *noun*
Gemini, the Twins, is one of the **constellations** of the **Zodiac**. The two brightest stars are the twins, Castor and Pollux. Both stars are of the first **magnitude**. Castor is a **multiple star**. Gemini is a constellation in the **northern hemisphere**. There is also a very bright **open cluster** of stars in Gemini.
The Milky Way passes through Gemini.

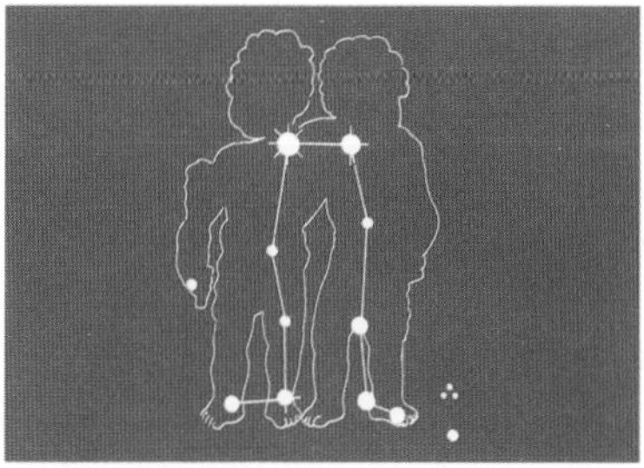

Gemini Project *noun*
The Gemini Project was part of the programme in the United States of America to send an **astronaut** to the **Moon**. Gemini was the name given to a series of **spacecraft** launched from 1964 to 1966. Each spacecraft carried two men. During the project, astronauts practised meeting and **docking** spacecraft, **extra-vehicular activity**, and using tools in space. The Gemini Project was very successful.
During the Gemini Project 10 two-man spacecraft were launched.

Geminids *noun*
The Geminids are a **meteor shower**. They can be seen from **Earth** in December. The shower is most active around 13 December. The Geminids are one of the best and brightest meteor showers. There is a maximum of 50 **meteors** an hour in the Geminid shower.
The Geminids appear to begin in the constellation Gemini.

galaxies *noun*

A galaxy is a very large group of **stars**. The stars are held together by **gravitational** pull. Small galaxies, such as dwarf galaxies, may only have about 100,000 stars in them. The largest galaxy known has about 3,000 billion stars in it. There are three types of galaxy — **elliptical**, **spiral** and **irregular**.

The Hubble classification arranges galaxies according to their shape.

Elliptical galaxies are oval-shaped and made up of old stars. They do not have arms.

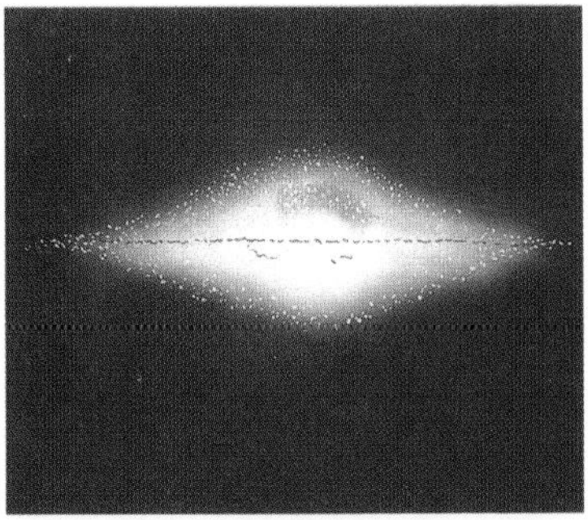

elliptical galaxy

Spiral galaxies are disc-shaped and include both old and young stars. Arms bending round in a spiral shape stretch out from a central mass.

barred spiral galaxy

The two types of spiral galaxy are the barred spiral galaxies and the normal spiral galaxies.

normal spiral galaxy

cluster of galaxies

The largest cluster of galaxies known lies in the constellation Virgo. The cluster contains up to 3,000 galaxies.

irregular galaxy

Irregular galaxies have no regular shape. A quarter of all known galaxies are irregular galaxies. They are full of young stars.

Edwin Powell Hubble's classification of galaxies

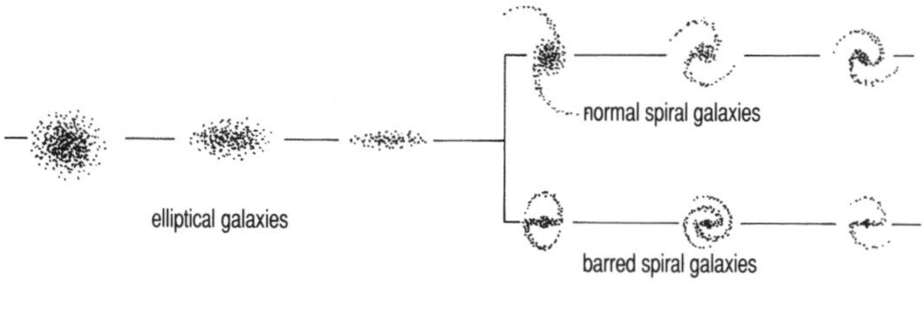

Galaxy *noun*

The Galaxy, with a capital G, is the way scientists refer to the galaxy to which the Sun belongs. This Galaxy can be seen at night as the **Milky Way**. It is a **spiral galaxy** and there may be about 200 billion stars in it. The Sun and the solar system lie about 28,000 light years from the galactic centre, on one of the spiral arms.

The Sun takes about 220 million years to orbit once around the centre of the Galaxy.

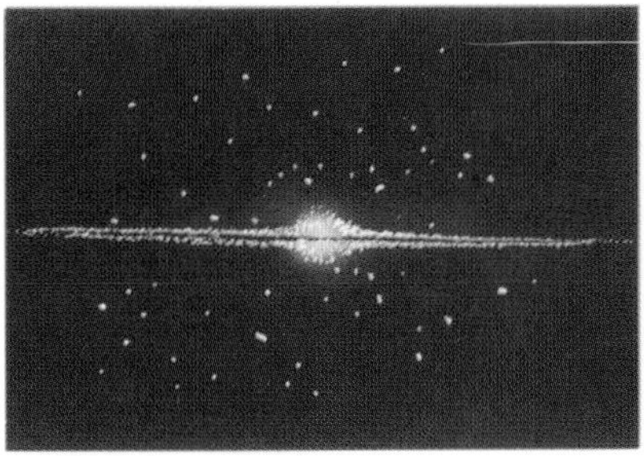

the Milky Way Galaxy from the side

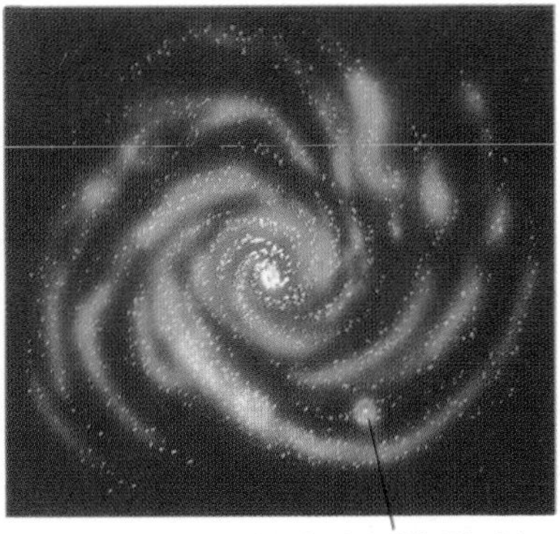

the position of the Sun in the Milky Way Galaxy

the Milky Way Galaxy as seen from Earth

geocentric theory ► Ptolemaic theory

Geostationary Operational Environmental Satellites (GOES) *noun*
The Geostationary Operational Environmental Satellites are a series of **weather satellites** launched by the United States of America. They are in **geosynchronous orbit** above the **Equator**. The satellites track weather systems on the west and east coasts of the United States.
Every half hour, the GEOS send a picture of the weather back to Earth.

geostationary orbit ► geosynchronous orbit

geostationary satellite *noun*
A geostationary satellite is a **satellite** in a geostationary, or **geosynchronous**, orbit. It appears not to move.
Weather satellites are usually geostationary satellites.

geosynchronous orbit *noun*
A geosynchronous orbit is an **orbit** in which a **satellite** appears to be stationary at a point over the surface of **Earth**. A satellite in geosynchronous orbit is orbiting the Earth at a height of 35,900 kilometres. The satellite turns about the Earth in exactly the same time that it takes the Earth to turn on its **axis**. A geosynchronous orbit can also be called a geostationary orbit.
The Intelsat communications satellites are in geosynchronous orbit.

Get-away Special *noun*
The Get-away Special is a programme run by **NASA**. It allows small **payloads** to be put on to **space shuttles**. Often the main payload on a shuttle does not take up all the room. Get-away Specials can be added. Schools, colleges, businesses and ordinary people can send Get-away Specials.
The Get-away Special programme makes people more knowledgeable about space.

giant planet *noun*
Giant planet describes the four **planets Jupiter**, **Saturn**, **Uranus** and **Neptune**. They are very much bigger than the small, rocky planets, such as **Pluto** and **Mars**.
The giant planet Jupiter has a diameter of 142,700 kilometres, compared with rocky Mercury's diameter of 4,878 kilometres.

gibbous *adjective*
Gibbous describes one of the **phases of the Moon**. It is the time between **half Moon** and **full Moon**. Gibbous Moons can be seen when the Moon is **waxing** and when it is **waning**.
A gibbous Moon seems to bulge.

Giotto *noun*
Giotto was a **space probe** launched by the **European Space Agency** in 1985. Giotto's **mission** was to meet **Halley's comet**. Giotto travelled closer to the **nucleus** of the comet than any other spacecraft. Giotto took many pictures of the comet, using a **charge-coupled device**. It also studied the chemicals that made up the comet.
Giotto is now in orbit round the Sun.

globular cluster *noun*
Globular clusters are groups of densely-packed **stars**. Globular clusters are usually sphere-shaped. They can contain millions of stars. There are about 100 globular clusters in the **Galaxy**. They contain some of the Galaxy's oldest stars.
Globular clusters form a halo round the outside of the Galaxy.

Goat ► Capricornus

gravitation *noun*
Gravitation is the pull, or attraction, that exists between all objects with **mass**. An object with strong gravitation, such as the **Earth**, will pull towards it an object with weaker gravitation, such as the **Moon**. Gravitation and its laws help us to understand how the **universe** works.
Newton's Laws of Gravitation and Einstein's Theory of Relativity both explain how gravitation works.
gravitational *adjective*

gravitational collapse *noun*
Gravitational collapse can happen at the end of the life of a massive **star**. The **temperature** at the **core** of the star falls. There is no longer any internal pressure pushing outwards. The outward pressure no longer balances the forces of **gravitation** which push inwards. The star collapses very suddenly. This releases huge amounts of **energy** and the star turns into a **supernova**.
Gravitational collapse is a step on the way to a supernova.

gravity *noun*
Gravity is the gravitational pull between **Earth** and a body on its surface, or within its field of gravity. The **weight** of a body is caused by gravity. Gravity also causes bodies to fall to Earth at a regular rate of **acceleration**. To stay in **orbit**, a satellite has to reach a **velocity** which is equal to the force of gravity.
Gravity caused the satellite to fall to Earth.

gravity assist *noun*
Gravity assist is used in the **orbit** of a **space probe**. The space probe is launched to pass near a **planet**. The gravity of that planet will pull on the space probe and speed it up. Gravity assist allows a space probe to use less fuel when changing course.
Voyager 2 used gravity assist to hop from planet to planet on its journey to Neptune.

Great Bear ► Ursa Major

Great Dark Spot *noun*
The Great Dark Spot is a dark patch on the **planet Neptune**. It was discovered by the **Voyager** 2 **space probe**, which flew by Neptune in 1989. Scientists think that the Great Dark Spot is a storm system in Neptune's atmosphere. They think it is like the **Great Red Spot** on Jupiter.
The Great Dark Spot is about 12,000 kilometres long.

Great Red Spot *noun*
The Great Red Spot is a large, red patch on the **planet Jupiter**. The spot seems to have been on Jupiter for at least 300 years. It turns round, or **rotates**, in an anti-clockwise direction, once every six days. Most scientists think that the Great Red Spot is the centre of a huge storm.
The Great Red Spot is about 40,200 kilometres long, and 32,000 kilometres wide.

Greek alphabet *noun*
The Greek alphabet is used by **astronomers**, mathematicians and scientists. It is used to name stars in a **constellation**. The brightest star is given the first letter, alpha. The second brightest star is given the second letter, beta. Using the Greek alphabet gives scientists an easy way to list stars.
The Greek alphabet was first used to name stars by Johann Bayer in 1603.

The Greek alphabet

alpha	α	iota	ι	rho	ρ
beta	β	kappa	κ	sigma	σ
gamma	γ	lambda	λ	tau	τ
delta	δ	mu	μ	upsilon	υ
epsilon	ε	nu	ν	phi	φ
zeta	ζ	xi	ξ	chi	χ
eta	η	omicron	ο	psi	ψ
theta	θ	pi	π	omega	ω

greenhouse effect *noun*
The greenhouse effect describes a state in which a **planet** becomes hotter because it cannot lose heat. If the **atmosphere** of a planet is full of carbon dioxide **gas**, it traps heat. Heat should be able to escape in the form of **infra-red radiation**. Venus suffers from the greenhouse effect because heat from the Sun is trapped by the dense atmosphere.
Scientists are afraid that the Earth may suffer from a greenhouse effect.

ground station *noun*
A ground station is a place on the **Earth** which **transmits** information to **spacecraft**, and receives information from spacecraft. Ground stations form a network with **mission control**. All over the world, ground stations track spacecraft using radio **antennae**. When the turning, or **rotation**, of the Earth carries a mission control out of direct touch with a spacecraft, there is always a ground station that can reach it.
Ground stations keep in touch with all the satellites that orbit Earth.

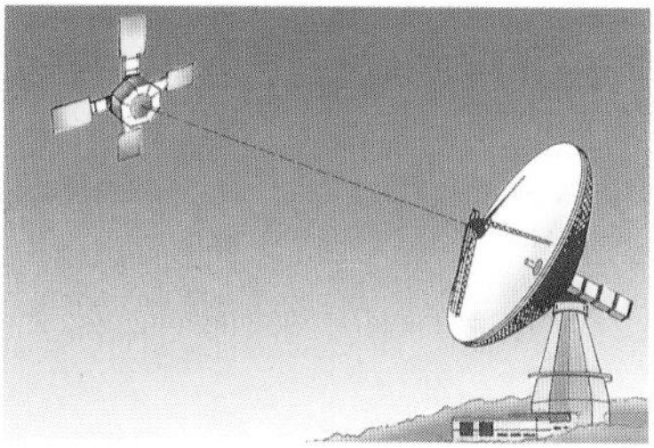

H

Hale Observatories *noun*
The Hale Observatories is the name now given to two **observatories** in the United States of America. Since 1970, the observatories at Mount Palomar and Mount Wilson in California have worked together as the Hale Observatories. They also run the Big Bear Solar Observatory, and the Las Campanas Observatory in Chile. The headquarters of the Hale Observatories is at Pasadena, California.
The Hale Observatories are amongst the most famous observatories in the world.

half Moon *noun*
Half Moon is one of the **phases of the Moon**. It is the time when the **Moon** is half-way between new and full. A half Moon can be seen when the Moon is **waxing** or **waning**. A half Moon can be a first quarter or a third quarter.
A half Moon can be seen once a fortnight.

Halley's comet *noun*
Halley's comet is the most famous of all **comets**. It is a **short-period comet**, which orbits the Sun once every 76 years or so. Halley's comet was last seen in 1986. Five **space probes**, two from the Soviet Union, two Japanese and one European, were launched to study the comet. **Giotto** passed within 605 kilometres of the **nucleus** of the comet. It found that the comet was made of ice and dust. The tail of dust can be several hundred million kilometres long.
Halley's comet is named after Sir Edmond Halley, who first worked out the expected time of its orbit.

heat-resistant tiles *noun*
Heat-resistant tiles are part of the **space shuttle**. They protect the shuttle from the fierce heat of **re-entry** to the **Earth's atmosphere**. There are about 27,000 tiles on the wings and body of the shuttle.
Heat-resistant tiles can withstand temperatures up to 978 degrees kelvin.

heat shield *noun*
A heat shield is a protection. It is designed to protect a **spacecraft** from the fierce heat of re-entering **Earth's atmosphere**. Early heat shields, such as the one on the **satellite** Vostock, were designed to burn away, or **ablate**, as the spacecraft came down. Later heat shields are made from materials that can stand up to great heat without damage.
Heat shields are coatings on the outside of spacecraft.

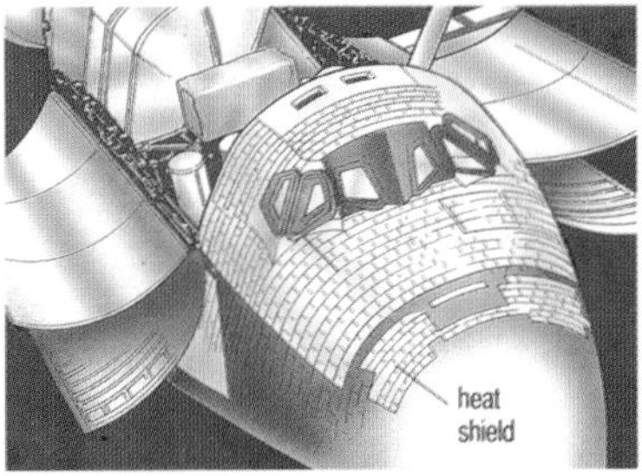

heliocentric theory ► Copernican theory

helium *noun*
Helium is a **gas**. Some scientists think that helium was formed from particles about three minutes after the **Big Bang**. They have worked out that the **universe** should be about 23 per cent helium. Helium is made from **hydrogen** in the **cores** of **stars**, such as the **Sun**. This happens by **thermonuclear reaction** at very high **temperatures**. The action of making helium releases huge amounts of **energy**.
Helium is an element.

hemisphere *noun*
A hemisphere is half a hollow ball, or sphere. Scientists imagine the sky as a sphere around the Earth. They divide it into two parts by the celestial **equator**.
Constellations and other bodies can be placed on the hemisphere in such a way that maps can be made of them.

Hermes space shuttle *noun*
Hermes is a plan for a **space shuttle**. It is being developed by the **European Space Agency**, led by France. It will be a small shuttle, launched using the **Ariane** rocket.
Hermes should be launched before the end of the century.

Hertzsprung-Russell diagram *noun*
The Hertzsprung-Russell diagram is a way of sorting and grouping **stars**. Stars are placed on a chart according to their colour and temperature, and their brightness. The Hertzsprung-Russell diagram shows that most stars fall into a band called the Main Sequence.
Almost all stars fall into clearly-marked groups on the Hertzsprung-Russell diagram.

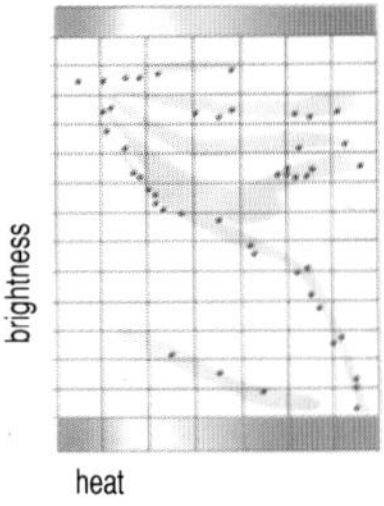

High Energy Astrophysical Observatory (HEAO) *noun*
The High Energy Astrophysical Observatory was three American **observatories** launched between 1977 and 1979. Two of the **satellites** were for X-ray astronomy, and one was for gamma-ray astronomy.
HEAO-2 was known as the Einstein Observatory.

Hipparchos *noun*
Hipparchos is a **satellite** built by the **European Space Agency**. It was designed to measure the positions of the **stars**. Hipparchos was launched in 1989. Scientists hope that it will find stars that are so far unknown. Hipparchos may also find **planets** orbiting other stars. Some scientists also think that the **Sun** may have a companion star, orbiting half-way between the Sun and Alpha Centauri. They call this star Nemesis. If Nemesis exists, Hipparchos should find it.
Information from Hipparchos will lead to a better star map of the region round the Sun than there has ever been.

hold *verb*
To hold means to stop something happening, maybe for a short time. Holding something is usually only done if there is a problem, or danger, that must be sorted out.
After the Challenger disaster, the space shuttle programme was held for two years.

horizon *noun*
The horizon is the furthest point that an observer can see in any direction. It appears as a distant, curved line where the Earth and sky meet. The horizon is usually at 90 degrees from the observer's **zenith**.
The astronomer could not see the stars that lay below his horizon.

Horizontal Take-Off and Landing (HOTOL) *noun*
Horizontal Take-Off and Landing describes a new **spacecraft**. HOTOL is being developed in Great Britain. It will be able to take off and land like a plane, but also be able to fly in space. HOTOL will have a new kind of engine. It will work like a jet in the atmosphere, and like a rocket in space. HOTOL has smaller wings than the **space shuttle**, but a longer body. HOTOL will be used at first to launch **satellites**.
Unlike the space shuttle, HOTOL is a single vehicle.

Horsehead nebula *noun*
The Horsehead nebula is a **nebula** in the **constellation** Orion. The horse's head is a dark nebula, made up of dust. It can be clearly seen against a background of glowing cloud that is part of an emission nebula.
The Horsehead nebula can easily be recognized by its shape, when seen in a photograph.

Hubble classification *noun*
The Hubble classification is a way of sorting and grouping **galaxies**. It uses the shape of the galaxy. The Hubble classification has three main groups of galaxies — elliptical galaxies, spiral galaxies and barred spiral galaxies. It is widely used, as it is a simple way of describing galaxies.
The Hubble classification was worked out by the American astronomer Edwin Hubble.

Hubble Space Telescope ► page 68

Huyghens space probe ► **Cassini spacecraft**

Hyades *noun*
The Hyades is a **star cluster**. It is an open cluster in the **constellation** Taurus, the Bull. Hyades is the nearest star cluster to Earth. It is 130 light years away.
The brightest stars in the Hyades cluster form a V-shape.

hydrogen *noun*
Hydrogen is a **gas**. It is the most common gas in the **universe**. Scientists think that hydrogen first started to form about one million years after the **Big Bang**. Clouds of hydrogen have been found all over the universe. Most **stars** are huge masses of burning hydrogen.
Hydrogen is an element.

Hubble Space Telescope *noun*
The Hubble Space Telescope is an orbiting **observatory**. It was built in the United States of America by **NASA** and the **European Space Agency**. The telescope was put into **orbit** in April 1990 from the **space shuttle**. It quickly became clear that there was a fault in one of the mirrors, and it would not **focus** sharply. Other instruments worked well, so some information could be got from the telescope.
The Hubble Space Telescope communicates through the Tracking and Data Relay Satellite System.

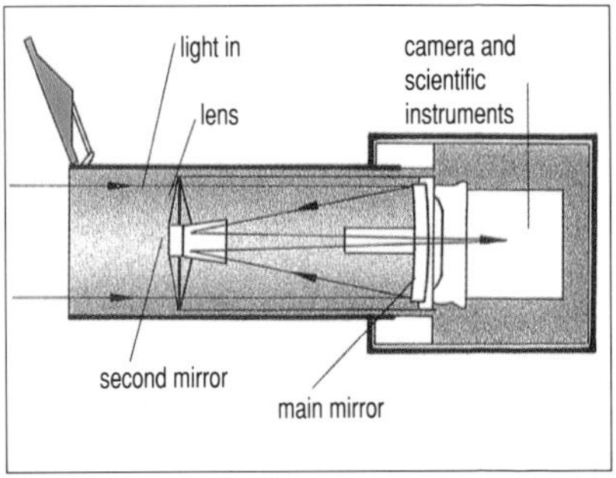

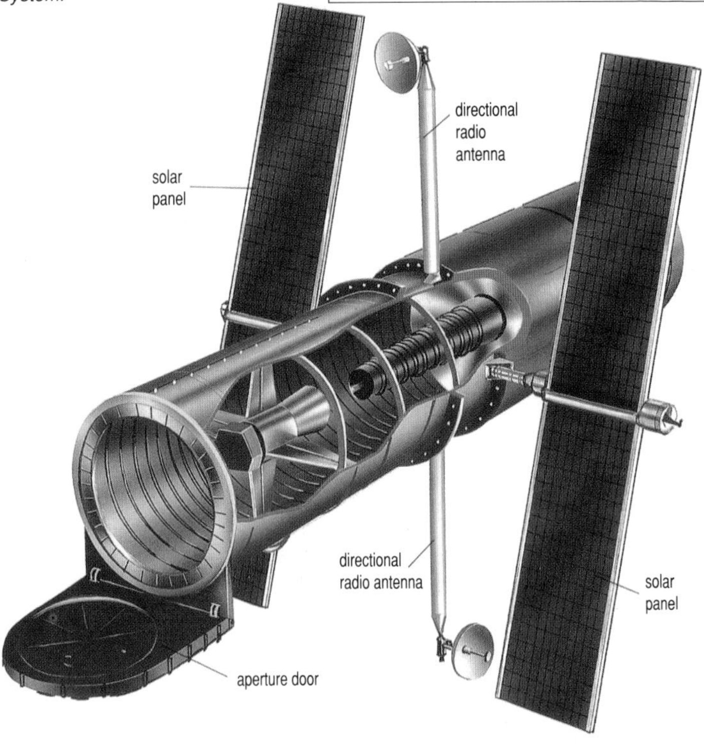

I

Iapetus *noun*
Iapetus is one of the 18 **moons** of **Saturn**. It is one of the furthest from the planet. The diameter of Iapetus is unknown.
Iapetus is more than two million miles from the centre of Saturn.

ignition *noun*
Ignition is the lighting of the **fuel** in a **rocket** motor. After ignition, the rocket blasts off.
The visitors saw smoke and flames pouring from the base of the rocket on ignition.

image *noun*
An image is a kind of picture. You see an image when you look in a mirror, through a **lens** or at a screen. It also describes the appearance of an object through the eyepiece of a **telescope** or a pair of binoculars.
Through the telescope, she saw a clear image of the planet Venus.

image intensifier *noun*
An image intensifier is a device which allows faint light signals in a **telescope** to be studied more closely. It contains an electronic tube which changes the signals into a bright picture on a screen.
The image intensifier made the faint light from a star show clearly on the screen.

inclination *noun*
An inclination is the angle between the **axis** of a planet and the plane of its orbit. It is measured in degrees.
The inclination of the Earth's axis with respect to its orbital plane is 66.5°.

inertial guidance *noun*
Inertial guidance is a method of keeping a **rocket** on course. It contains three gyroscopes which resist the forces trying to change the rocket's speed or direction. The gyroscopes send signals to a computer which works out any corrections of speed or direction that are necessary.
The rocket's inertial guidance system kept it on its planned course.

inferior planets ► inner planets

Infra-Red Astronomical Satellite (IRAS) *noun*
An Infra-Red Astronomical Satellite is an artificial **satellite** which was put into **orbit** beyond the Earth's atmosphere in 1983. It carried special **telescopes** which measured **infra-red radiation** from stars, planets and other objects in space. This radiation was photographed and sent back to Earth as television pictures.
The Infra-Red Astronomical Satellite showed the presence of many stars that were unknown before.

infra-red astronomy *noun*
Infra-red astronomy is the study of the heavens by the use of infra-red photography. **Infra-red radiation** produces 'heat pictures' of distant objects which cannot be seen by visible light.
Infra-red astronomy is carried out by special telescopes on Earth and on satellites in space.

infra-red radiation *noun*
Infra-red radiation is a term which describes a special kind of electromagnetic wave. The **wavelengths** of infra-red light are longer than those of visible light, and we cannot see them. Infra-red radiation can be recorded on film with a special camera.
Infra-red radiation is part of the electromagnetic spectrum, which also includes radio waves.

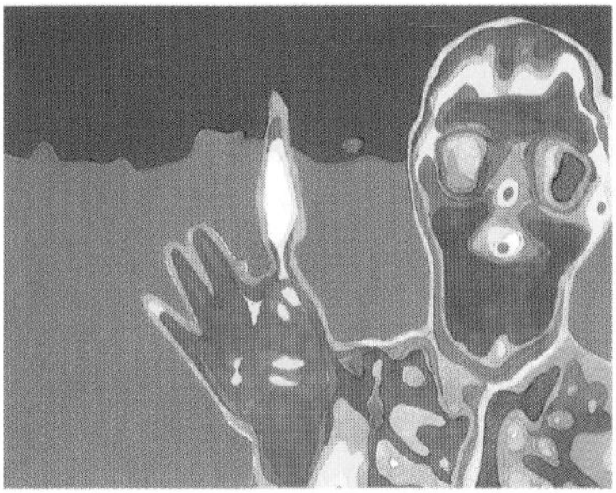

Infra-Red Space Observatory (ISO) *noun*
The Infra-Red Space Observatory is the name of a large **satellite** which has been designed to carry on the work of the Infra-Red Astronomical Satellite. It will pick up infra-red rays from distant objects in space and send them back to Earth. Scientists hope that the Infra-Red Space Observatory will help them make many new discoveries.
The Infra-Red Space Observatory should be launched in 1993.

infra-red telescope *noun*
An infra-red telescope is a special kind of **telescope**. It picks up **infra-red radiation** from objects in space. Infra-red light is light which you cannot see, but you can feel it as radiant heat.
A camera in the infra-red telescope recorded on film the heat from distant stars.

Inmarsat *noun*
Inmarsat is the name of a group of communications **satellites**. It allows ships and offshore drilling rigs to communicate by radio with each other and with radio stations on land.
The ship's captain sent a message by Inmarsat to say that his voyage was delayed.

inner planet noun
An inner planet is one of the four planets in the **solar system** that are closest to the Sun. The inner planets are **Mercury**, **Venus**, **Earth** and **Mars**. Mercury is the closest to the Sun of all the planets. Then come Venus, Earth and Mars.
Of the four inner planets, Mars is furthest from the Sun.

instrument *noun*
An instrument is a tool used to carry out an action. The word is usually used to describe tools made for scientific work, or for careful measurements. **Telescopes** are instruments that are very important for **astronomers**.
An antenna is an instrument used to receive radio waves.

Intelsat *noun*
Intelsat is the name of a series of communications **satellites**. The first was launched in 1965. Intelsat provides a world-wide system of telephone circuits and television channels.
News film can be flashed from one side of the world to the other by Intelsat.

interferometer *noun*
An interferometer is a group of **optical** or **radio telescopes**. They are arranged in a pattern which is called an array. An interferometer produces sharper, clearer images than a single large telescope and can be used to measure distances between objects in space.
An interferometer is a special kind of observatory.

International Astronomical Union (IAU) *noun*
The International Astronomical Union is an organization of **astronomers** from all over the world. It issues reports of new discoveries and gives early warning of **comets** and other astronomical events.
Anyone can be a member of the IAU and receive its circulars full of astronomical news.

International Ultraviolet Explorer (IUE) *noun*
The International Ultraviolet Explorer is a **satellite**. It was launched in 1978 to study **ultraviolet radiation** from the Sun. It carries a 45-centimetre **reflecting telescope**. Its equipment studies the ultraviolet radiation and sends the results back to Earth.
The International Ultraviolet Explorer was part of a joint European and American project.

interstellar matter *noun*
Interstellar matter is a term which describes gas and dust between the stars of a **galaxy**. This gas and dust sometimes forms into clusters which are called **nebulae**.
Interstellar matter prevents astronomers from seeing some objects clearly.

Io *noun*
Io is the name of one of the 16 moons of the planet **Jupiter**. It is one of the **Galilean satellites**. Io is the second closest moon to the planet. It is about the same size as the Earth's Moon.
Through a telescope, Io's surface seems to be covered with light and dark patches.

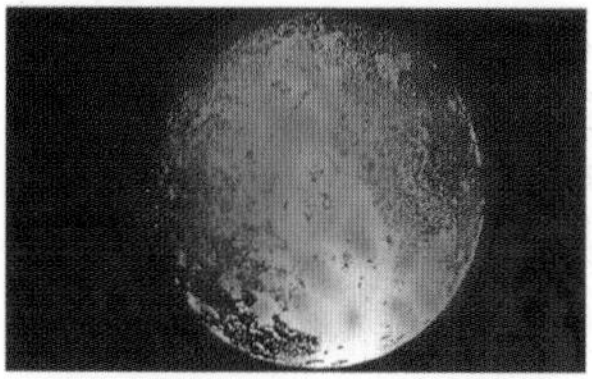

ion *noun*
An ion is usually an atom that has lost one or more of its **electrons**. It has a positive electric charge. An atom which has gained an electron becomes an ion with a negative charge.
Atoms can become ions when they collide with other atoms.

ionization *noun*
Ionization describes what happens when an ion loses or gains electrons.
The presence of radioactivity is one cause of ionization.
ionize *verb*

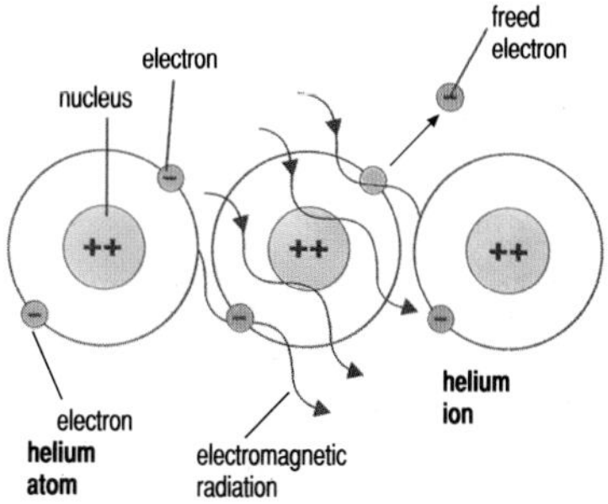

ionosphere *noun*
The ionosphere is a layer of ions in the **atmosphere**. It is between 80 and 640 kilometres above the surface of the Earth. The electric charges in the ionosphere send back, or reflect, **radio waves** to Earth. The charges change from day to night and are affected by sunspots.
The ionosphere is caused by ultraviolet radiation and X-rays from the Sun.

irregular galaxy *noun*
An irregular galaxy is the kind of **galaxy** that forms a shapeless mass. Other galaxies are in the shape of spirals or ellipses.
Like other galaxies, irregular galaxies are collections of stars, gas and dust.

Jupiter *noun*
Jupiter is a planet in the **solar system**. It is the largest of the planets, 11 times the size of **Earth**. It is the fifth planet from the **Sun**. Jupiter is a giant ball of gas and liquid hydrogen. The planet rotates quickly. This causes the gas and liquid to flatten out at the poles, and bulge at the equator. **Pioneers** 10 and 11 and **Voyagers** 1 and 2 have flown past Jupiter. Jupiter has a magnetic field 4,000 times as strong as Earth's. From it, scientists have picked up radio waves. There is no life on Jupiter.
Jupiter may have a very small core of rock.

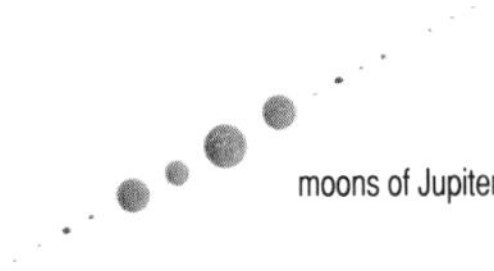

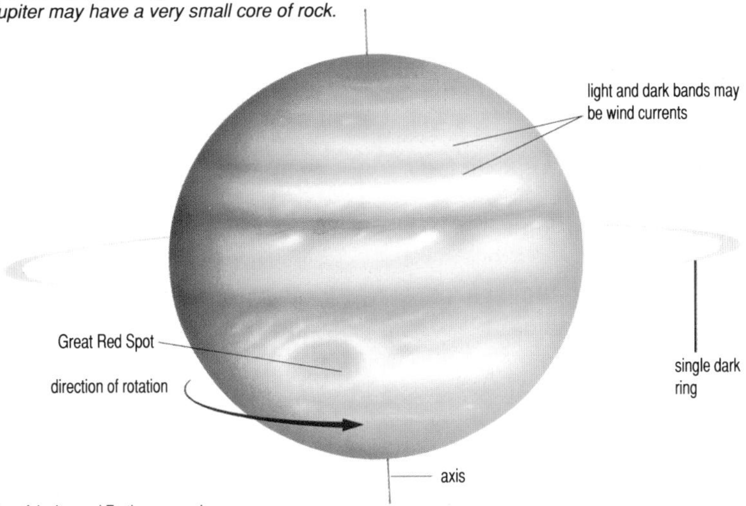

size of Jupiter and Earth compared

Planetary facts
Diameter: 142,700 kilometres
Distance from Sun: 778,400,000 kilometres
Nearest distance to Earth: 628,760,000 kilometres
Orbits the Sun in 12 earth years
Rotates on axis once in 9 hours, 55 minutes
Temperature at cloud tops: –130 degrees Celsius
Atmosphere: yes, a thick atmosphere of hydrogen and helium
Magnetic field: yes, a very strong one
Satellites: 16, including Io, Callisto, Europa and Ganymede

J

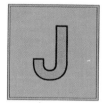

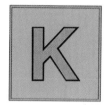

jettison *verb*
Jettison describes the throwing or falling away of objects that are no longer needed. In a space launch, the **rockets** which carry out the launch are jettisoned when they have done their work. They burn up as they fall through the **atmosphere**.
The space control centre made the spacecraft jettison its third stage rocket.

Jewel Box *noun*
The Jewel Box is the name of a cluster of stars which are part of the **constellation** called the Southern Cross. It is invisible from the northern hemisphere. The brightest star in the Jewel Box is a blue **supergiant** called Kappa Crucis.
The distance of the Jewel Box from Earth is 7,800 light years.

Jodrell Bank Observatory *noun*
Jodrell Bank Observatory is a radio astronomy **observatory** near Manchester, in England. Its large dish **antenna** collects **radio signals** from objects in space.
Jodrell Bank Observatory was opened in 1957 and picked up signals from the first Soviet satellite, Sputnik 1.

Juno *noun*
Juno is the name of a bright **asteroid** which is in **orbit** round the Sun. It is about 240 kilometres in diameter. Juno was first discovered in 1804.
Juno's orbit passes between the orbits of Mars and Jupiter.

Jupiter ► page 72

K

kelvin scale *noun*
The kelvin scale is a scale for the measurement of **temperature**. The kelvin scale starts from absolute zero, which is the same as –273.16 degrees Celsius.
One degree kelvin is the same as one degree Celsius.

Kennedy Space Centre *noun*
The Kennedy Space Centre is a part of the **Cape Canaveral** rocket launching site in the United States of America. Cape Canaveral is the main base for United States space exploration. **Space shuttles** take off from, and land at, the Kennedy Space Centre **launch pads**.
The Kennedy Space Centre has a special runway where returning space shuttles land.

Kepler's laws *plural noun*
Kepler's laws are a set of rules about the way **planets** move. They were laid down by the German **astronomer** Johannes Kepler between 1609 and 1618. Kepler proved that the planets revolve round the Sun in egg-shaped, or elliptical, **orbits**.
Kepler's laws were based on many years of study of the movements of the planets.

Kitt Peak National Observatory *noun*
The Kitt Peak National Observatory is an **observatory** near Tucson in the United States of America. It is built at the top of the 2,000-metre high Kitt Peak. It was founded in 1958 by a group of American universities.
Kitt Peak National Observatory has the largest collection of optical telescopes.

L

Lagoon nebula *noun*
The Lagoon nebula is a mass of **gas** and **dust** in outer space. Astronomers give it the name M8. The Lagoon nebula is 4,850 **light years** from Earth.
The Lagoon nebula can easily be seen with a good telescope or pair of binoculars.

Landsat *noun*
Landsat is the name of a series of **satellites**. They are used to make accurate maps of the Earth's surface and to study resources such as minerals. Landsat can take photographs of both **visible light** and invisible, **infra-red** light.
Pictures from Landsat satellites can show where vegetation is diseased or dying.

last quarter *noun*
The last quarter is a term which describes a **phase of the Moon**. At the start of the last quarter, there is a half Moon. Over a period of just over seven days, this shrinks to nothing and a new Moon starts, followed by first quarter.
Only half of the Moon's surface can be seen when it is in its last quarter.

latitude *noun*
Latitude is an imaginary line around the Earth, parallel to the **Equator**. It is used to measure distance from the Equator in units called **degrees**. Lines of latitude run east and west above and below the Equator.
Lines of latitude are used by sailors to help them work out their position.

launch ► page 76

launch pad *noun*
A launch pad is the place from which **satellites** and **spacecraft** lift off. Fuelling and final checks to the equipment are carried out on the launch pad.
The space shuttle lifted off from the launch pad on its journey into space.

launch vehicle *noun*
A launch vehicle is the **rocket** which sends a **satellite** or **spacecraft** into space. Once the craft is safely launched, the launch vehicle drops away, or is **jettisoned**.
Some launch vehicles are fitted with parachutes so that they can be used again.

lens *noun*
A lens is a piece of clear glass or plastic with curved sides. Lenses can be concave or convex. They are used in **telescopes**, cameras, binoculars and other optical instruments. A lens concentrates or bends rays of light so that they produce a clear **image** which can be seen through an eyepiece or photographed.
Large astronomical telescopes contain both lenses and mirrors.

Leo *noun*
Leo, or the Lion, is one of the **constellations** of the **Zodiac**. It lies close to the Great Bear, or **Ursa Major**. Its brightest star is called Regulus.
Leo can be seen north of the celestial equator.

Leonids *plural noun*
Leonids is the name astronomers give to a shower of bright **meteors** or 'shooting stars'. The shower takes place every year, but can be seen clearly only every 33 years. The Leonids appear in the **constellation Leo**. The Leonid shower can be seen around 17 November. There are up to 10 meteors in an hour.
The next shower of Leonids will be seen in 1999.

Libra *noun*
Libra, or the Scales, is one of the **constellations** of the **Zodiac**. It is a group of four **stars** which make a shape called a quadrilateral. Libra lies south of the celestial equator, in the **southern hemisphere**. It is one of the constellations of the Zodiac that is the most difficult to see.
The name Libra comes from the Latin word for scales.

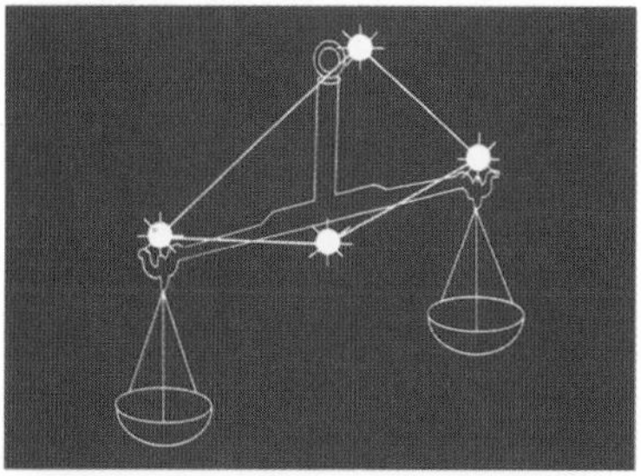

libration *noun*
A libration is an apparent movement of the **Moon**. Librations allow us to see more than 50 per cent of the Moon's surface. The area of the Moon's surface facing the Earth is not always exactly the same. Because of the Moon's librations, 59 per cent of its surface can be studied altogether over a period of time, but never more than 50 per cent at any one time.
Librations make the Moon appear to turn slightly if it is observed over a long period.

life support system *noun*
Life support system is a term which describes the resources which **astronauts** have to take into space with them. A life support system includes oxygen, food and water, as well as equipment to check on the astronauts' health.
Life support systems are necessary because there are no resources in space.

lift-off *noun*
Lift-off is the moment when a space vehicle leaves the surface of the Earth. Lift-off takes place when the rocket fuel has been ignited and the clamps which hold the vehicle in place are released.
Huge amounts of energy are used to achieve lift-off.

light *noun*
Light is a form of **energy**. Light waves are part of the **electromagnetic spectrum**. In the night sky, light comes directly from the **stars** and is reflected by the **Moon** and **planets**.
Light from the Sun is the source of all life on Earth.

light pollution *noun*
Light pollution is the name **astronomers** give to the light that interferes with their studies of the night sky. It is the light that is thrown up into the sky by street lamps and brightly-lit buildings in towns and cities. To avoid light pollution, observatories are built in places such as in deserts and on mountain tops.
Light pollution around the Earth can be seen by astronauts in space.

light year *noun*
A light year is a way of measuring the distance from the **Earth** of objects in space. It is the distance that light can travel in one year. This is about 9.46 million million kilometres.
The bright star Sirius is 8.6 light years away from the Earth.

launch *noun*
A launch describes the actions that allow a **spacecraft** to leave the Earth. Spacecraft are launched by **rockets** or **launch vehicles** that lift them off the Earth and carry them to the correct **orbit** in space. When the rocket engines are fired, a huge **thrust** lifts the launch vehicle upwards.
Lift-off is the moment during a launch when the rocket leaves the ground.

crawler with mobile launch pad

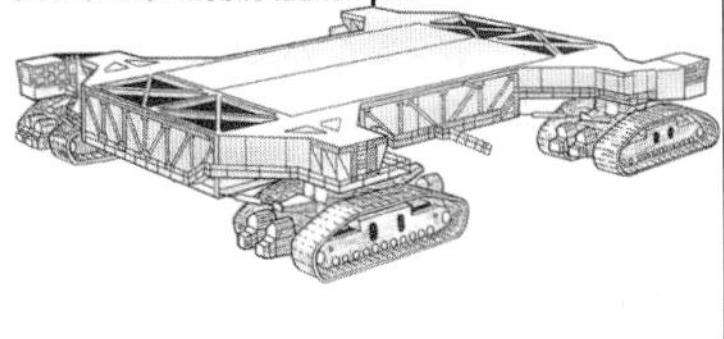

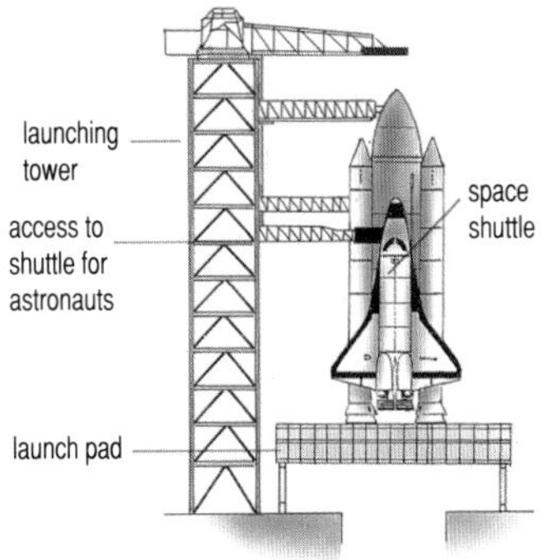

spaceport

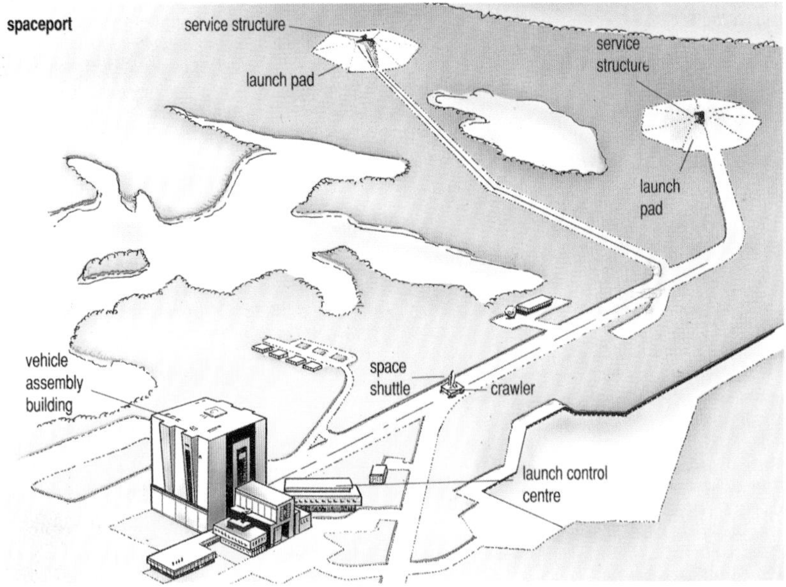

the shuttle is launched

limb *noun*
Limb is a word which describes the edge of the Sun, Moon or a planet.
A new Moon shows only part of its limb to people watching from Earth.

Lion ► Leo

liquid fuel *noun*
Liquid fuel is the kind of fuel that is used in **rockets** for **spacecraft**. It is usually **oxygen** or **hydrogen**. These are normally gases, but they are turned into liquid when they are placed under pressure.
Liquid fuel is used in rockets because it is easier than gas to pump and control.

Little Bear ► Ursa Minor

Little Dipper ► Ursa Minor

Local Group *noun*
The Local Group is a group of **galaxies**. Earth's **Galaxy** is a member of the Local Group. The Local Group contains about 25 galaxies, within a radius of about 2.4 million **light years**.
The Local Group of galaxies includes the Andromeda galaxy and the Milky Way.

longitude *noun*
Longitude is an imaginary line around the **Earth**. Lines of longitude run north and south. They start at the North Pole and finish at the South Pole.
By measuring latitude and longitude, any position on Earth can be found.

long-period comet *noun*
A long-period comet is a **comet** which is visible from the Earth regularly but at very long intervals. Comet Bennett is a long-period comet which is thought to appear only every 1,680 years. Its last appearance was in the year 1970.
Comet Bradfield is a long-period comet which can be seen from Earth only every 29,000 years.

long-period variable star *noun*
A long-period variable star is a **star** which varies in brightness over a period of time up to 400 days. Many long-period variable stars are very old.
The star Mira is a long-period variable star which is sometimes as bright as the Pole Star.

luminosity *noun*
Luminosity is a word which means the brightness of light shining from an object in space. Luminosity is measured in units called watts.
The luminosity of variable stars changes from time to time.
luminous *adjective*

Luna probes *plural noun*
Luna probes were a series of unmanned visits by **spacecraft** to the **Moon**. They were launched from the Soviet Union. Luna 1 was launched in 1959. In the same year, Luna 3 sent back the first pictures of the side of the Moon that is not visible from Earth.
Luna 2 was the first object from Earth to land on the Moon.

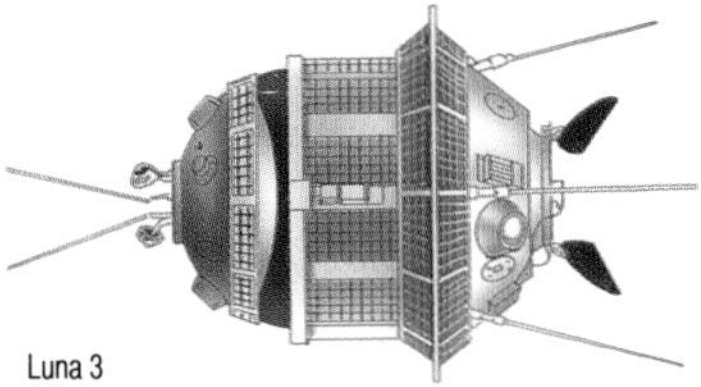
Luna 3

lunar eclipse ► eclipse

Lunar Excursion Module *noun*
A Lunar Excursion Module is a **spacecraft**. It is placed in **orbit** round the **Moon**, attached to another spacecraft. The Lunar Excursion Module can be separated and make journeys on its own, taking **astronauts** to the surface of the Moon.
In 1969, the first men set foot on the Moon from a Lunar Excursion Module.

Lunar Orbiters *plural noun*
Lunar Orbiters were a series of American space **probes**. They were **satellites** which were placed into **orbit** round the Moon and sent information back to Earth. There were five Lunar Orbiter probes. The first was launched in 1966.
Photographs sent back by Lunar Orbiters allowed detailed maps of the Moon to be made.

Lunar Roving Vehicle *noun*
The Lunar Roving Vehicle is a vehicle designed for journeys on the surface of the **Moon**. It is powered by electric motors, which are driven by batteries, and it can carry two passengers.
In 1971, two astronauts went for three drives on the Moon in their Lunar Roving Vehicle.

lunar surface *noun*
The lunar surface is the surface of the Moon. Mountains and valleys on the lunar surface make the dark shapes which we call 'the man in the Moon'.
Lunar probes have shown that the lunar surface is rocky.

lunation *noun*
Lunation is the period of time between one new Moon and the next. Lunation lasts for 29 days, 12 hours and 44 minutes.
Another term for lunation is Synodical month.

Lunik probes ► Luna probes

Lunokhod *noun*
A Lunokhod is an unmanned vehicle designed to make journeys on the **Moon**. The first Lunokhod was landed on the Moon from a Soviet **Luna probe** in 1970. It had eight wheels and was battery-powered.
Lunokhods are guided and steered by radio signals from Earth.

Lyrids *plural noun*
Lyrids are **meteor showers** which appear in the **constellation** Lyra. As many as 15 meteors can be seen in one hour.
Lyrids can be seen in the month of June each year.

M

Magellanic Clouds *plural noun*
The Magellanic Clouds are two **galaxies** which are part of the **Local Group** of galaxies. There are two Magellanic Clouds, the Large Cloud and the Small Cloud. They are irregular galaxies.
From the Earth, the Magellanic Clouds look like detached parts of the Milky Way.

magnetic field *noun*
A magnetic field is an invisible layer of **energy** which surrounds some objects in space. The **Earth** has a large magnetic field. It traps charged particles, such as **ions** and **electrons**, to form the **Van Allen belts**.
Several planets have a magnetic field shaped like that of a bar magnet.

magnetometer *noun*
A magnetometer is an instrument designed to measure changes in the strength of the Earth's **magnetic field**. Some space probes carry a magnetometer to measure the magnetic field of other planets.
Magnetometers show that the Earth's magnetic field is always changing shape and strength.

magnetosphere *noun*
The magnetosphere is part of the Earth's **atmosphere**. It is a band of electrically-charged particles beyond the **ionosphere**. The magnetosphere extends from about 640 kilometres to about 65,000 kilometres above the Earth's surface.
The particles in the magnetosphere are held there by the Earth's magnetic field.

magnitude *noun*
Magnitude describes the brightness of an object in space as seen by the **naked eye.** Magnitude is measured in numbers. The lower the number, the brighter the object shines and the greater its magnitude.
The magnitude of the brightest star, Sirius, is –1.4.

Manned Manoeuvring Unit (MMU) *noun*
A Manned Manoeuvring Unit is a jet-propelled backpack. It allows an **astronaut** to make space walks unconnected to the spacecraft. The Manned Manoeuvring Unit is powered by jets of **nitrogen** gas.
The first Manned Manoeuvring Unit was used in a space shuttle flight in 1984.

manned space flight ► page 82

mare (plural **maria**) *noun*
A mare is a large, dark patch on the surface of the **Moon**. **Astronomers** once thought that these patches were seas. The maria are now known to be craters filled with dark rock.
Mare is the Latin word for 'sea'.

Mariner ► page 84

Mariner probes *plural noun*
Mariner probes were a series of unmanned American **probes** which flew past **Venus**, **Mars** and **Mercury**. The first Mariner probe was launched in 1962.
In December 1973, Mariner 10 flew past Mercury and sent pictures back to Earth.

Mars ► page 86

mass *noun*
Mass describes the amount of material an object contains. All objects have mass and take up space. When an object goes into space away from the Earth's **gravitational** pull, its mass stays the same but its weight becomes less.
Astronauts in space have no weight, but their mass is the same as on Earth.

Mauna Kea Observatory *noun*
Mauna Kea Observatory is an **observatory** in Hawaii, in the United States of America. It is built on top of an old volcano where the air is clear and dry. There are both **optical telescopes** and **infra-red telescopes** at the Mauna Kea Observatory.
The largest infra-red telescope is at Mauna Kea.

Mercury ► page 87

meridian *noun*
A meridian is a line of **longitude** which runs north and south round the Earth through the North and South poles. Lines of longitude are numbered east and west from the meridian, which runs through Greenwich, England.
All meridians meet at the poles.

Messier's catalogue *noun*
Messier's catalogue is a list of objects in the sky. It was made by the French **astronomer**, Charles Messier, more than 200 years ago. Astronomers still use Messier's catalogue. The objects in it are known by the letter M and a number.
Astronomers know the Andromeda Spiral by the Messier number M.31.

meteor *noun*
A meteor is a particle of matter from space which enters the Earth's **atmosphere**. Most meteors burn up in the atmosphere, leaving a streak of light behind them.
Meteors are often wrongly called 'shooting stars'.

meteorite *noun*
A meteorite is a body of matter from space. It is large enough to reach the Earth without burning up in the **atmosphere**. Meteorites may be made of stone, iron, or a mixture of the two. Most meteorites are no larger than small rocks, but one that landed in Siberia in 1908 weighed many hundreds of tonnes. It made a huge **crater**.
A meteorite's blazing trail across the sky is called a 'fireball.'

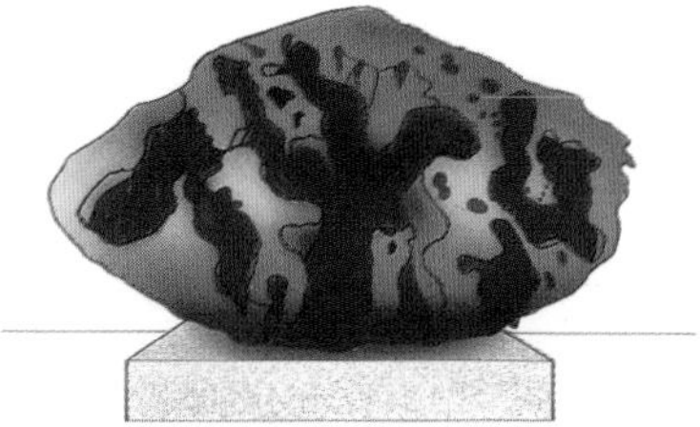

meteoroid *noun*
Meteoroid describes a **meteor** or a **meteorite** while it is still outside the Earth's **atmosphere**. All meteoroids are made of matter left over from the beginning of the **solar system** or they are part of the tails of **comets**.
It was once feared that meteoroids would be a danger to spacecraft.

meteorologist *noun*
A meteorologist is a person whose job is to study the weather. Meteorologists gather information about conditions in the Earth's **atmosphere**. They use instruments, such as thermometers, on the ground, and information sent back to Earth by **weather satellites**.
Weather satellites allow meteorologists to forecast the weather for a long period ahead.

manned space flight *noun*
Manned space flight describes all the space programmes and **spacecraft** that have taken human beings beyond Earth's **atmosphere** and into space. The first manned space flight was made by a Russian cosmonaut, Yuri Gagarin, in 1961. Also in 1961, the United States of America successfully launched an astronaut. Manned space flights include the **Apollo project**, in which men landed on the Moon, the use of **space stations**, and the work of the **space shuttle**.
The first manned space flight lasted for 1 hour and 48 minutes.

Yuri Gagarin, 1934-1968, a cosmonaut from the Soviet Union, was the first man to travel in space in the spacecraft Vostok 1, in 1961.

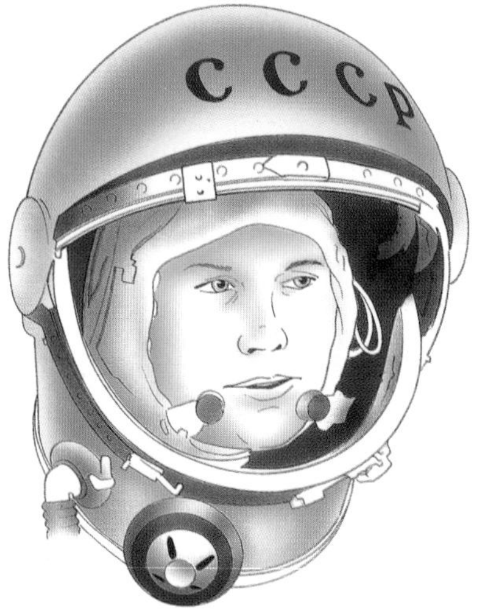

Valentina Tereshkova (born 1937), a cosmonaut from the Soviet Union, was the first woman in space, in 1963.

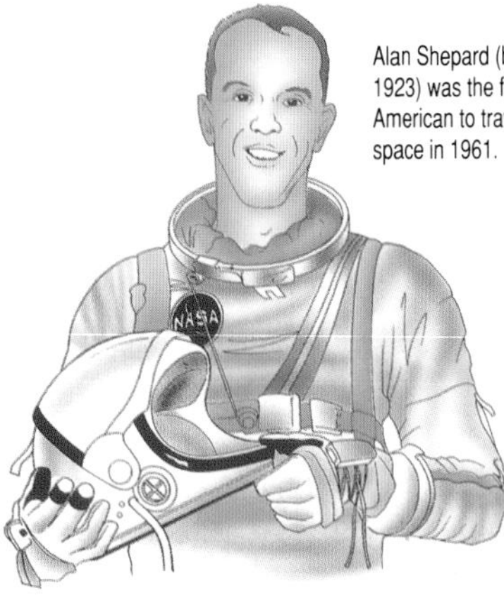

Alan Shepard (born 1923) was the first American to travel in space in 1961.

The first men on the Moon — Edwin 'Buzz' Aldrin (born 1930) and Neil Armstrong (born 1930), astronauts from the United States of America, were the first people to set foot on the Moon. The command module was piloted by Michael Collins (born 1930).

The crew of the ill-fated Challenger, which exploded on take-off, 26 January 1986: front (left to right) Michael Smith, Dick Scobee and Ronald McNair back (left to right) Ellison Onizuka, Christa McAuliffe, Gregory Jarvis, Judy Resnik

Mariner *noun*
Mariner was the name given to a series of 10 **space probes** launched by the United States of America from 1962 to 1973.
The Mariner **spacecraft** explored **Venus**, **Mercury** and **Mars**. Mariner 10 was the first space probe to visit two planets. It flew by Mercury and Venus. The Mariner spacecraft collected information about the three planets, such as the surface **temperatures** and the gases in the **atmosphere** of Venus.
Mariners 11 and 12 are better known as Voyager 1 and Voyager 2.

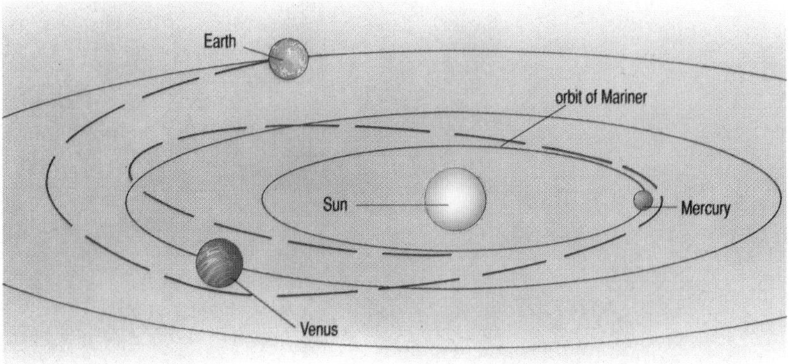

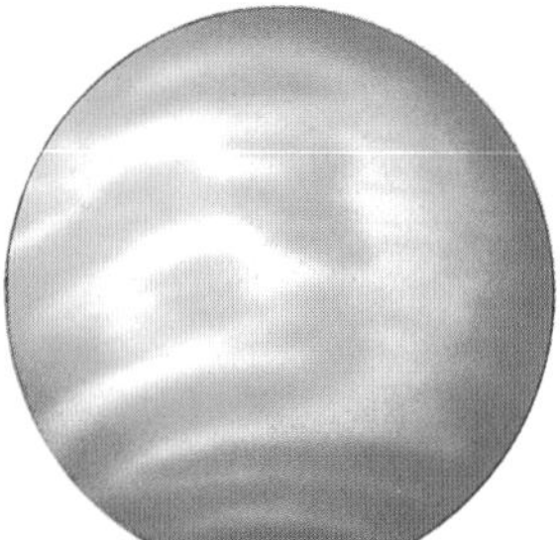

Venus

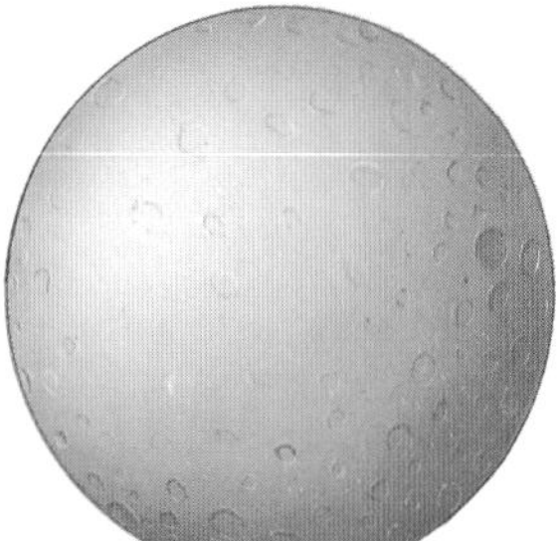

Mercury

Mariner 6 flew by Mars in July 1969. It passed within 2,120 miles of the planet, and took 75 photographs.

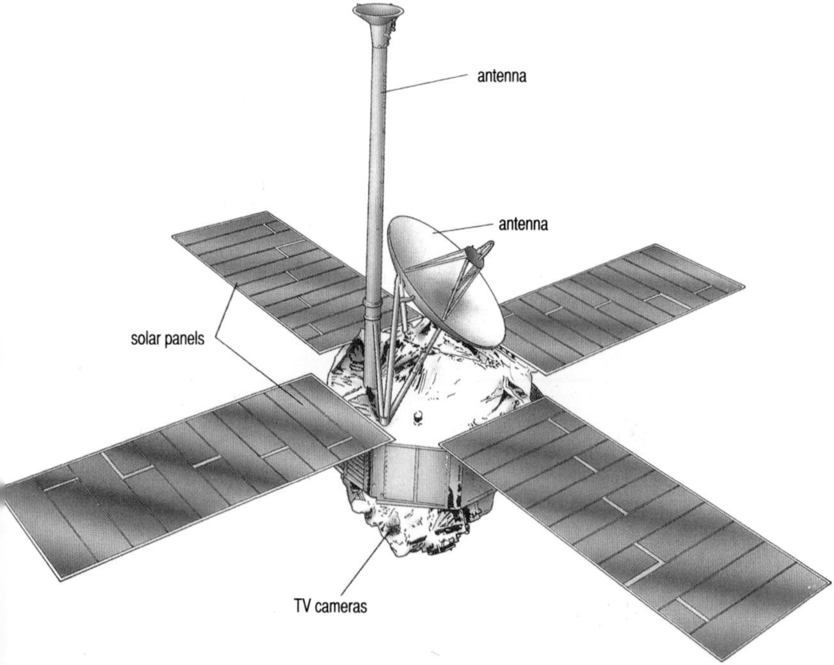

Mariner took photographs of Venus which showed swirling clouds. They never break to show the surface.

Mariner took photographs of Mercury which showed a rocky surface covered with craters, very like the Moon.

Mars *noun*
Mars is a planet in the **solar system**. It is the fourth nearest planet to the **Sun**. Four **Mariner spacecraft** have flown by Mars, and **Vikings** 1 and 2 have landed on the surface. The polar regions are covered with thin ice caps, made up of frozen water and frozen carbon dioxide. Clouds can often be seen in the atmosphere, and strong winds cause large dust storms. Rocks on the surface are rich in iron, which has turned to rust. This gives the planet a red colour. No life has so far been found on Mars.
Scientists think that the core of Mars is made of iron.

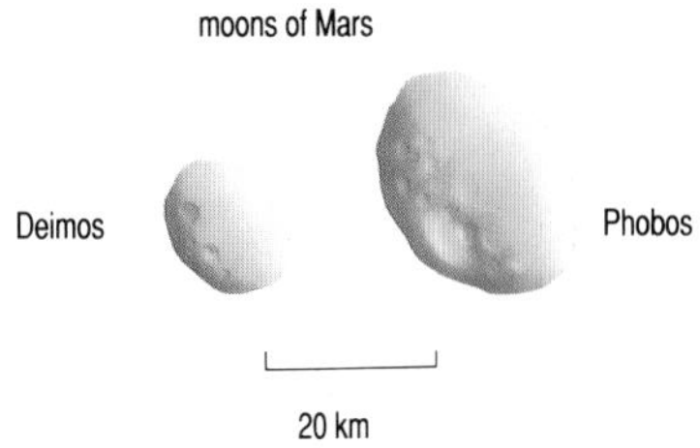

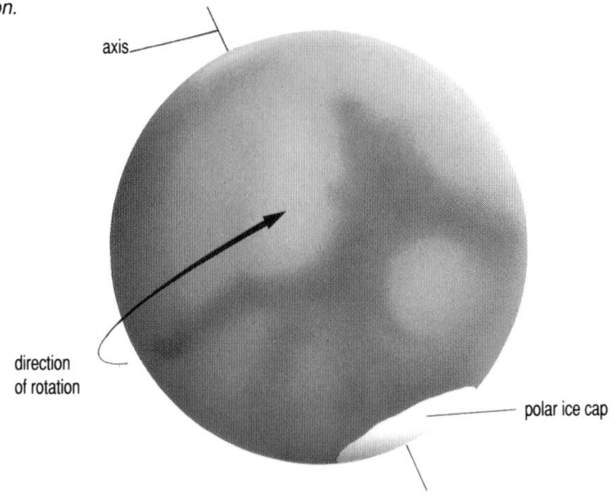

size of Mars and Earth compared

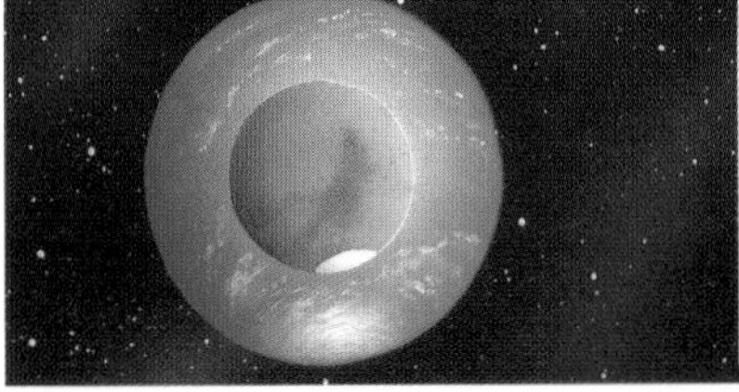

Planetary facts
Diameter: 6,790 kilometres
Distance from Sun: 228,000,000 kilometres
Nearest distance to Earth: 78,390,000 kilometres
Orbits the Sun in 687 earth days
Rotates on axis once in 24 hours, 37 minutes
Coldest temperature: –124 degrees Celsius
Hottest temperature: –31 degrees Celsius
Atmosphere: yes, a thin atmosphere, mostly carbon dioxide
Magnetic field: yes, a very weak one
Satellites: two, Phobos and Deimos

Mercury *noun*

Mercury is a planet in the solar system. It is the second smallest planet, and lies nearest to the **Sun**. For many years, little was known about Mercury. Its **orbit** lies so close to the Sun that it was hard for **astronomers** to see it with **telescopes**. In 1974 and 1975, the spacecraft **Mariner** 10 flew past Mercury three times. It photographed the planet, showing a rocky surface with many craters. Mercury has a very thin atmosphere, mostly made up of the gas helium. Scientists think that at the centre of the planet is a large, iron core. There is no life on Mercury.

Mercury turns round very slowly on its axis.

the surface of Mercury

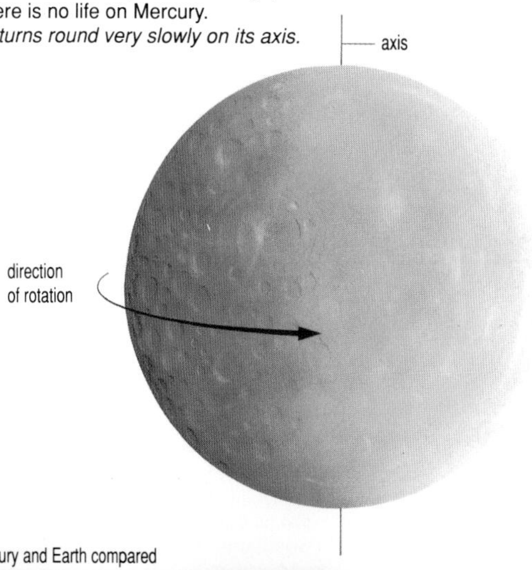

size of Mercury and Earth compared

Planetary facts
Diameter: 4,878 kilometres
Distance from Sun: 57,900,000 kilometres
Orbits the Sun in 88 earth days
Rotates on axis once in 59 earth days
Coldest temperature: –170 degrees Celsius
Hottest temperature: 430 degrees Celsius
Atmosphere: yes, a very small amount of helium
Magnetic field: yes, a very small one

meteor shower *noun*
A meteor shower is a stream of **meteors** that seems to rain down on the Earth.
A meteor shower happens when the Earth passes through a cloud of meteors that are orbiting the Sun.
Meteor showers are often seen in the late autumn.

Meteosat *noun*
Meteosat is the name of a **weather satellite** which provides information for **meteorologists** working in Europe. It takes television pictures of cloud formations. The pictures are used to forecast storms.
Information from Meteosat is sent from weather stations to ships in European waters.

methane *noun*
Methane is a **gas**. It can explode when it is mixed with air. The **atmospheres** of the four largest planets, Jupiter, Saturn, Uranus and Neptune, are made up mainly of methane.
Living things cannot survive in an atmosphere of methane.

microprocessor *noun*
A microprocessor is a very small circuit which contains a single silicon chip. Microprocessors are used in the controls of **satellites** and **spacecraft**.
Microprocessors carry out instructions which they receive from a computer program.

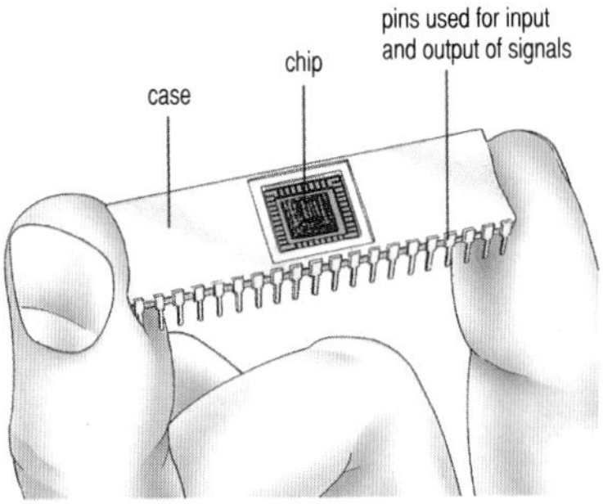

microwave *noun*
Microwaves are part of the **electronic spectrum**. They are **radio waves** with a very high **frequency**. Microwaves are used for communications to and from **spacecraft** and **satellites**.
Microwaves can be aimed very accurately along narrow beams.

Milky Way *noun*
1. The term Milky Way is sometimes used to describe the whole of our **Galaxy** which is made up of about 100,000 million stars.
The galaxy of the Milky Way includes the Earth, the other planets and the Sun.
2. The Milky Way is also used to describe the band of light which stretches across the night sky, containing millions of stars.
The stars in the Milky Way seem to be close together because we see it from the side.

Mimas *noun*
Mimas is the name of one of the **moons** of **Saturn**. It is about 390 kilometres in diameter.
Mimas is one of Saturn's 13 inner moons and has a very cold atmosphere.

minor planet ► asteroid

Mir *noun*
Mir is the name of a Soviet **space station** which was launched in 1986. It was designed so that **crews** and scientists could live on board for several months.
Spacecraft can visit Mir, bringing food, fuel and visitors.
Mir allows scientists to carry out experiments over a long period of time.

Mira star ► long-period variable star

Miranda *noun*
Miranda is the name of one of the **moons** of **Uranus**. It is 500 kilometres in diameter. Miranda has high mountains and cliffs overlooking deep valleys.
Miranda is made of ice and rock.

mirror *noun*
A mirror is a sheet of glass which is silvered so that it reflects **light**. **Reflecting telescopes** use mirrors to collect light and change its direction.
The main mirror of the world's largest reflecting telescope is six metres in diameter.

mission *noun*
Mission is a word which describes a **space probe** and the tasks it has to perform.
The first manned space mission was made in 1961 by Yuri Gagarin of the Soviet Union.

mission control ► page 90

Molniya *noun*
Molniya is the name of a series of Soviet communications **satellites**. Molniya satellites orbit high over CIS territory.
Molniya satellites provide radio, television and telecommunications links.

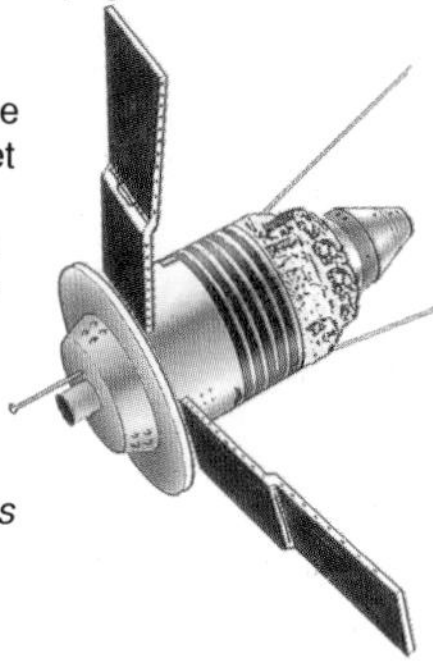

moon *noun*
The moons of a planet are natural **satellites** which travel with their planet in **orbit** round the Sun. Some planets, like **Mercury**, have no moons. Others, like **Uranus**, have many. **Saturn** has at least 23 moons.
Astronomers are not sure how many moons Uranus has, but it is at least 15.

Moon ► page 91

Mount Wilson Observatory *noun*
Mount Wilson Observatory is an **observatory** in California in the United States of America.
It was at the Mount Wilson Observatory that Edwin Hubble discovered that the universe is still expanding.

M-type star *noun*
M-type stars are those **stars** in the nebulae, galaxies and spirals that are listed in the **Messier catalogue**. They are identified by a number with the letter M in front of it.
The stars in the Andromeda galaxy, M.31, are M-type stars.

Multi-Element Radio-Linked Interferometer Network (MERLIN) *noun*
The Multi-Element Radio-Linked Interferometer Network is a group of radio dishes linked to the **Jodrell Bank Observatory** in the United Kingdom. The five dishes are aimed at the same part of the sky.
The five dishes of MERLIN are more powerful than one large dish would be.

multi-stage rocket *noun*
A multi-stage rocket is a **rocket** which has more than one rocket engine. The engines are arranged one above the others. The lowest rocket is fired first, and the others are fired in turn. This gives a **spacecraft** extra **thrust** to push it into space.
A multi-stage rocket was used to launch the United States' Apollo mission to the Moon.

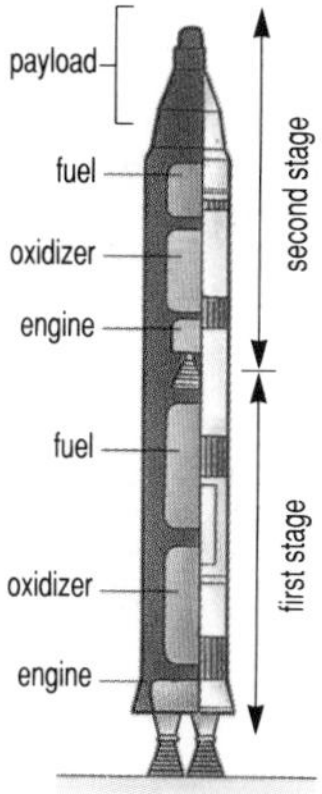

multiple star *noun*
A multiple star is a group of three or more **stars** that **orbit** each other. They are held together by **gravitation**. Sometimes **binary stars** are included in the group of multiple stars.
Rigel, in the leg of Orion, is a multiple star system made up of five stars.

mission control *noun*
Mission control is the place from which a **space mission** is controlled and directed. Scientists at mission control can send signals to **spacecraft** and receive signals back.
Mission Control for the American space shuttles is at the Johnson Space Centre in Texas.

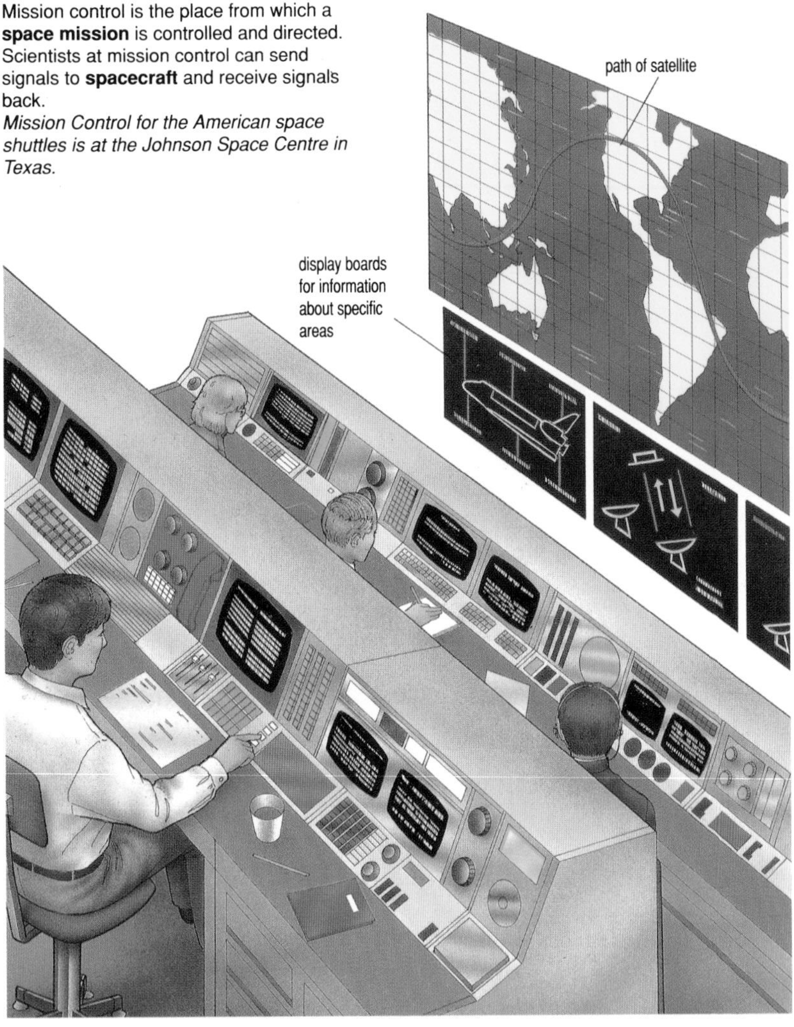

Moon *noun*

The Moon is the Earth's **satellite**. It **orbits** the Earth. The Moon is the brightest object that can be seen in the sky. The Moon shines by reflecting light from the Sun. As the position of the Moon and Sun change in the sky, different parts of the Moon are lit up. These changing shapes are called the **phases of the Moon**. The Moon orbits the Earth in such a way that only one side, or face, of the Moon can be seen.

Men have landed on the Moon, travelling in the Apollo series of spacecraft.

a lunar landscape

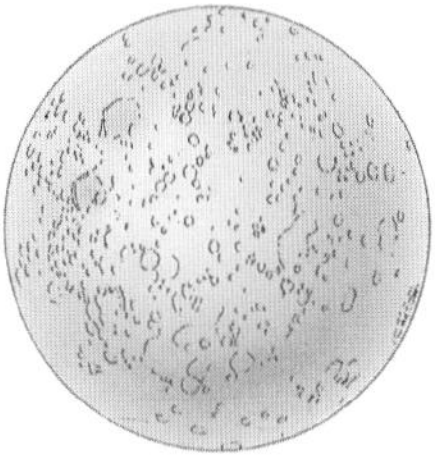

the far side of the Moon mapped from spacecraft

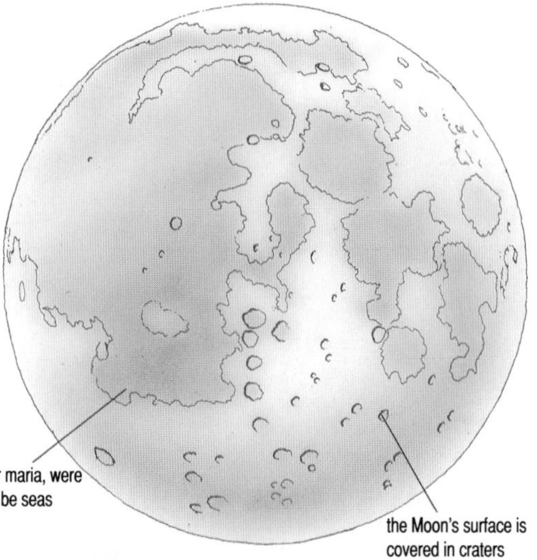
dark patches, or maria, were once thought to be seas
the Moon's surface is covered in craters

size of the Moon and Earth compared

Moon facts

Diameter: 3,476 kilometres
Distance from Earth: 384,403 kilometres
Orbits the Earth in: 27 days, 7 hours, 43 minutes
Rotates on axis once in: 27 days, 7 hours, 43 minutes
Hottest temperature: 127 degrees Celsius
Coldest temperature: –173 degrees Celsius
The Moon's day and night is 24 earth days long

N

nadir *noun*
The nadir is the point on the **celestial sphere** immediately under the observer. The observer cannot, of course, see the nadir.
The nadir is opposite to the zenith, which is the point directly overhead.

naked eye *noun*
The naked eye describes the way of looking at objects without the help of a **telescope** or binoculars. Objects in space which are visible to the naked eye can be seen simply by looking at the sky on a clear night.
Millions of stars can be seen with the naked eye.

nanometre *noun*
A nanometre is a unit of measurement. It is one thousand-millionth of a metre. A nanometre is used to measure the **wavelengths** of **light** and other forms of **electromagnetic radiation**.
The abbreviation for nanometre is nm.

National Aeronautics and Space Administration (NASA) *noun*
The National Aeronautics and Space Administration, NASA for short, is a United States government agency. It is responsible for all American **space flights**, space **probes** and **satellites**. NASA carries out research and operates launch sites and control centres in several parts of the USA. Its headquarters are in Washington, DC. The National Aeronautics and Space Administration began work in October 1958.
NASA runs the Get-away Special programme for small, private payloads.

National Space Development Agency (NASDA) *noun*
The National Space Development Agency is a Japanese government agency. It is responsible for Japan's space programme. The Agency is known as NASDA for short.
NASDA works closely with similar agencies in other countries.

natural satellite ► moon

Navstar *noun*
Navstar is the name of a navigation **satellite**. It was launched by the United States of America in 1978. Navstar broadcasts continuous time and position signals.
Navstar is short for Navigation System Using Time and Ranging.

neap tide *noun*
A neap tide is a **tide** which happens twice each month when the **Moon** is half-full. At a neap tide, high-water level is at its lowest point in the tidal cycle.
Neap tides take place soon after the Moon's first and third quarters

nebula ► page 94

Neptune ► page 93

Nereid *noun*
Nereid is the name of the smaller of the **moons** of **Neptune**. It is the moon that is furthest away from the planet. Nereid is about 170 kilometres in diameter.
Nereid was discovered in 1948 by an amateur astronomer, William Lassell.

neutrino *noun*
A neutrino is a tiny particle of matter that is given out when a **radioactive** atom decays. A neutrino has no electric charge and no **mass**. It travels in space at the **speed of light**.
The existence of neutrinos was discovered in 1956.

Neptune *noun*

Neptune is a planet in the **solar system**. It is usually the eighth planet from the Sun, but until 1999 Pluto's **orbit** brings Pluto into eighth place, and Neptune is ninth. Neptune was discovered in 1846. Scientists know that the outer layers of Neptune's **atmosphere** are made up of the gases hydrogen, helium and methane. They do not yet know what may lie beneath. The spacecraft **Voyager** 2 flew by Neptune in 1989. Neptune has a magnetic field, and radio waves have been recorded from it.
Neptune has four very faint rings.

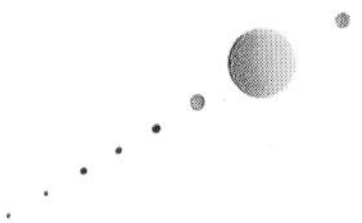

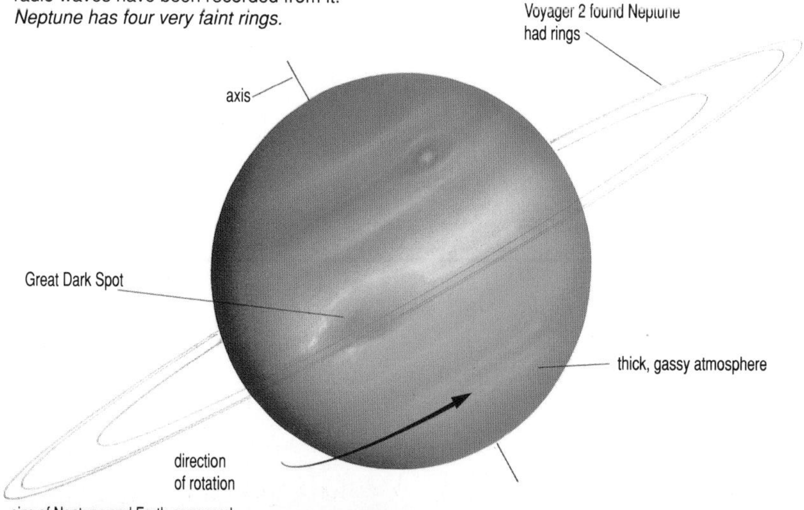

size of Neptune and Earth compared

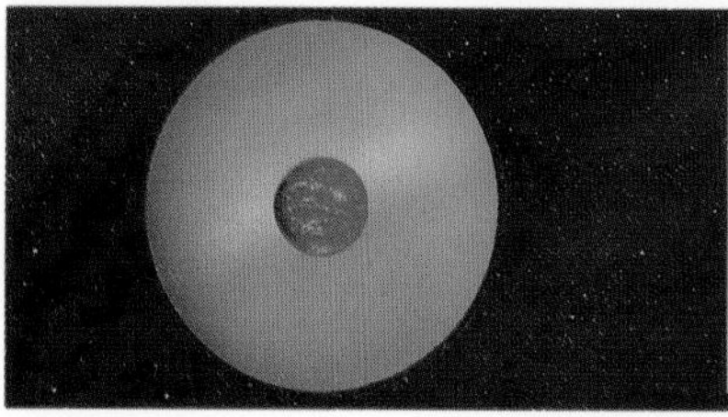

Planetary facts
Diameter: 48,600 kilometres
Distance from Sun: 4,486,100,000 kilometres
Nearest distance to Earth: 4,350,000,000 kilometres
Orbits the Sun in 165 earth years
Rotates on axis once in 18 to 20 hours
Temperature: –218 degrees Celsius at cloud tops
Magnetic field: yes
Atmosphere: contains hydrogen, helium, methane
Satellites: eight

nebula (plural **nebulae**) *noun*
A nebula is a mass of **gas** and **dust** in space. Some nebulae are made **luminous** by **electromagnetic radiation**. Others are dark and can only be seen because there is a bright nebula or star field behind them. A planetary nebula is a ring of gas thrown off by a **red giant** when it becomes a **white dwarf** in the process of **stellar evolution**.
Over millions of years, new stars are formed out of the material in a nebula.

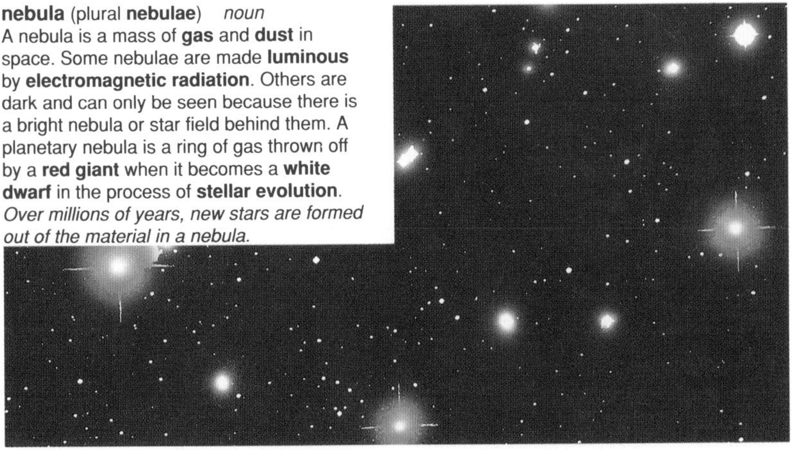

▲ All the stars in this open cluster are young and have formed at the same time out of the same gas cloud, or nebula.
▼ The Ring nebula is a shell of glowing gas in the constellation Lyra.

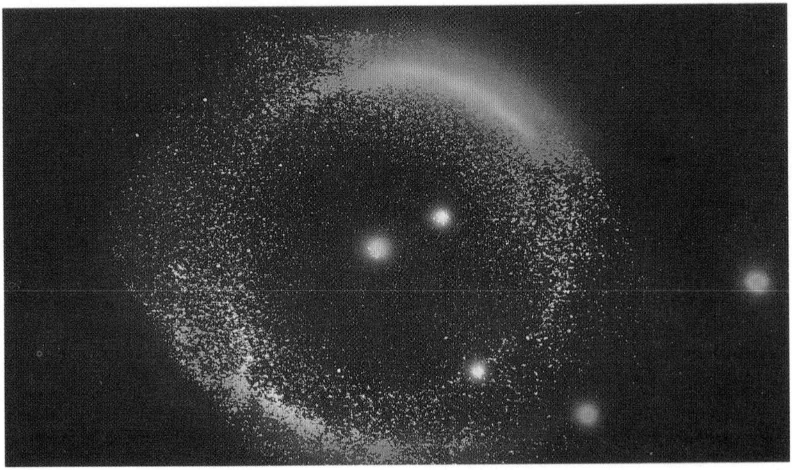

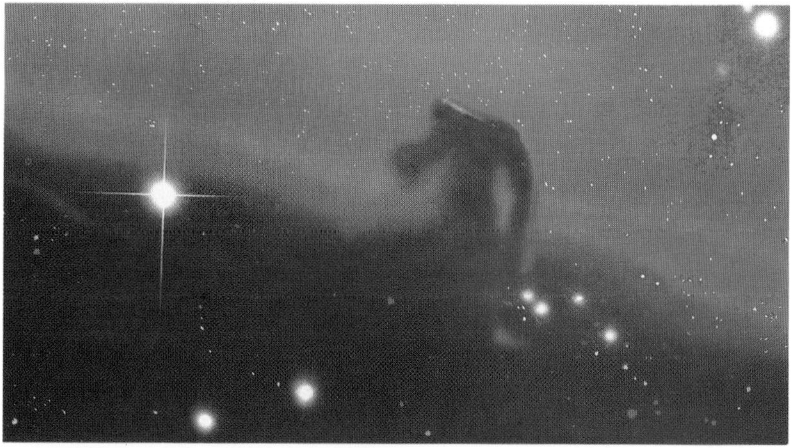

▲ The Horsehead nebula is a dark nebula. It is a dust cloud in the constellation Orion and is lit by the bright nebula behind it.

▼ The Eta Carina nebula is a cloud of gas lit by a large star inside it.

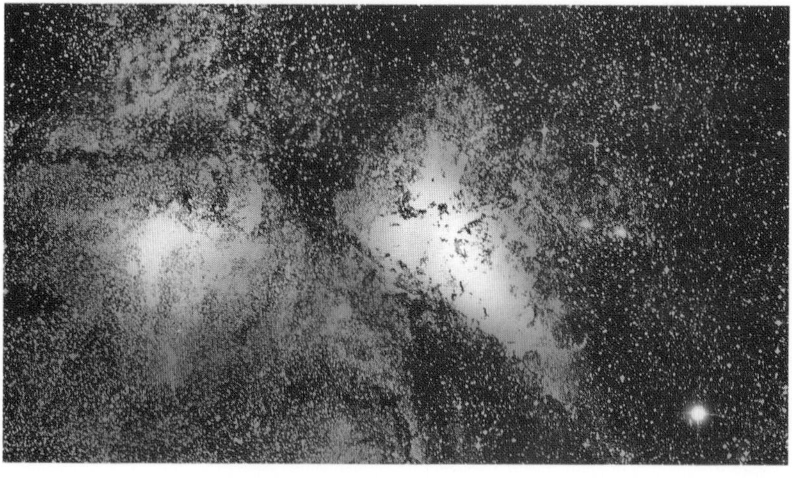

neutron *noun*
A neutron is one of the particles that make up the **nucleus** of an atom. It has no electric charge.
Neutrons are present in all atoms except hydrogen atoms.

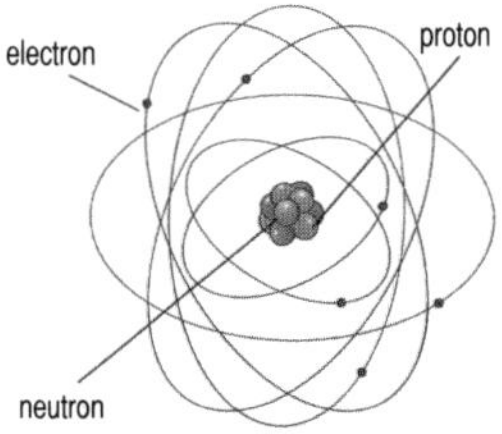

neutron star *noun*
A neutron star is a **star** which is mostly or entirely made up of neutrons. In the life of a star, neutron stars are old stars which form after **supernova** explosions. They have almost burned themselves out and so are of low brightness, or **luminosity**. Neutron stars are only about 10 kilometres across.
Most scientists believe that the radio stars called pulsars are neutron stars.

New General Catalogue *noun*
The New General Catalogue is a list of objects in space. It was started in 1888. There are over 13,000 objects in the list. Over 12,000 of these are **galaxies**.
Objects in the New General Catalogue are identified by a number and the prefix NGC.

new Moon *noun*
The new Moon is the start of the **lunar cycle**. It is followed by the Moon's **first quarter**.
The new Moon is visible as a thin, crescent-shaped line of light reflected from the Sun.

Newtonian telescope ► telescope

Newton's laws of motion *noun*
Newton's laws of motion were laid down by the English scientist, Sir Isaac Newton, in the late 1600s. They describe how moving objects behave.
Newton's laws of motion explain inertia, acceleration and reaction.

Newton's theory of gravitation *noun*
Newton's theory of gravitation was worked out by the English scientist, Sir Isaac Newton, in the late 1600s. He discovered that the force which holds objects to the Earth is the same as the force which keeps the Moon and planets in their **orbits.**
The force described in Newton's theory of gravitation is called gravity.

nitrogen *noun*
Nitrogen is a **gas**. The Earth's **atmosphere** contains about 78 per cent of nitrogen. There is nitrogen around Venus.
Nitrogen was discovered by the British scientist, Daniel Rutherford, in 1772.

node *noun*
A node is the point where the **orbit** of a planet, a comet or a moon crosses the plane of the Earth's orbit.
There are two nodes in an orbit, and the line joining them is called the line of nodes.

North Star ► Polaris

northern hemisphere ► page 97

Northern Lights ► aurora borealis

nova (plural **novae**) *noun*
A nova is a **star** which suddenly flares up and shines far more brightly than before. It may continue to shine brightly for many months. The flare-up of a nova is caused by exploding **gases**.
Astronomers once thought that novae were new stars, so they described them by the Latin word for 'new'.

northern hemisphere *noun*
The northern hemisphere is the half of the **Earth** which is north of the **Equator**. **Latitudes** in the northern hemisphere are measured in degrees North. The northern hemisphere of the sky is the part of the sky that can be seen from the northern hemisphere of the Earth. It includes the **constellations of the northern hemisphere**, nebulae, galaxies and other bodies.
The star Polaris appears to be at the centre of the northern hemisphere of the sky.

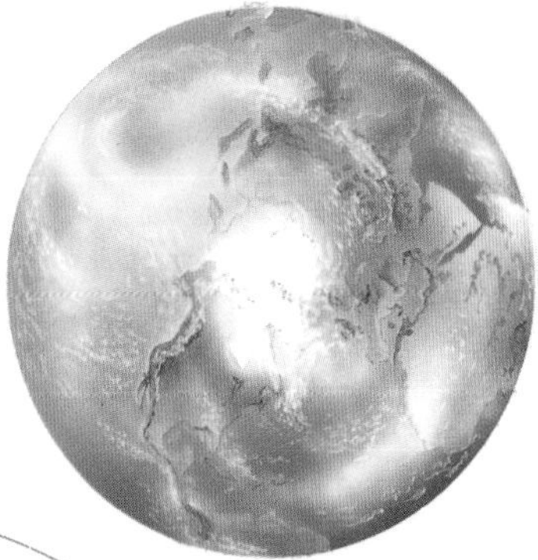

the northern hemisphere of Earth

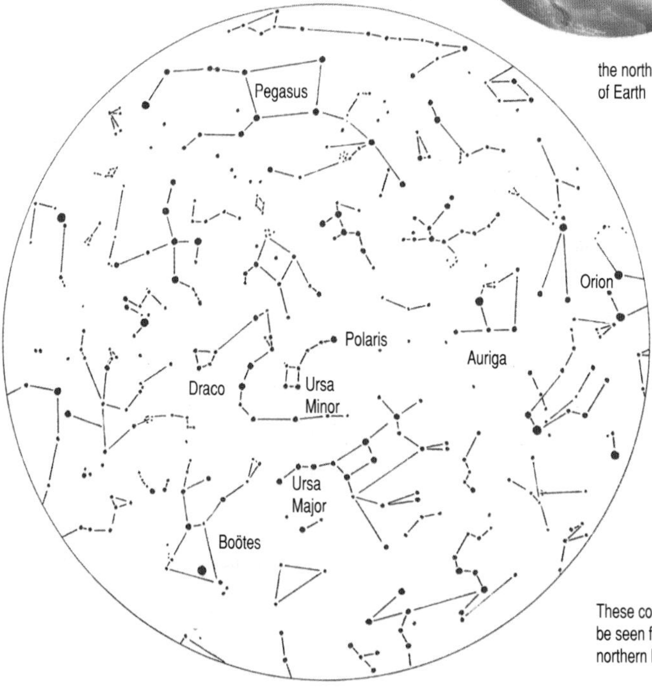

These constellations can be seen from the northern hemisphere.

nuclear energy *noun*
Nuclear energy is a kind of **energy**. It is released when changes are made to the particles in the **nucleus** of an atom. There are three forms of nuclear energy, **nuclear fission**, **nuclear fusion**, and **thermonuclear reaction**. Heat and radiation are given out, or emitted, by nuclear energy. *Many space probes are fuelled by nuclear energy.*

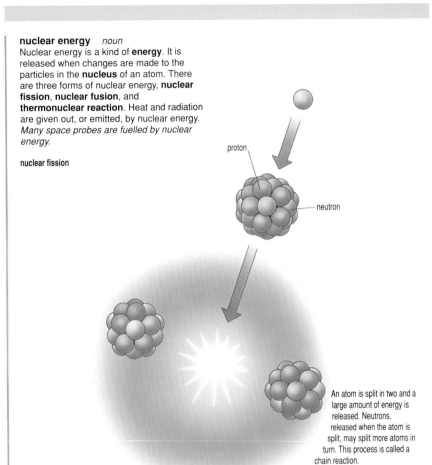

nuclear fission

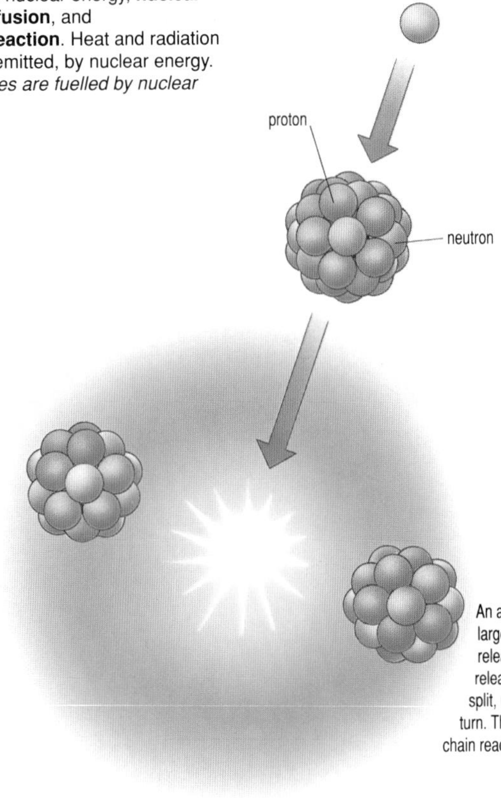

An atom is split in two and a large amount of energy is released. Neutrons, released when the atom is split, may split more atoms in turn. This process is called a chain reaction.

nuclear fusion

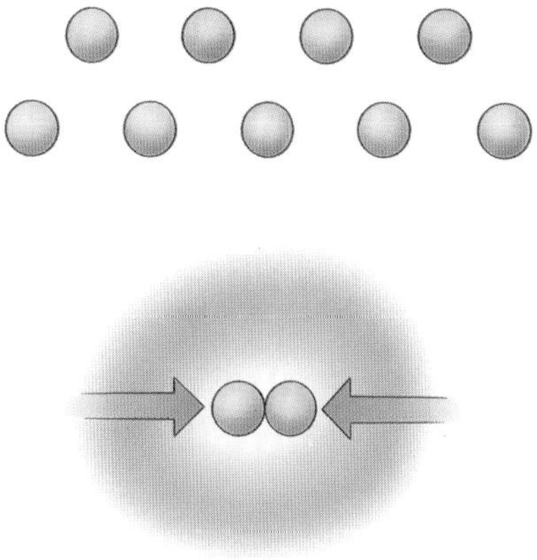
atoms of light elements, such as hydrogen
Two hydrogen atoms fuse together to form a helium nucleus. One helium atom weighs less than two hydrogen atoms. The lost matter has become heat energy.

thermonuclear reaction

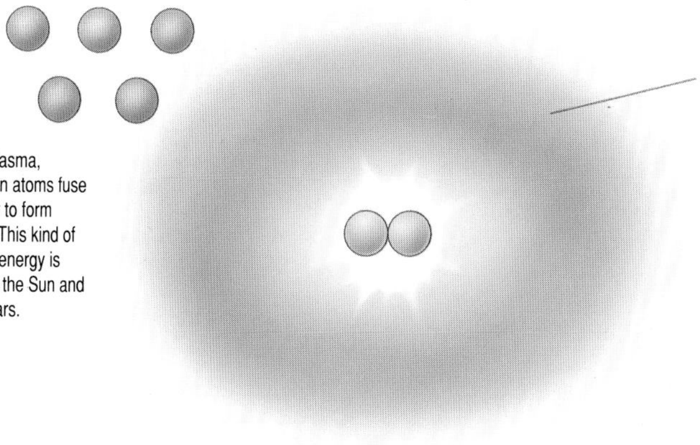

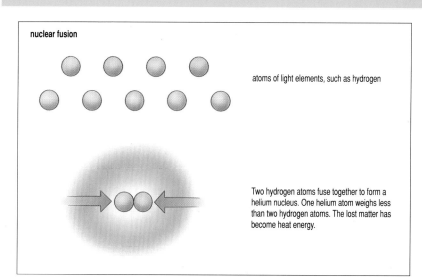

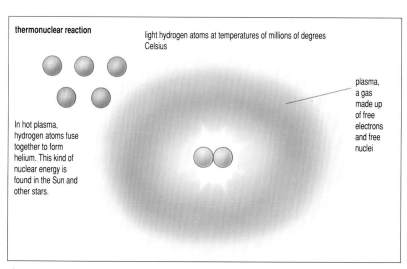

nuclear *adjective*
Nuclear is a word which describes changes that take place in the centres of atoms. These centres are called **nuclei**.
Nuclear energy is made by splitting nuclei of uranium or plutonium in a process called nuclear fission.

nuclear energy ► page 98

nuclear fission *noun*
Nuclear fission is a kind of **energy**. It describes the process of using a **neutron** to split the **nucleus** of an atom into two pieces. Heat energy and radiation are released when this happens.
Nuclei of elements such as uranium are used in nuclear fission.

nuclear fusion *noun*
Nuclear fusion is a kind of **energy**. It describes the process of making **nuclei** of one **element** by melting together, or fusing, nuclei of another element. Usually the nuclei of the light element **hydrogen** are fused to make atoms of the element **helium**. In nuclear fusion there is a loss of mass, and this is changed into energy.
Nuclear fusion only happens at very high temperatures.

nucleus (plural **nuclei**) *noun*
A nucleus is the heavy centre of an atom. It is made up of **protons** and **neutrons**. The nucleus of an atom contains **energy** which, when it is released, is called **nuclear energy**.
The nucleus of a hydrogen atom contains only one proton.

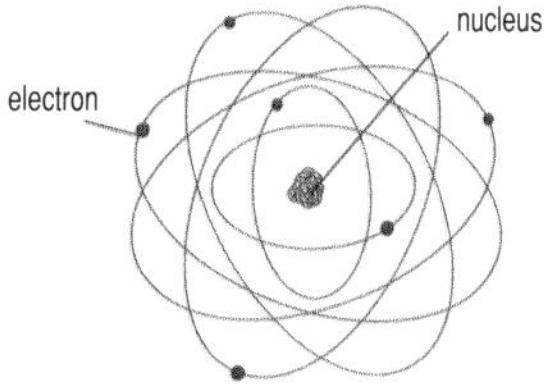

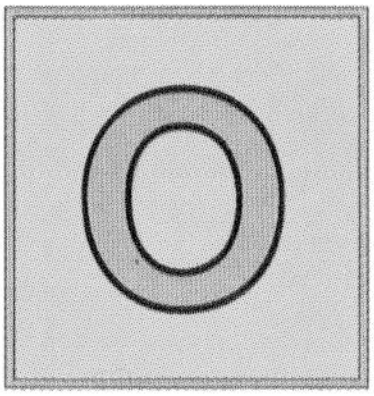

Oberon *noun*
Oberon is the name of one of the **moons** of **Uranus**. It is 1,600 kilometres in diameter.
Oberon is almost 600,000 kilometres from Uranus.

object glass *noun*
An object glass is part of a **refracting telescope**. It is the **lens** nearest to the object being viewed.
An object glass is sometimes called the objective.

observatory ► page 102

observer *noun*
An observer describes someone who looks at, or watches, something. The word observer is often used to describe an **astronomer** looking at heavenly bodies.
The observers watched the comet through their telescopes.

Odyssey *noun*
Odyssey was the name of the **command module** of the United States' Apollo 13 mission to the Moon. The mission had to be abandoned because of an explosion, but Odyssey returned the three astronauts safely to Earth.
Odyssey was launched on 11 April 1970 and spent six days in space.

Omega nebula *noun*
The Omega nebula is a cloud of **gas** and **dust** in space. It was discovered in 1746.
The Omega nebula can be easily seen with the help of binoculars.

open cluster *noun*
An open cluster is a group of many hundreds of **stars** together with **gas** and **dust**. Open clusters change their shape over a period of time.
With the naked eye, open clusters look like faint, blurred patches of light.

open universe *noun*
Open universe is an idea. It is a theory of what the **universe** is like. The open universe theory states that the universe is increasing in size and will go on doing so for ever.
According to the open universe theory, our own universe is the only one that exists.

optical astronomy *noun*
Optical astronomy is the study of objects in space using **optical telescopes**.
The first discoveries about stars and planets were made by optical astronomy.

optical telescope *noun*
An optical telescope is a **telescope** which gathers **light** and magnifies **images** of objects. It produces an image in an eyepiece which can be viewed by an **astronomer** or photographed by a camera.
Reflectors and refractors are two different types of optical telescope.

orbit ► page 104

orbital velocity *noun*
Orbital velocity is the speed at which one object **orbits** round another object.
The orbital velocity of the Moon is 3,680 kilometres per hour.

Orbiting Astronomical Observatory (OAO) *noun*
The Orbiting Astronomical Observatory is a **satellite**. It is equipped with **telescopes** and measuring instruments. The OAO is also called Copernicus.
The Orbiting Astronomical Observatory sends information about outer space back to Earth by radio.

Orion *noun*
Orion is the name of a **constellation**. It contains many bright **stars** and can be seen with the naked eye. One of Orion's stars, **Betelgeuse**, is yellowish-red in colour.
Parts of Orion can be seen in both the northern and southern hemispheres.

Orionids *plural noun*
The Orionids are a meteor shower. They are made up of matter which was once part of **Halley's comet**.
Orionids are seen around 21 October, even if Halley's comet is not visible.

Orion nebula *noun*
The Orion nebula is a cloud of dust and gas in the **constellation** of Orion. It is made up of stars which are in the process of being formed. It can easily be seen with the naked eye.
The Orion nebula is one of the nebulae closest to the Earth.

oscillating universe *noun*
The oscillating universe is the name astronomers give to one theory about what the **universe** is like. According to this theory, the universe has grown larger and smaller in waves over billions of years. The oscillating universe is sometimes called the cyclic universe.
According to the theory of the oscillating universe, the universe is now expanding.

observatory *noun*
An observatory is a place where **astronomers** study objects in space with the use of large **telescopes**. **Optical telescopes** produce images or photographs of the objects being studied. **Radio telescopes** pick up and record **radio signals** from space.
Some observatories collect information sent back to Earth from satellites.

1. Yerkes
2. Palomar
3. Kitt Peak
4. Socorro
5. Arecibo
6. La Palma
7. Jodrell Bank
8. Effelsberg
9. Zelenchukskaya
10. Nobeyama
11. Mauna Kea
12. Siding Spring
13. Cape of Good Hope
14. Cerro Tololo

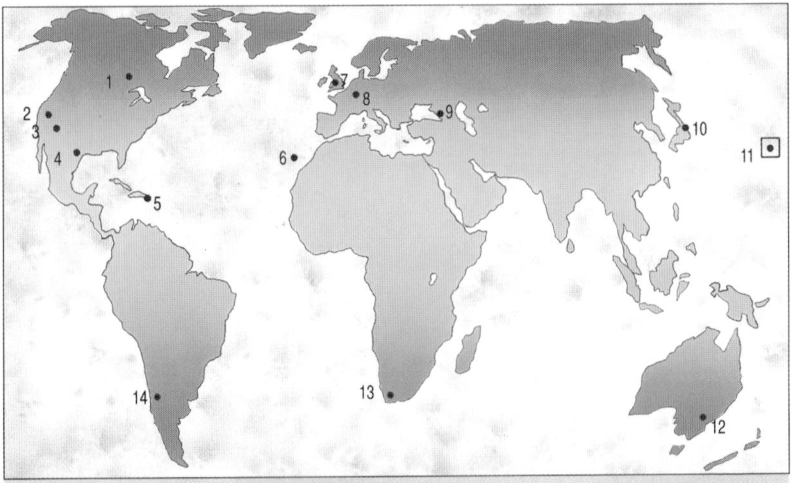

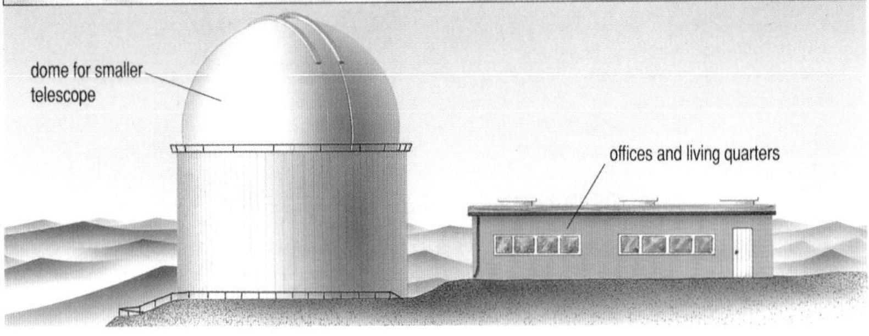

Observatories are usually built on a mountain top to avoid light pollution.

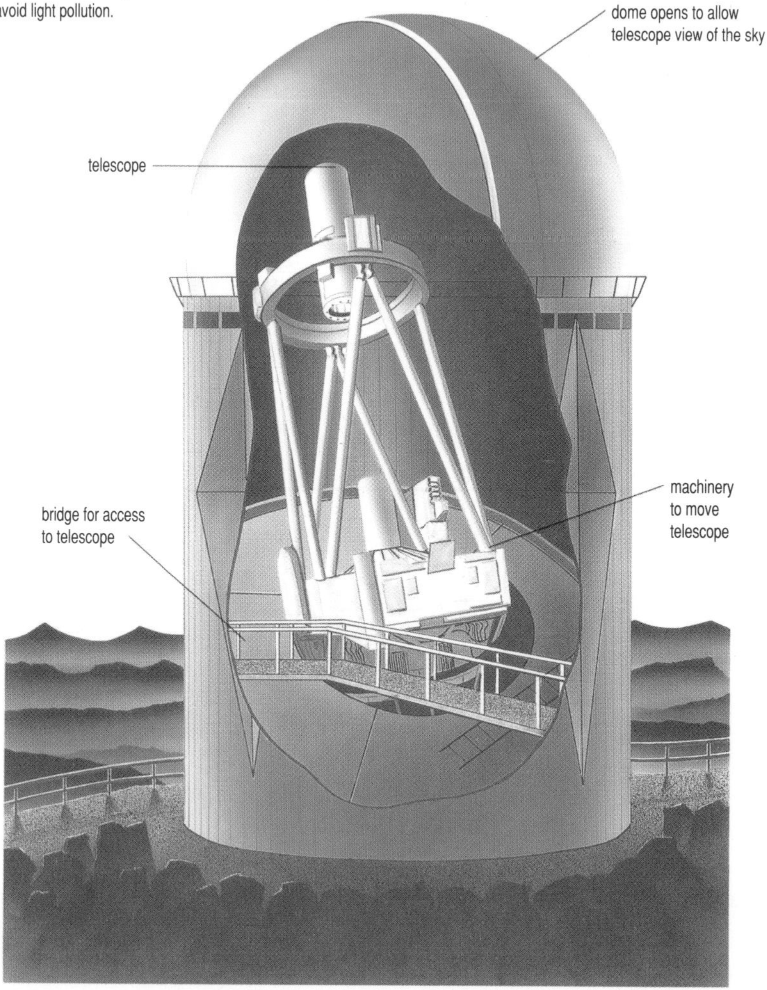

orbit noun

An orbit is the path taken by a natural or artificial object in space. Most orbits are **elliptical**, but a **geosynchronous orbit** takes a circular path. Satellites are held in orbit by the **gravitational** pull of the body they move around. The lower the orbit, the faster the satellite must travel to resist the gravitational pull. The planets in the **solar system** are in orbit round the Sun.

Our own Moon and the moons of other planets are in orbit round their hosts.

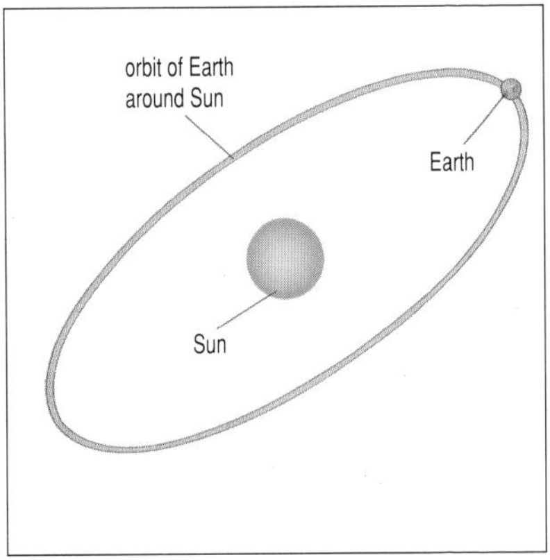

Eccentric orbit

The Soviet Union sent many satellites into eccentric orbits.

Polar orbit

A satellite in a polar orbit can survey the whole Earth as the Earth turns below the satellite. It is used for survey and spy satellites.

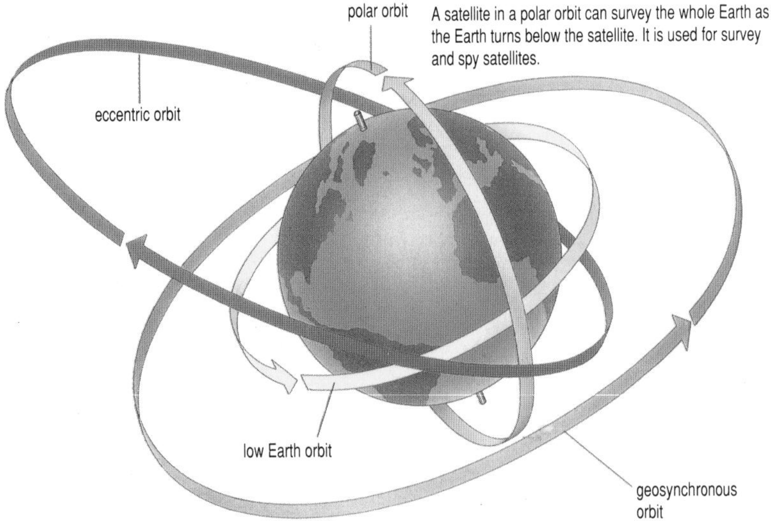

Low Earth orbit

A low Earth orbit is about 300 kilometres above the Earth. This is the level where the space shuttle and the Mir space station orbit.

Geosynchronous orbit

A satellite positioned at 35,880 kilometres above the Equator takes exactly 24 hours to orbit the Earth. It seems to hover over one point on the Earth's surface. Weather and communications satellites use geosynchronous orbits.

oscillation *noun*
Oscillation describes a kind of movement. Oscillation is a movement backwards and forwards between two points. Each movement takes the same amount of time as the movement before. Oscillation can be seen in all forms of **electromagnetic radiation**.
She measured the oscillation of a pendulum.

oxygen *noun*
Oxygen is a chemical **element**. The Earth's **atmosphere** contains about 20 per cent oxygen. Oxygen is also present in water and in living things.
Life on Earth would not be possible without oxygen.

ozone *noun*
Ozone is a **gas**. It is formed in the upper **atmosphere** when a molecule of **oxygen** joins with an extra atom of oxygen. Ozone absorbs harmful **ultraviolet radiation** from the Sun.
Ozone is a colourless gas with a strong smell.

ozone layer *noun*
The ozone layer is a band of ozone about 25 kilometres up in the Earth's **atmosphere**. It filters out harmful **ultraviolet radiation** from the Sun and prevents it from reaching the Earth's surface.
Scientists are worried that holes in the ozone layer may allow dangerous amounts of ultraviolet radiation to reach the Earth.

P

Pallas *noun*
Pallas is the name of an **asteroid**. It was discovered in 1802.
Pallas is the third largest of all the asteroids, with a diameter of 474 kilometres.

parallax *noun*
Parallax is a word which describes how an object appears to move when it is observed from two different directions. This apparent movement can be used to measure the distance from Earth of objects in outer space.
The line joining two points from which parallax is observed is called the baseline.

Parkes Observatory *noun*
The Parkes Observatory is the Australian National Radio Astronomy Observatory.
The Parkes Observatory contains the largest radio telescope in the southern hemisphere.

parking orbit *noun*
A parking orbit is an **orbit** which is taken for a time by a **satellite** or **spacecraft**. Signals from Earth can instruct the object in a parking orbit to move out of it into space or back to Earth.
The command modules of the Apollo missions went into parking orbit round the Moon.

parsec *noun*
A parsec is a unit of measurement. It is used to measure the distance of **stars**. One parsec is equal to 3.26 **light years**.
Every star except the Sun is more than one parsec away from the Earth.

partial eclipse ► eclipse

payload *noun*
The payload, or cargo, is part of the **space shuttle**. It is all the equipment contained in the space shuttle orbiter's **payload bay**. It is also other equipment found in the orbiter that belongs to a crew member and is not part of the shuttle's usual flight equipment. Experiments carried into orbit by the shuttle are part of the payload, but the astronauts' spacesuits are not.
One payload was an experiment to see if a spider could spin a web in space.

payload bay *noun*
The payload bay, or cargo bay, is part of the **space shuttle**. It is the unpressurized mid-part of the shuttle orbiter behind the crew cabin. The payload bay is used for carrying **satellites** that are to be released into **orbit**, experiments and other equipment. The bay is large enough to hold the **Spacelab** module, and has carried large observatories, such as the **Hubble Space Telescope**.
The payload bay will also hold parts for the space station, Freedom.

penumbra *noun*
1. The penumbra describes the outer parts of a **sunspot**.
The penumbra of a sunspot glows brightly.
2. The penumbra describes the outer edges of the shadow of the Earth.
During a lunar eclipse, the Moon moves through the penumbra into the Earth's main shadow, or umbra.

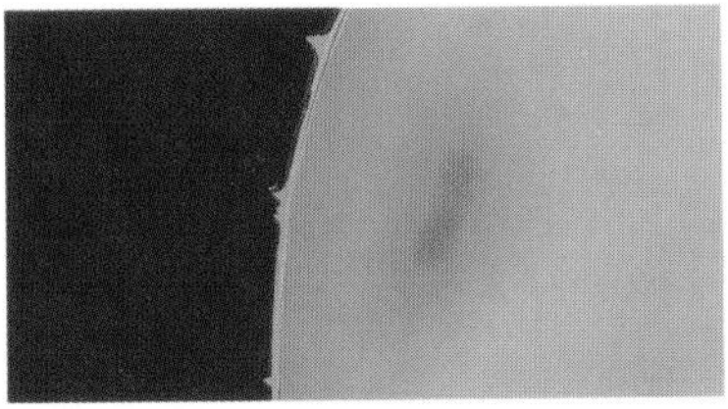

periodic comet *noun*
A periodic comet is a **comet** which is in **orbit** close to the Earth at regular intervals.
Halley's comet is a periodic comet which can be seen from the Earth every 75 to 76 years.

Perseids *plural noun*
The Perseids are a **meteor shower**. They are seen every August. The shower is most active around 12 August. The Perseids seem to originate in the constellation Perseus. They are the best and brightest meteor shower.
The Perseids can contain as many as 65 meteors per hour.

phases of the Moon ► page 91

Phobos *noun*
Phobos is the name of the larger of the two **moons** of **Mars**. Phobos is very small. It is only 27 kilometres long and 20 kilometres wide.
Phobos has an uneven outline and there are many craters on its surface.

Phobos mission *noun*
The Phobos mission was an unmanned Soviet **mission** which went into **orbit** round **Mars**. It was launched in 1989.
The Phobos mission investigated conditions on Phobos as well as on Mars.

photoelectric photometry *noun*
Photoelectric photometry is a way of measuring the strength, or intensity, of **light**. It uses a photoelectric cell, which produces an electric current when light falls on it. Light is projected on to the cell from a **telescope**.
Photoelectric photometry measures variations in the light from stars as well as their brightness.

photometer *noun*
A photometer is a device for carrying out **photoelectric photometry**.
A photometer measures light in units called watts.

phases of the Moon *noun*
The phases of the Moon are the different appearances that the **Moon** passes through when seen from **Earth**. The crescent Moon is the first phase of a new Moon. The crescent grows, or waxes, until it is a full Moon. Then it becomes smaller, or wanes, until it disappears completely and another new Moon begins.
All the phases of the Moon are completed in just over 29 days.

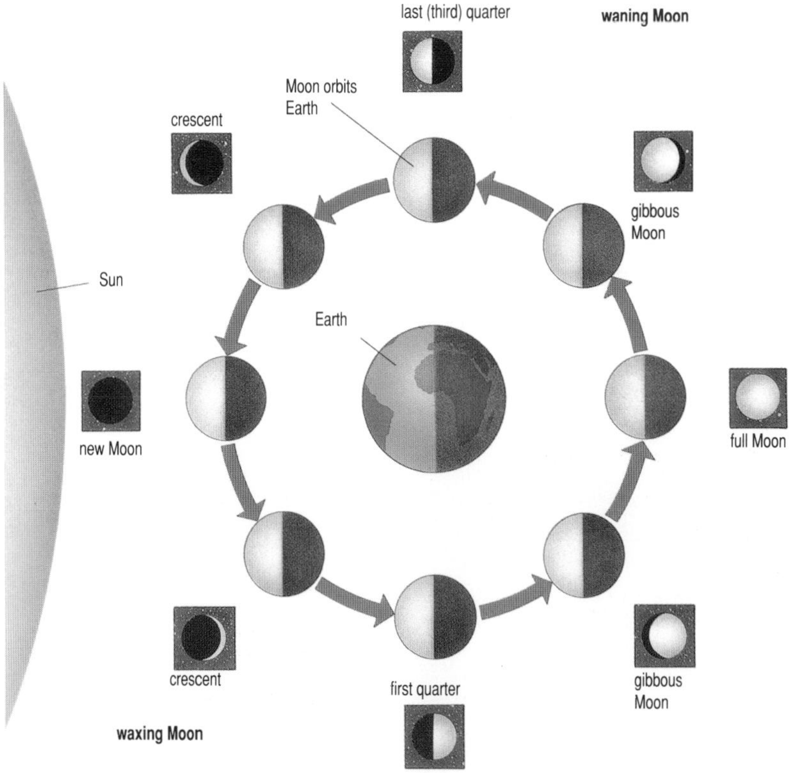

photon *noun*
A photon is a particle of **electromagnetic radiation**. Electromagnetic waves are made up of groups of packets called photons.
Another name for a photon is a light quantum.

photosphere *noun*
The photosphere is the name for the bright surface of the **Sun**. Its temperature is about 6,000 degrees kelvin.
Electromagnetic energy radiating from the photosphere gives the Earth its heat and light.

Pioneer space probe *noun*
The Pioneer space probes were a series of unmanned **probes** which visited **Venus**, **Jupiter** and **Saturn**. Some of them moved into outer space and are heading for the distant **stars**.
A Pioneer probe produced the first map of the surface of Venus.

Pisces *noun*
Pisces, or the Fish, is one of the **constellations** of the **Zodiac**. It is a rather faint constellation.
Pisces is named after the Greek for 'fish'.

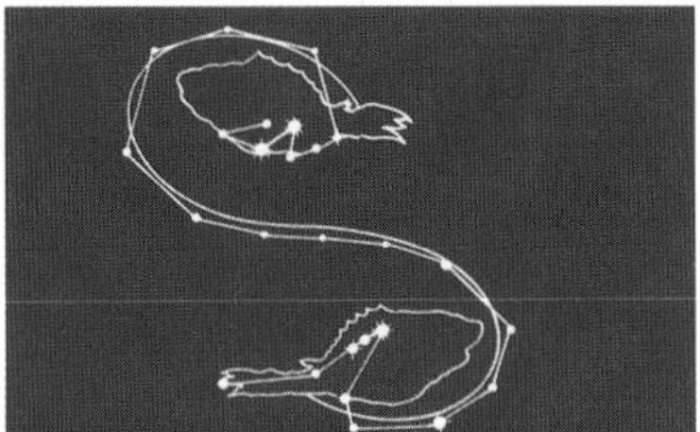

Piscis Austrinus *noun*
Piscis Austrinus is the name of a **constellation** which can be seen only in the **southern hemisphere**. It contains only one bright star, called Fomalhaut.
Piscis Austrinus is sometimes called the 'Southern Fish'.

planet *noun*
The planets are bodies in space which are not **luminous**. There are nine main planets in our **solar system**, which are Mercury, Venus, Earth, Mars, Jupiter, Saturn, Uranus, Neptune and Pluto. There are also thousands of very small ones which are often called **asteroids**.
Mercury is the planet which is closest to the Sun.

planetarium *noun*
A planetarium is a dome with an artificial sky on the inside. A projector throws images of the stars and planets onto the sky.
A planetarium can show what the night sky will look like in many years' time.

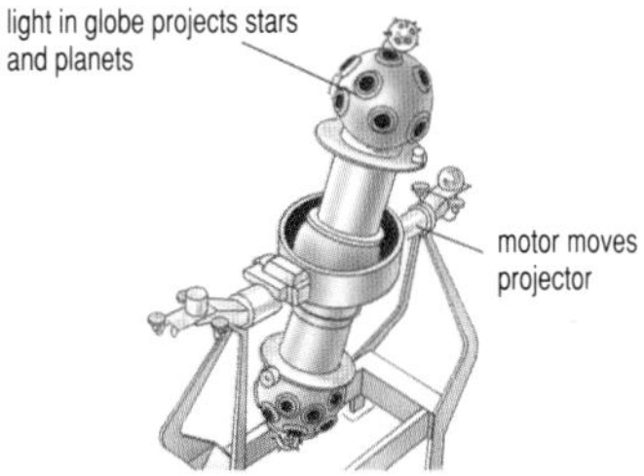
light in globe projects stars and planets
motor moves projector

plasma *noun*
Plasma is the name given to a cloud of gas which contains **ions** and free **electrons**.
Plasma has no overall electric charge, but it is a good conductor of electricity.

Pleiades *plural noun*
The Pleiades are a loose **star cluster**. Seven of the stars of the Pleiades, including the brightest, Alcyone, can be seen with the **naked eye**. Another 50 can be seen with a small **telescope**.
The Pleiades are sometimes called the Seven Sisters.

Plough ► Ursa Major

Pluto ► page 106

polar orbit *noun*
A polar orbit is a path round the **Earth** taken by a **satellite**. A polar orbit passes over both the North and South poles.
Most satellites designed to observe the Earth are placed in polar orbit.

Polaris ► **Pole Star**

poles *noun*
The poles are two points on the surface of the Earth. The North Pole is in the Arctic at **latitude** 90 degrees north, and the South Pole is in the Antarctic at latitude 90 degrees south.
Both poles are covered by a thick layer of ice.

Pole Star *noun*
The Pole Star is the star nearest the north celestial pole of the sky when seen from the northern hemisphere. It is the brightest star in the **constellation Ursa Minor**. It can easily be found by following the line from the stars Merak and Dubhe in **Ursa Major**.
Until recent times, sailors navigated at night by using the Pole Star as a marker.

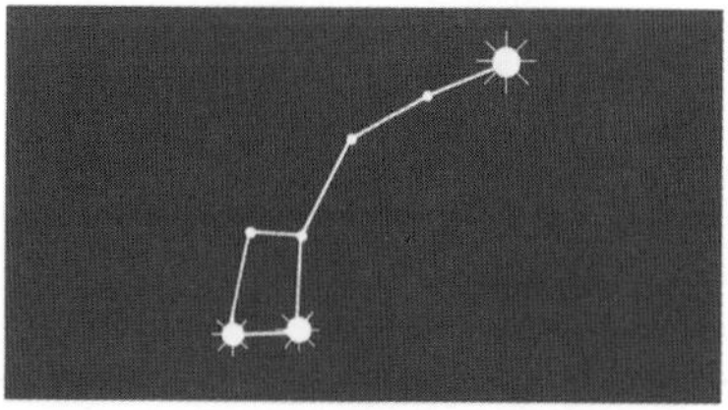

probe ► **space probe**

Procyon *noun*
Procyon is one of the brightest stars in the night sky. It is one of the stars in Canis Minor, close to the **constellation** of **Orion**.
Procyon, the eighth brightest star, can be seen from everywhere on Earth.

prominence *noun*
A prominence is a mass of glowing **gas** above the surface of the **Sun**. Prominences may take place in the **chromosphere** or the **corona**. They can be seen only when there is a total **eclipse** of the Sun.
Some prominences, which are called eruptive prominences, swirl like clouds in a violent storm.

proper motion *noun*
Proper motion describes the apparent movement of a star in the sky. Stars are so far away that their proper motions are small.
Some stars are so remote that their proper motions are too small to be measured.

proton *noun*
A proton is a particle with a positive electric charge. Protons are found in the **nucleus** at the centre of an atom.
The atoms of different elements have different numbers of protons.

Proxima Centauri *noun*
Proxima Centauri is a **star** in the **constellation** of Centaurus. It is the closest known star to our solar system. Proxima Centauri is about 4.3 **light years** away from Earth. Proxima Centauri is a **flare star**. It is the third star in the group called **Alpha Centauri**.
Proxima Centauri can easily be seen with binoculars.

Pluto *noun*
Pluto is a planet in the **solar system**. It is the smallest planet. Pluto is usually the ninth planet from the Sun, but it has an unusual **orbit**. This means that from 1979 until 1999, Pluto lies closer to the Sun than **Neptune**. Pluto's orbit is very sharply angled to the path of the Sun. The angle is more than 17 degrees. Scientists have found frozen methane on Pluto's surface. They think this may mean that Pluto has a rocky surface, with a solid core of rock and iron.
Pluto was discovered in 1930.

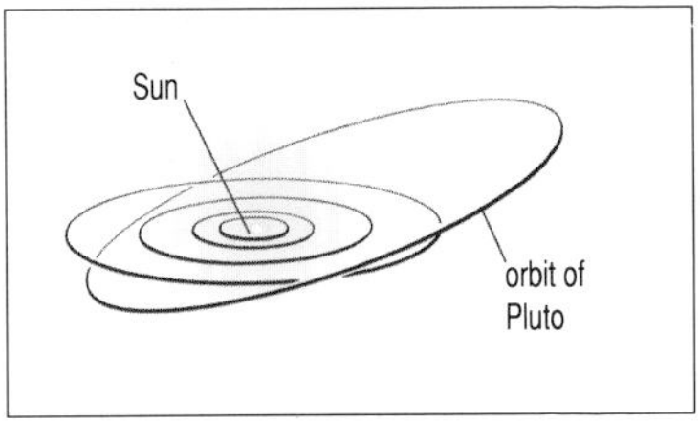

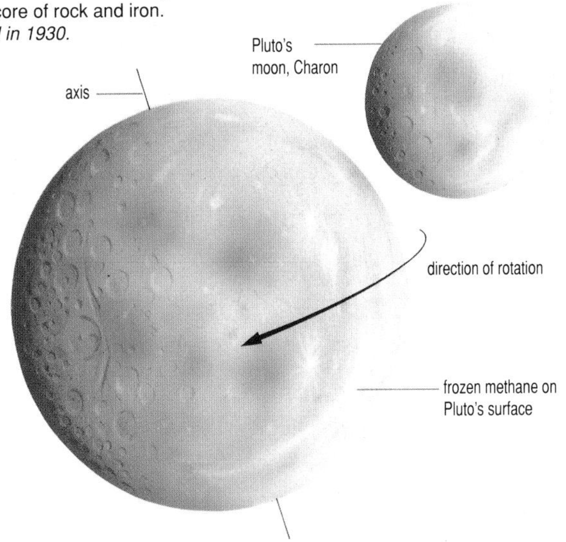

size of Pluto and Earth compared

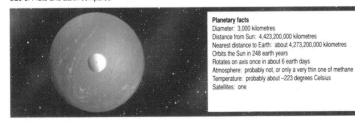

Planetary facts
Diameter: 3,000 kilometres
Distance from Sun: 4,423,200,000 kilometres
Nearest distance to Earth: about 4,273,200,000 kilometres
Orbits the Sun in 248 earth years
Rotates on axis once in about 6 earth days
Atmosphere: probably not, or only a very thin one of methane
Temperature: probably about –223 degrees Celsius
Satellites: one

Ptolemaic theory *noun*
The Ptolemaic theory is a view of the solar system put forward by the Greek mathematician and astronomer Ptolemy, about 1,900 years ago. Ptolemy believed that the planets moved round the Earth, but also had separate orbits which he called epicycles.
It was 1,500 years before astronomers realized that the Ptolemaic theory was incorrect.

pulsar *noun*
A pulsar is a **star** which is a source of **radio signals** from space. A pulsar is a piece of matter which results from the explosion of a **supernova**. It spins round in space and, as it spins, the beam of its signal can be picked up by a **radio telescope**.
The signals from pulsars seem to switch on and off as their beam passes across the Earth.

Q

Quadrantids *plural noun*
The Quadrantids are a **meteor shower**. They appear in the first few days of January each year.
The number of meteors per hour in the Quadrantids varies between 20 and 80.

quantum theory *noun*
The quantum theory describes the way in which the energy of **electromagnetic radiation** is given out by atoms. The quantum theory suggests that this energy is not continuous but is given out in bursts which are called groups of quanta, or **photons**, which are rather like packets of energy.
The development of quantum theory in the early 1900s changed scientists' ideas about radiation.

quasar *noun*
Quasar is short for quasi-stellar radio source. Quasars are **galaxies** which are far out in space. They send out strong **visible light** and strong radio signals.
Quasars are so far away that the light and signals received on Earth left them many hundreds of millions of years ago.

quasi-stellar radio source ► quasar

R

radar astronomy *noun*
Radar astronomy is the study of objects in the **solar system** by collecting radar echoes from them. The echoes are sent from Earth and bounced back by the object.
In radar astronomy, the distance of an object from Earth can be found by measuring the time a radar signal takes to return.

Radar Ocean Reconnaissance Satellite (RORSAT) *noun*
The Radar Ocean Reconnaissance Satellite is a **satellite** in **orbit** above the Earth. It sends out radar pulses which find the position and size of warships at sea.
The Radar Ocean Reconnaissance Satellite is known as RORSAT for short.

radiation *noun*
1. Radiation describes how **energy** moves in waves through space. Light, heat and other forms of electromagnetic energy all travel by radiation.
Radiation from the Sun warms the Earth.
2. Radiation is a kind of energy which moves in waves.
Radio waves are an example of radiation.
radiate *verb*

radioactivity *noun*
Radioactivity is a form of **energy**. It is given out when the nucleus of a radioactive atom throws out one or more of its particles, such as **protons** or **neutrons**. This releases particle, or radioactive, energy.
Huge amounts of radioactivity were released when the universe was created.
radioactive *adjective*

radio astronomy *noun*
Radio astronomy is the study of the **radio waves** sent out by objects in space. The radio waves are collected by **antennae** and then increased in sound, or amplified, so that they can be recorded.
Radio astronomy has been used to study our Sun, some planets, special stars, galaxies and the early universe.

radio galaxy *noun*
A radio galaxy is a **galaxy** which sends out very powerful radio signals. About one galaxy in a million is a radio galaxy. **Cygnus A** is a typical example of a radio galaxy.
Radio astronomers record the signals from radio galaxies so that they can be studied.

radio interferometer *noun*
A radio interferometer is a kind of **radio telescope**. It is a device which allows radio **astronomers** to pick up very faint signals from space. It is made up of a group of dishes or other kinds of **antennae**, which is called an **array**. Each part of the array covers a different section of space.
The world's largest radio interferometer is at Socorro, New Mexico, and contains 27 large dishes.

radio source *noun*
A radio source is a **star** or another kind of body in space which sends out **radio waves**.
Radio astronomers gather and study the signals from radio sources.

radio telescope *noun*
A radio telescope is a device for collecting radio signals from space. Most radio telescopes have a dish **antenna** which can be turned in any direction, towards any part of space. An amplifier and a detector are connected to the antenna.
Radio telescopes can detect signals from objects which are too far away to be seen by optical telescopes.

radio waves *plural noun*
Radio waves are part of the **electromagnetic spectrum**. They are a form of **energy**. Radio waves occur naturally, for example, those that are given out by objects in space. They can also be created by radio **transmitters**.
Radio waves carry messages between satellites and receiving stations on Earth.

Ram ► Aries

red giant *noun*
A red giant is one of the stages in the life of a **star**. Some stars swell, or expand, towards the end of their lives and become red giants. Then they shrink to become **white dwarfs** which give out only faint light.
A red giant is a star that can be 300-400 times the size of the Sun.

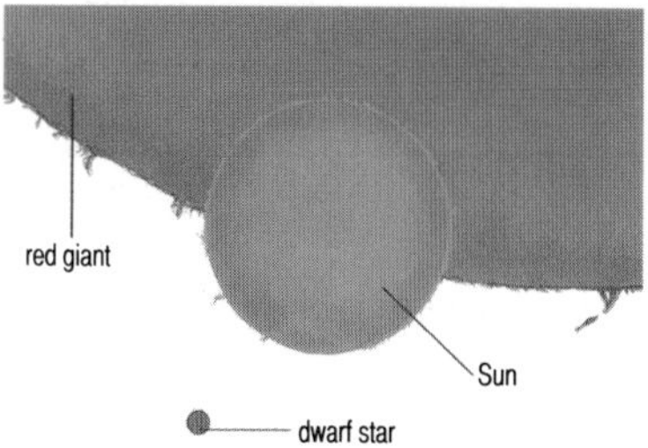

Red Planet ► Mars

red shift ► Doppler effect

Red Spot ► Great Red Spot

re-entry *noun*
Re-entry describes the return of a landing **capsule** or **space shuttle** from space. When an object re-enters the Earth's atmosphere, it becomes very hot due to the air rubbing against it. This is called friction.
Re-entry vehicles are protected with heat-resisting materials.

reflecting telescope *noun*
A reflecting telescope is a **telescope** which collects light by means of a mirror. The light is then reflected through a series of **lenses** to an eyepiece or on to a screen.
The world's largest telescopes are reflecting telescopes.

refracting telescope *noun*
A refracting telescope is a **telescope** which collects light through a lens called the **object glass** or objective.
The image collected by the lens of a refracting telescope is focused and magnified by lenses in the eyepiece.

refraction *noun*
Refraction is a word which describes an alteration in the direction of rays of light.
A **lens** changes the direction of light passing through it because it alters the speed of the light.
Many optical instruments, such as refracting telescopes, work by refraction.
refract *verb*

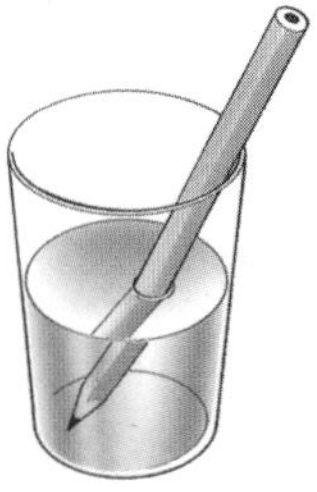

relativity *noun*
Relativity describes the links between space, time and movement. If an object moves at speeds approaching the **speed of light**, time appears to 'slow down'. The shape of the fast-moving object also appears to change, and its **mass** increases.
The theory of relativity was worked out by a German physicist, Albert Einstein.

rocket *noun*
A rocket is a powerful engine which uses a mixture of fuel and oxygen to produce gas. The gas is expelled with great force, which pushes, or **thrusts**, the rocket upwards. A rocket is used to launch **spacecraft** and **satellites**.
Rockets carry their own oxygen supply and so they can propel craft in space.

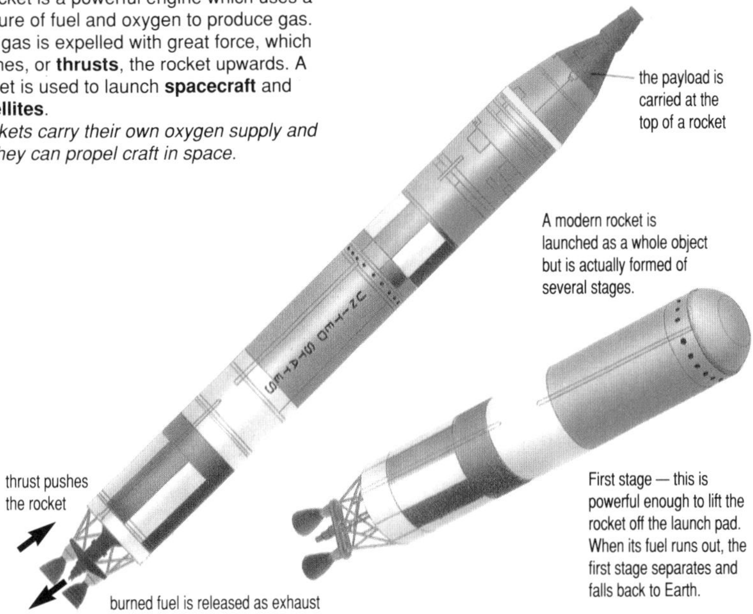

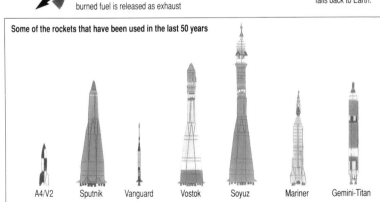

the payload is carried at the top of a rocket
A modern rocket is launched as a whole object but is actually formed of several stages.
thrust pushes the rocket
burned fuel is released as exhaust
First stage — this is powerful enough to lift the rocket off the launch pad. When its fuel runs out, the first stage separates and falls back to Earth.

Some of the rockets that have been used in the last 50 years

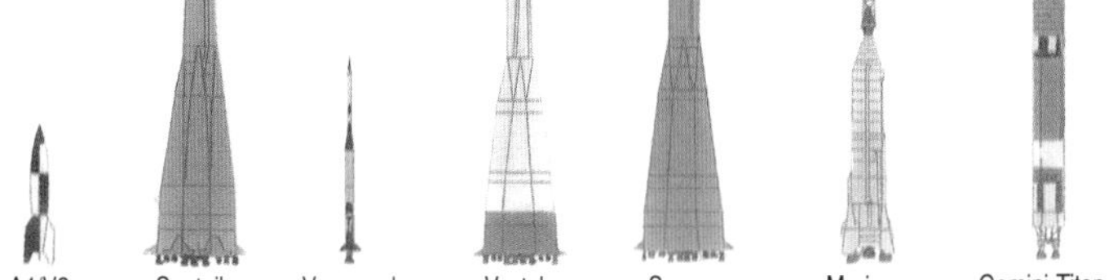

A4/V2
Sputnik
Vanguard
Vostok
Soyuz
Mariner
Gemini-Titan

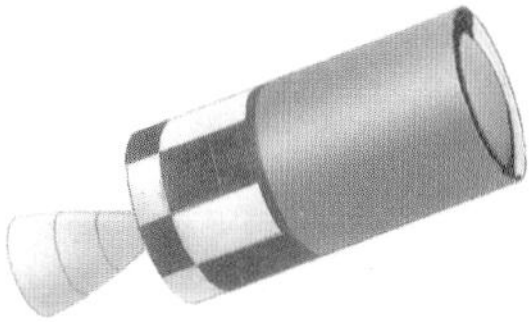

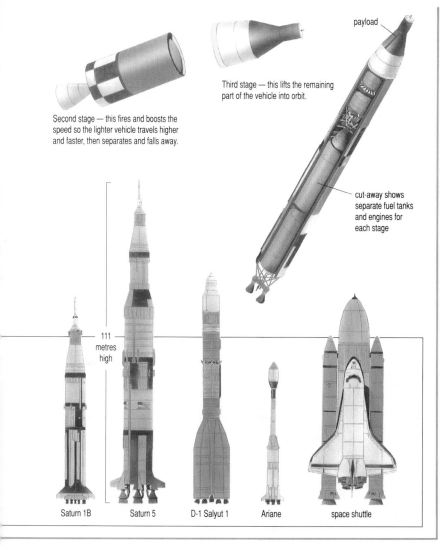

Second stage — this fires and boosts the speed so the lighter vehicle travels higher and faster, then separates and falls away.

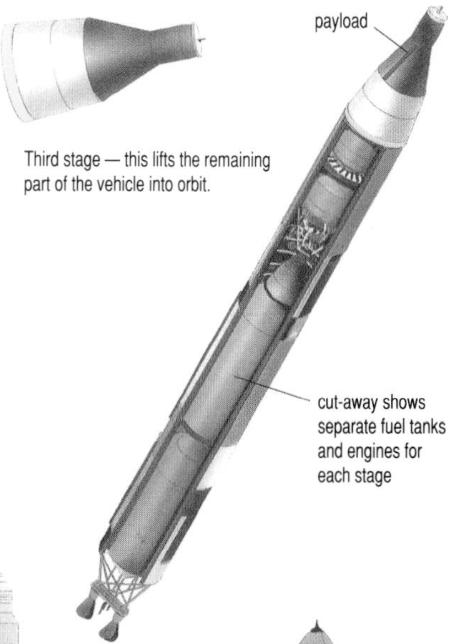

Third stage — this lifts the remaining part of the vehicle into orbit.

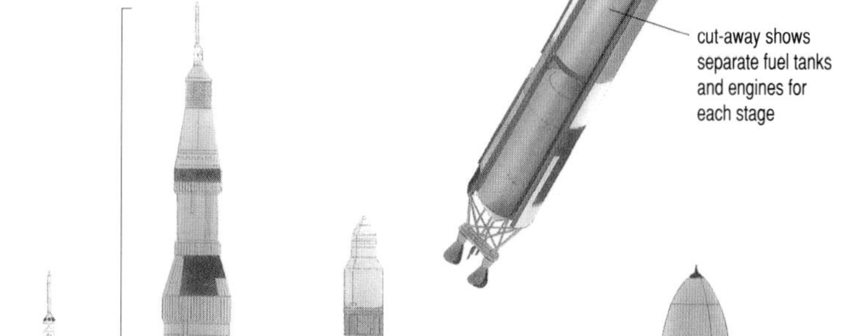

relay satellite *noun*
A relay satellite is a **satellite** which receives signals from one Earth station and reflects them towards another.
Satellite television comes to us from relay satellites.

retardation *noun*
Retardation is the difference between the times of two successive moonrises.
Retardation usually lasts for about one hour.

retrograde motion *noun*
Retrograde motion describes the movement of an object in space. The movement is retrograde if it is in the opposite direction to the movement of the Earth in **orbit**.
Objects in retrograde motion appear to move from east to west.

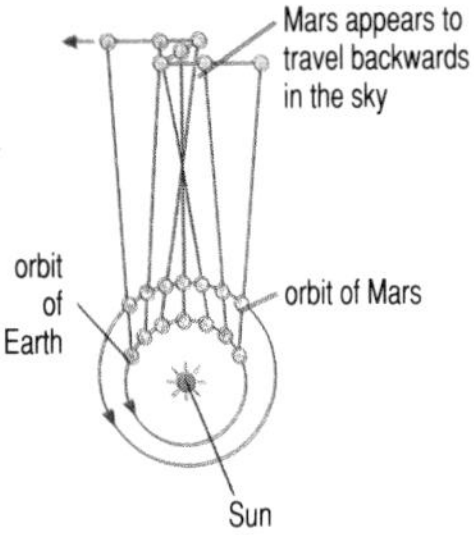

retro-rocket *noun*
A retro-rocket is a small **rocket** fitted to a **spacecraft** or a space **capsule**. It can be fired to slow the vehicle down or change its direction of travel.
Retro-rockets are used when astronauts carry out small movements in space.

Rhea *noun*
Rhea is the name of one of the **moons** of **Saturn**. It is the largest of the inner moons, and the second largest satellite of Saturn. **Voyager** 1 flew by Rhea and found it had an icy surface covered with craters. Some bright streaks were also seen on the surface.
Rhea has a diameter of 1,530 kilometres.

Rigel *noun*
Rigel is one of the brightest **stars**. It can easily be seen with the **naked eye**. Rigel is in the **constellation** of **Orion**.
Rigel is 900 light years away from Earth.

ring *noun*
A ring decribes a circular band of material that can be found surrounding some planets. **Saturn** has many thousands of rings made of rocks, pebbles and dust. They are only one kilometre thick. **Jupiter**, **Uranus** and **Neptune** also have rings.
Scientists think that rings are material that did not form into moons.

rings of Saturn ► **Saturn**

rocket ► page 114

Rosette nebula *noun*
The Rosette nebula is a cloud of **gas** and **dust** which is part of our **Galaxy**.
The Rosette nebula is bright and close enough to the Earth to be seen with an optical telescope.

rotation *noun*
Rotation describes the circular movement of an object round its own **axis**.
A complete rotation of the Earth takes place once each day.
rotate *verb*

Royal Greenwich Observatory *noun*
The Royal Greenwich Observatory is an **observatory** in south-east London, England. It was opened in 1675, and until 1958 it was Britain's major observatory.
Longitudes are measured from a line called the Greenwich meridian which runs through the Royal Greenwich Observatory.

RR Lyrae stars *plural noun*
RR Lyrae stars are **variable stars**. They are too dim to be seen with the **naked eye**.
RR Lyrae stars have periods ranging from 1 to about 30 hours.

S

Sagittarius *noun*
Sagittarius, or the Archer, is a **constellation**. It is one of the constellations of the **Zodiac**. Sagittarius can be seen in the **southern hemisphere**, and in southerly regions of the **northern hemisphere**. It covers a large region of the sky, and includes many bright stars. Sagittarius also includes a large number of star **clusters** and **nebulae**. Among these are the **Trifid nebula** and the **Lagoon nebula**.
The centre of the Milky Way Galaxy lies behind Sagittarius.

Sagittarius A *noun*
Sagittarius A is the name of a **radio source**. The radio source seems to be connected with the centre of the **Galaxy**. It seems to have at least four parts. The signals from Sagittarius A are not as strong as those from sources such as radio galaxies, even though it is closer to us.
Sagittarius A is only one of many interesting objects to be found in the constellation Sagittarius.

Sakigake *noun*
Sakigake was a **space probe** launched by Japan. It was designed to collect information about **Halley's comet**. Sakigake flew past the comet in 1986. It found out about the **magnetic field** of the comet, and took pictures with an **ultraviolet** camera.
Sakigake is a Japanese word meaning 'pioneer'.

Salyut space station *noun*
Salyut was the name of seven **space stations** launched into Earth's orbit by the Soviet Union from 1971 to 1987. The space stations were built as laboratories, where the **cosmonauts** could live and work. One of their main tasks was to study **weightlessness** over a long time.
Two cosmonauts spent 237 days on the Salyut 7 space station, long enough for a flight to Mars.

satellite ► page 118

Satellite Pour l'Observation de la Terre (SPOT) *noun*
The Satellite Pour l'Observation de la Terre is a **satellite** launched into Earth's **orbit** by France. It studies the resources of Earth. From photographs taken by the satellite, scientists can find out about minerals, crops, water and other resources.
The Satellite Pour l'Observation de la Terre has taken many very detailed photographs of Europe.

Saturn ► page 120

Scales ► Libra

scintillation *noun*
Scintillation describes the twinkling of the **light** from a **star**. It is caused by light passing through disturbances in the **atmosphere**. When they are watched, stars seem to change in brightness very quickly.
Scintillation can make it very difficult to see a star clearly with a small telescope.

satellite *noun*
A satellite is a body in **orbit** around a larger body. There are two kinds of satellite. Artificial satellites have been placed in orbit deliberately. Natural satellites, or **moons**, have been found orbiting many planets.
The Moon is a satellite of the Earth.

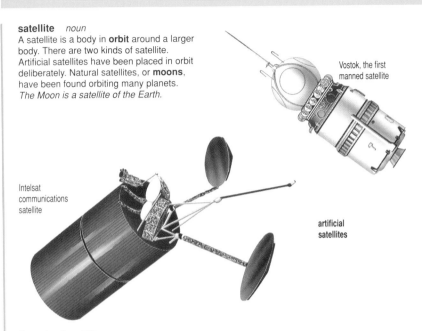

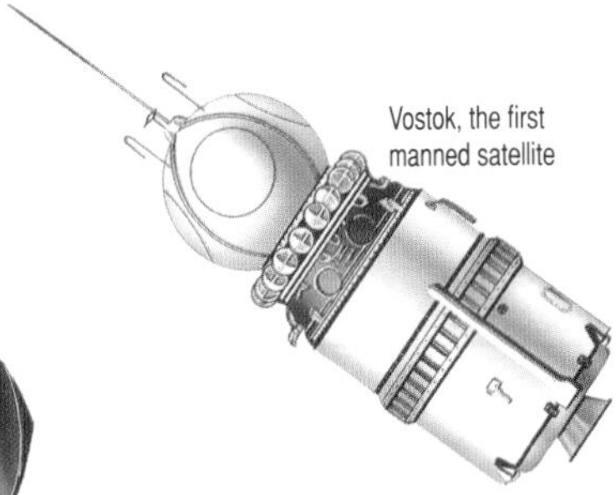
Vostok, the first manned satellite

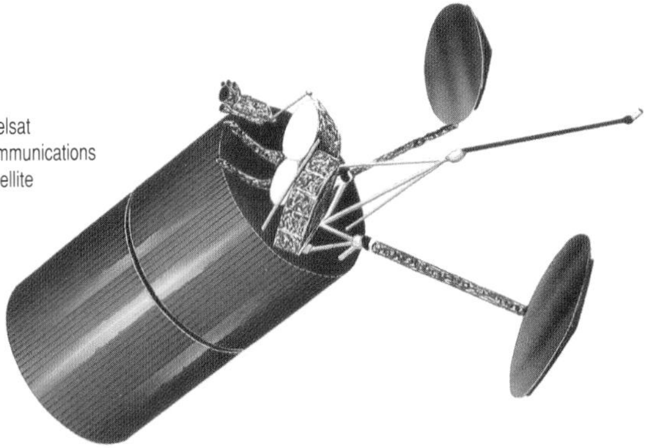
Intelsat communications satellite

artificial satellites

Meteosat weather satellite

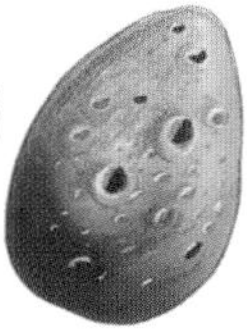

Deimos, moon of Mars

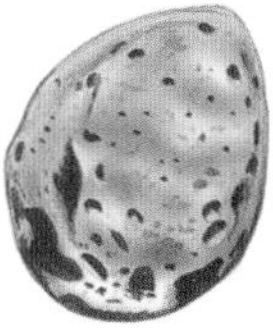

Phobos, moon of Mars

Enceladus, moon of Saturn

Dione, moon of Saturn

natural satellites

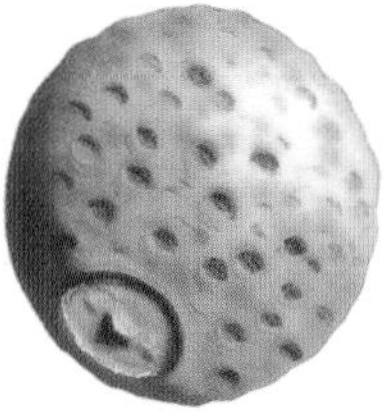

Mimas, moon of Saturn

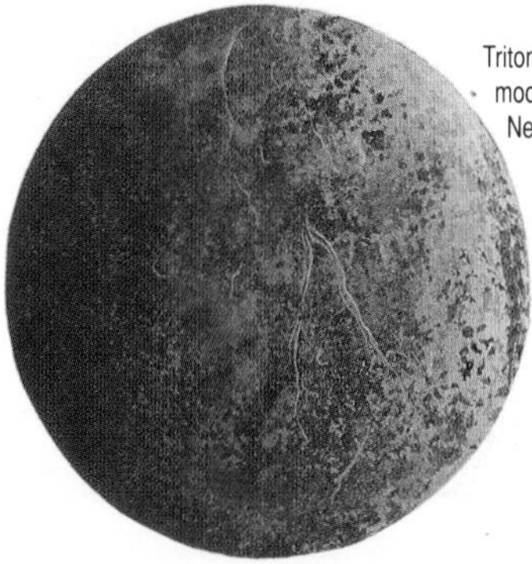

Triton, moon of Neptune

Miranda, moon of Uranus

Saturn *noun*

Saturn is a planet in the **solar system**. It is the second largest planet, over nine times the size of **Earth**. Saturn is the sixth planet from the **Sun**. It is a ball of hydrogen and helium gas. The spacecraft **Voyagers** 1 and 2 have flown past Saturn. They have shown that the light and dark bands that can be seen on the planet are caused by winds. The most beautiful feature of Saturn is a system of **rings** that circle the planet at the level of the **equator**. There is no life on Saturn.

Scientists think Saturn may have a massive iron core.

size of Saturn and Earth compared

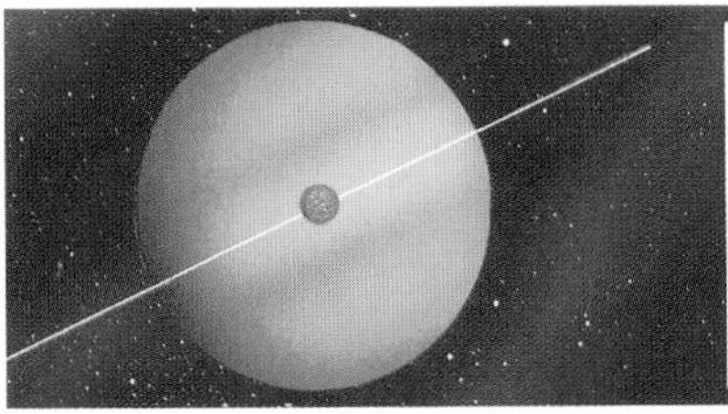

Planetary facts
Diameter: 120,600 kilometres
Distance from Sun: 1,424,600,000 kilometres
Nearest distance to Earth: 1,277,400,000 kilometres
Orbits the Sun in 29.50 earth years
Rotates on axis once in 10 hours, 39 minutes
Temperature at cloud tops: –185 degrees Celsius
Atmosphere: yes, a thick atmosphere of hydrogen and helium
Magnetic field: yes, a very strong one
Satellites: 23 known for certain, probably 3 more

Scorpion ► Scorpius

Scorpius *noun*
Scorpius, or the Scorpion, is one of the constellations of the **Zodiac**. Scorpius is mostly in the **southern hemisphere**. Part of it lies in the **northern hemisphere**. It has many bright stars, including a very large, red **supergiant** called Antares, which is a **double star**. There are many globular and open **star clusters** in Scorpius.
Many people think that Scorpius actually looks like a scorpion.

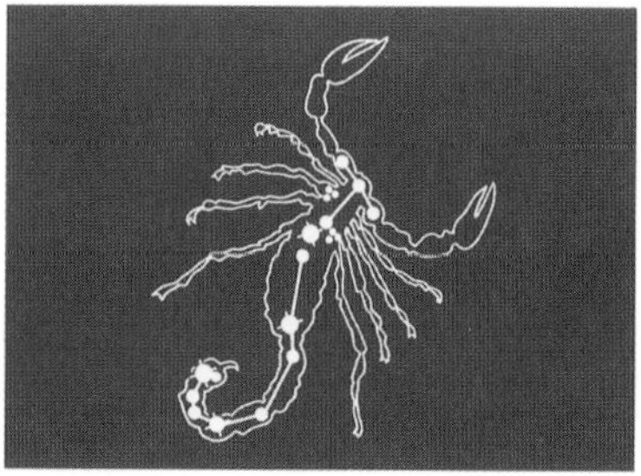

Scorpius X-1 *noun*
Scorpius X-1 is an **X-ray** source. It is the brightest X-ray source in the sky. Scorpius X-1 is a **binary star**.
The scientists studied the X-ray signals from Scorpius X-1.

Search for Extra-Terrestrial Intelligence (SETI) *noun*
The Search for Extra-Terrestrial Intelligence has been going on for many years. Scientists have listened for radio signals that might be in a pattern that could be a message. The **radio telescope** at **Arecibo Observatory** was used in 1974 to send a message into space. The message gave details of where Earth was, and who lived on it. More messages were placed in the **Pioneer** and **Voyager** space probes.
Scientists working on SETI hope that one day aliens will answer their messages.

second contact *noun*
Second contact is one of the stages of an **eclipse**. In an eclipse of the **Moon**, second contact is the time when the Moon is just covered completely by the shadow, or **umbra**, of the **Earth**. In an eclipse of the **Sun**, second contact is the time when the edges of the Moon and the surface of the Sun just touch at the beginning of the total eclipse.
She took many photographs of the second contact stage of the eclipse.

selenography *noun*
Selenography is the study of the **Moon**. It is the study of the surface of the Moon, and includes making maps of all the features.
The student of selenography made a map of the craters of the Moon.

selenology *noun*
Selenology is the study of the rocks of the **Moon**. It also looks at the surface and the inside, or interior, of the Moon.
Selenology is the name given to the lunar form of geology.

sensor *noun*
A sensor is part of an instrument. It is the part that changes a signal that has been received into a form that can be measured by another part of the instrument. Sensors can be used to find out about heat, cold or the speed of a wind.
Sensors on Voyager 2 found that the temperature of the moon Triton was 38 degrees kelvin.

service module *noun*
A service module is part of a **spacecraft**. In a manned spaceflight, the service module stores fuel, water and electrical **energy** for the **astronauts** to use. It is usually attached to the **command module**.
The service module for the Apollo spacecraft was 6.6 metres long.

Seven Sisters ► Pleiades

Seyfert galaxy *noun*
A Seyfert galaxy is a kind of **galaxy**. It has a very bright centre, or **nucleus**. The arms of a Seyfert galaxy do not show up brightly. Many Seyfert galaxies are strong sources of **infra-red radiation**.
About two per cent of all galaxies are Seyfert galaxies.

shepherd moons *noun*
Shepherd moons are **natural satellites** of the **planet Saturn**. They **orbit** the planet in pairs. They are found one on each side of a **ring**, and seem to be keeping the ring in place by their **gravitational** pull.
Pandora and Prometheus are shepherd moons for part of the F ring.

shooting star ► meteor

short-period comet *noun*
A short-period comet is a **comet** that **orbits** the **Sun** once in a time of up to 25 years. Sometimes comets that take up to 200 years to complete one orbit are also included in the group of short-period comets. The comet with the shortest period is **Encke's comet**. The most famous short-period comet of all is **Halley's comet**, which takes about 76 years to complete one orbit.
Some scientists think short-period comets come from the Oort Cloud.

sidereal *adjective*
Sidereal describes anything to do with the **stars**.
Sidereal time is the time measured by the rotation of Earth with respect to the stars.

Siding Spring Observatory *noun*
Siding Spring Observatory is in Australia. It is an optical **observatory** and includes **reflecting telescopes** of 66 centimetres, 1 metre and 2.3 metres. The observatory is at an **altitude** of 1,000 metres, on Siding Spring Mountain in New South Wales.
Siding Spring Observatory is owned by the Australian National University.

signal *noun*
A signal is a kind of message. It carries information from one place to another. Different kinds of **electromagnetic radiation** can be received as signals by **antennae** and **dish aerials**. Scientists can use this information to find out where the signals have come from.
The scientist found that the signals were coming from a strong radio source.

simulator *noun*
A simulator is a machine that helps train **astronauts**. It copies the problems and conditions that can be met with during a flight. The simulator contains all the machinery and **instruments** that an astronaut would have. The astronaut can practise flying a spacecraft without leaving **Earth**. Powerful computers allow a space flight to be copied in a simulator.
Space shuttle pilots use simulators for their training.

Sirius *noun*
Sirius is a star in the **constellation** Canis Major, the Great Dog. It is the brightest star in the sky, and has a pure white colour. Sirius is 26 times as bright as the Sun. It is 8.5 light years from Earth. Sirius is a **binary star**. Its companion, Sirius B, is a **white dwarf**. Sirius can also be called the Dog Star.
Sirius is a Greek word meaning 'scorching'.

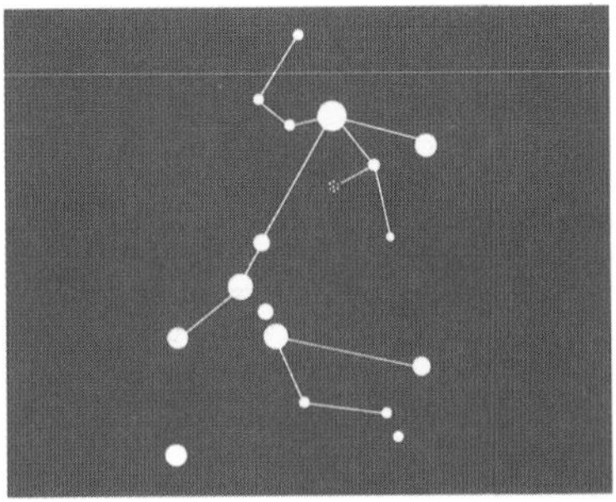

Skylab space station *noun*
Skylab was a **space station** put into **orbit** by the United States of America in 1973. Skylab was made from part of a **Saturn** rocket. It was turned into a work section and a place for three astronauts to live. Work done by the **crews** included observing the Sun and the Earth, and experimenting with materials such as metal and glass.
The Skylab space station burned up on re-entry in 1979.

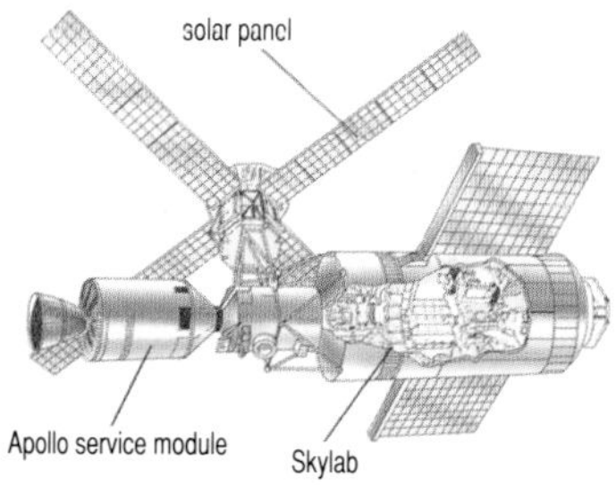

Small Astronomy Satellites *noun*
The Small Astronomy Satellites were three **satellites** launched by the United States of America. They were designed for **X-ray** and **gamma ray astronomy**, and were launched in 1970, 1972 and 1973.
The first Small Astronomy Satellite is better known as Uhuru.

solar *noun*
Solar means having to do with the **Sun**. Solar energy is energy from the Sun.
A solar eclipse is an eclipse of the Sun.

solar activity *noun*
Solar activity describes energetic activity of the Sun. It includes **sunspots**, **solar flares**, **faculae** and **prominences**. Scientists have found that solar activity runs in phases. For example, the number of sunspots changes over a period of 11 years.
Many scientists have studied solar activity.

solar cycle *noun*
A solar cycle describes a phase or cycle of **solar activity**. A solar cycle is most often used to describe **sunspot** activity. The cycle seems to be about 11 years.
At the beginning of a solar cycle, there are very few sunspots.

solar eclipse ► eclipse

solar flare *noun*
Solar flares are bursts of **energy** on the **Sun**. They seem to be linked with **sunspots**. A flare is an explosion that lasts a few minutes. **X-rays** and **radio waves** are sent out from the flare.
Aurorae seen on Earth are related to solar flares.

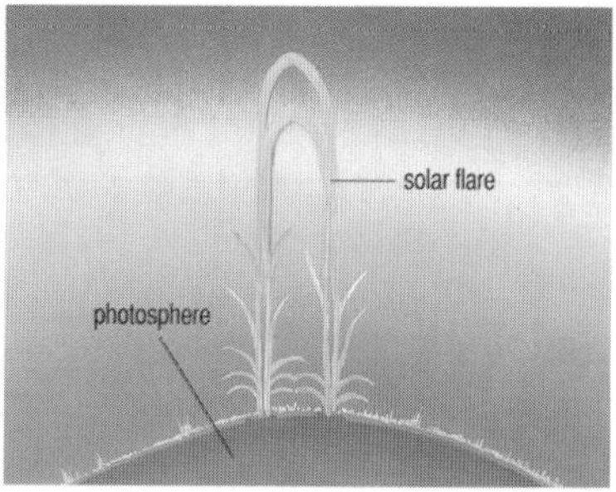

Solar Heliospheric Observatory (SOHO) *noun*
The Solar Heliospheric Observatory is a **satellite** that the **European Space Agency** plans to launch. It will carry 12 instruments. The information they will try and gather includes details of the **solar atmosphere**, solar **oscillations** and how the **Sun** is made up. SOHO will orbit the Sun at the point where the gravitational attraction of the Sun and the Earth are equal.
SOHO will increase our understanding of the Sun to a great extent.

Solar Maximum Mission *noun*
The Solar Maximum Mission was a **satellite** launched by the United States of America in 1980. It was going to study the **Sun** during a period of high **solar activity**. The satellite broke down after nine months in **orbit**. Astronauts from the Challenger **space shuttle** managed to catch the Solar Maximum Mission after several attempts. They were able to repair the satellite, so that it could carry on working until 1989.
The Solar Maximum Mission repair was carried out in 1984.

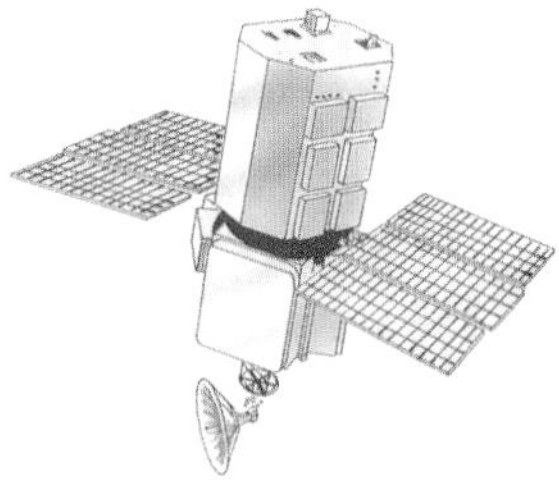

solar panel *noun*
Solar panels are a way of providing **energy** for **spacecraft**. There is plenty of sunlight in **space**, which can be used to make electricity. Solar panels on the outside of a spacecraft are covered with rows of cells, made of silicon. Each cell can make a tiny electric current from sunlight.
Solar panels can also be called solar arrays.

solar sailing *noun*
Solar sailing is an idea. Solar sailing would use the pressure of sunlight to drive spacecraft. The sunlight would fall on large sails made of very thin, light plastic. Over a period of time the spacecraft would accelerate without needing any rocket fuel.
Solar sailing might be the cheapest way of travelling in space.

solar system ► page 126

solar tower *noun*
A solar tower is a kind of **telescope**. It is designed to study the Sun. To get a good image of the Sun, scientists need a long distance between the **lens** or **mirror** of a telescope and the point where the image **focuses**. The **atmosphere** at ground level is often too disturbed to obtain clear pictures. To deal with these problems, scientists build towers that act as giant telescopes.
There is a solar tower at the Sacramento Peak Observatory in New Mexico.

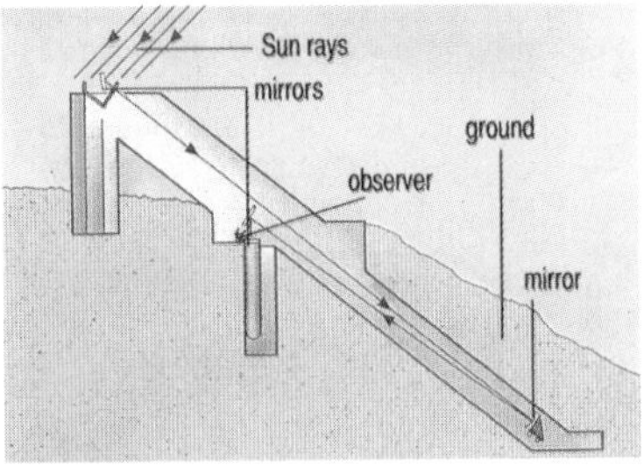

solar wind *noun*
The solar wind describes the stream of particles blown outwards from the **Sun**. The particles come from the **corona**. The hot **gases** that make up the corona become thinner as they get further from the Sun. The **gravitational** pull of the Sun cannot hold them, and they become the solar wind.
The particles in the solar wind have a velocity of about 500 kilometres a second by the time they reach Earth.

Southern Cross *noun*
The Southern Cross is a **constellation** in the southern hemisphere. It is the constellation nearest to the south celestial pole. The Southern Cross contains a beautiful **open cluster** known as the **Jewel Box**.
The Southern Cross is almost surrounded by the constellation Centaurus.

southern hemisphere ► page 128

Soyuz *noun*
Soyuz was the name of a series of **spacecraft** launched by the Soviet Union from 1967. The first Soyuz flights were used to experiment with meeting and **docking** techniques. Later Soyuz spacecraft were used as shuttles to the **Salyut space stations**. In 1975, Soyuz 19 docked with an **Apollo** spacecraft.
The Soyuz spacecraft normally held two cosmonauts.

space *noun*
Space describes the region between all the bodies in the **universe**. Space is not completely empty. It includes **magnetic fields**, **electromagnetic radiation**, clouds of **hydrogen gas**, and **dust** particles. Space is being explored, using telescopes, and satellites and space probes.
Space does not include the atmospheres of planets or stars.

Space Age *noun*
The Space Age is the name given to the last decades of the 1900s. It was at this time that humans were first able to build a **rocket** powerful enough to put a **satellite** into **orbit** around the **Earth**. The first satellite was launched by the Soviet Union on 4 October 1957. In the first half of the 1900s, many countries had worked on rockets. This work has sent men to the **Moon**, and launched **space probes** to study the furthest planets.
Today we all live in the Space Age.

spacecraft *noun*
A spacecraft is a vehicle that works in **space**. Each spacecraft has a **mission**. Spacecraft include their own supply of **energy**. They also include powerful computers, which communicate with **ground stations** and **mission control**. Many spacecraft **orbit** the Earth. Some are **interplanetary**. Spacecraft have many uses, including communications, watching the weather, and scientific observation.
A spacecraft can be manned or unmanned.

spaceflight *noun*
Spaceflight describes travelling in **space**. The first human to fly in space was a **cosmonaut** from the Soviet Union, in 1961. Since then, many spaceflights have taken place, including the **Apollo** missions to the Moon, and the experiments on the **Mir space station**. Spaceflight also describes the launching of any vehicle into space which returns to Earth or travels to the Moon or planets.
People imagined spaceflight long before the first spacecraft was launched.

Spacelab *noun*
Spacelab is a small, re-usable **space station** built by the **European Space Agency**. Spacelab fits into the **payload** of the **space shuttle**. It is a scientific laboratory. Spacelab missions have included medical studies and Earth observations.
Payload specialists work on Spacelab while the shuttle is in orbit.

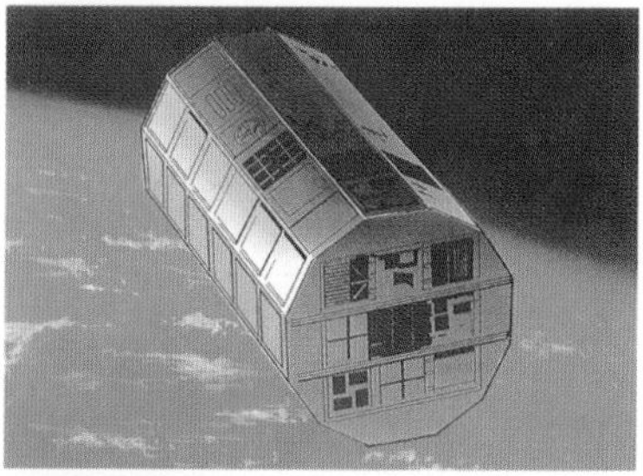

space probe *noun*
Space probes are unmanned **spaceflights**. They are **missions** to find out about **moons**, **planets** and other objects in the **solar system** and beyond. Space probes are also the vehicles that carry instruments to record and send back information. Probes to the closer planets use solar panels to supply energy. Probes to deep space are powered by **nuclear energy**.
Powerful radio transmitters allow ground stations to communicate with space probes.

solar system *noun*
The solar system describes the **Sun** and all the bodies that orbit the Sun, including the **planets**, **asteroids**, **moons**, **meteoroids** and **comets**. It also includes the **gas** and **dust** found in the space between larger bodies. Scientists think that the solar system formed from a rotating cloud of gas and dust. This surrounded the Sun when it formed about 5 billion years ago.
All the objects in the solar system are held in orbit by the gravitational pull of the Sun.

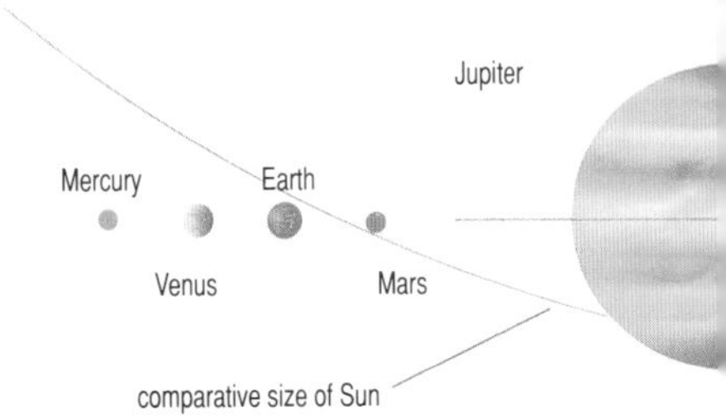

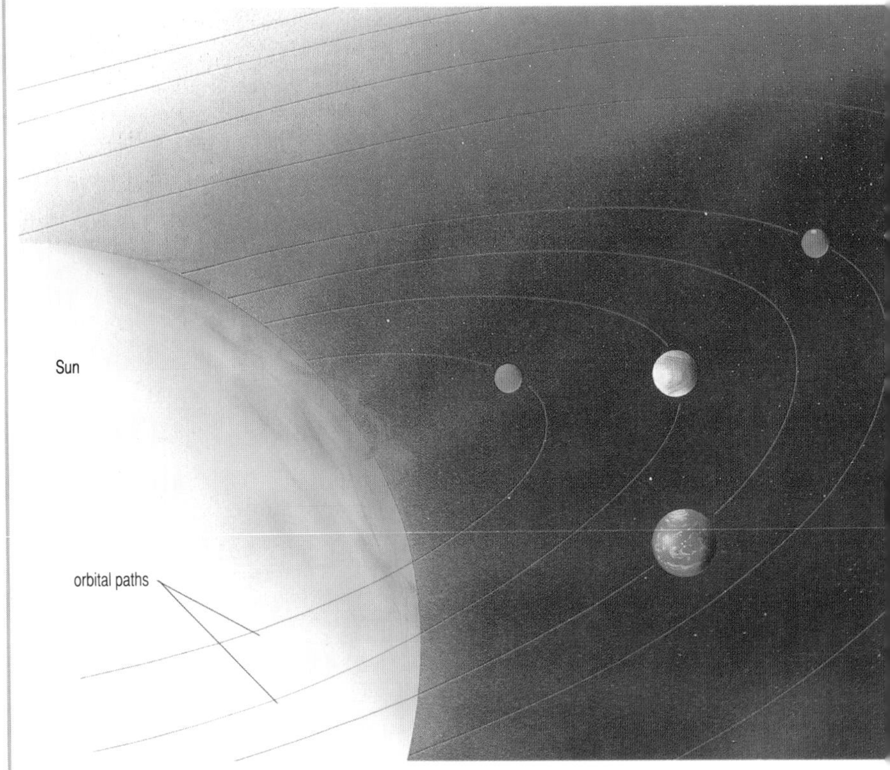

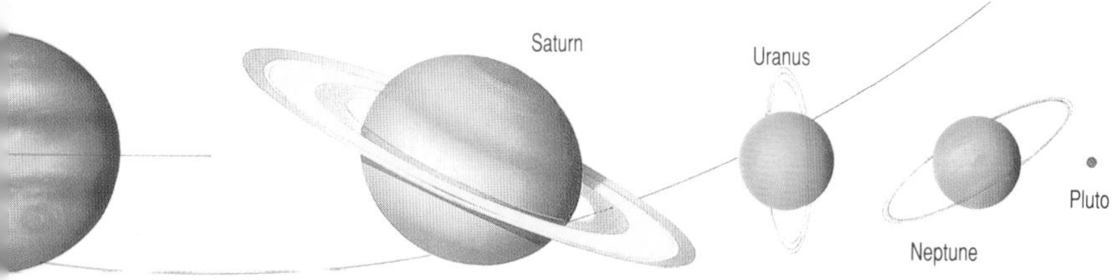
Saturn
Uranus
Pluto
Neptune

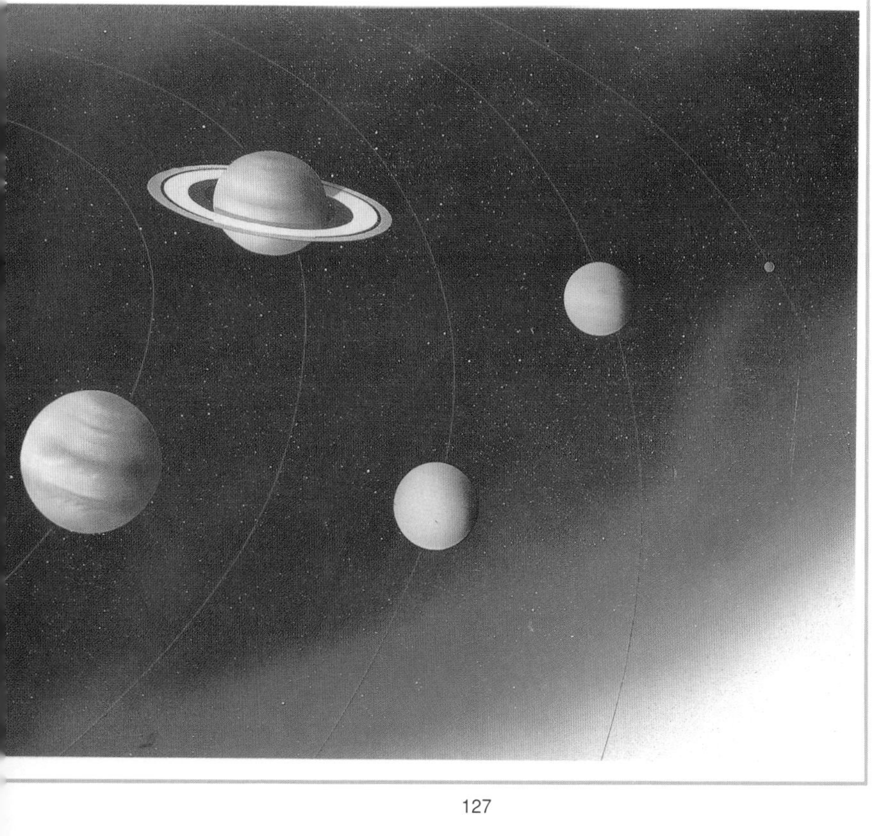

southern hemisphere *noun*
The southern hemisphere is the half of the **Earth** which is south of the **Equator**. **Latitudes** in the southern hemisphere are measured in degrees South. The southern hemisphere of the sky is the part of the sky that can be seen from the southern hemisphere of the Earth. It includes the **constellations of the southern hemisphere**, nebulae, galaxies and other bodies.
There are more constellations in the southern hemisphere of the sky than in the northern hemisphere.

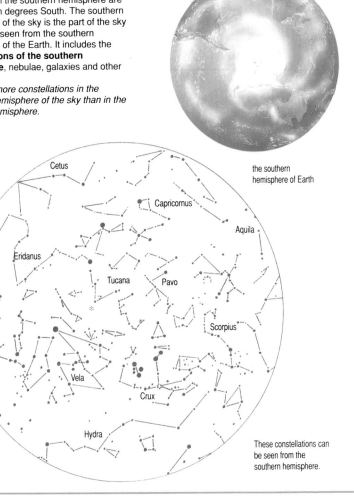

the southern hemisphere of Earth

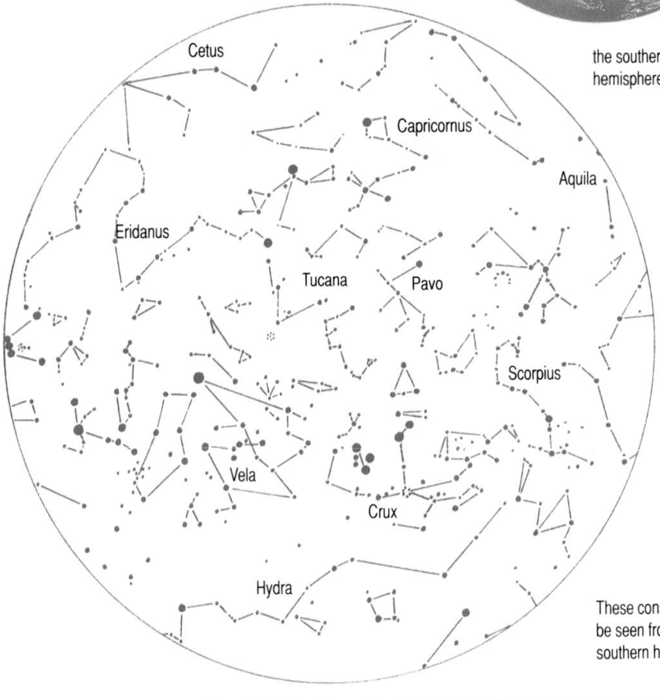

These constellations can be seen from the southern hemisphere.

space shuttle ► page 130

space station ► page 132

space suit ► page 133

space telescope ► **Hubble space telescope**

Space Transportation System (STS) *noun*
The Space Transportation System is the programme planned in the United States of America that includes the **space shuttle**. It includes developing **rockets**, **fuel tanks** and **spacecraft** that can all be re-used. If machinery can be re-used, it will help to keep the cost of space programmes down.
The Space Transportation System includes plans to lower the cost of working in space.

spacewalk ► **Extra-Vehicular Activity**

special relativity ► **relativity**

spectral class *noun*
Spectral class groups **stars** by the colours of their **spectra**. The spectral class runs from high **temperatures** to low temperatures. It is made up of 10 groups. Spectral class is one of the features of a star used on the **Hertzsprung-Russell Diagram**.
Scientists are still working on improvements to the spectral class system.

spectral lines *noun*
Spectral lines are lines that appear when starlight is split into a **spectrum**. When starlight passes through the cooler, outer **atmosphere** of the star, some **radiation** is taken in, or absorbed. It is absorbed by **chemicals** in the atmosphere. The missing **wavelengths** show up as black lines in the spectrum. Scientists can tell what chemicals are present in the atmosphere from the position of the spectral lines.
The spectral lines showed that there was calcium in the atmosphere of the star.

spectroheliosope *noun*
A spectrohelioscope is a kind of **spectroscope** used only to study the **Sun**. The spectrohelioscope takes an image of the Sun at one particular wavelength. A normal image is taken in white light, made up of mixed wavelengths. The image at a single wavelength allows scientists to study solar features they could not otherwise see.
The scientist used a spectrohelioscope to study hydrogen on the Sun's surface.

spectroscope *noun*
A spectroscope is an instrument used for breaking down **light** into a **spectrum**. The spectrum can be recorded, using a camera or a **charge-coupled device**. By using a spectroscope, a scientist can gain information about stars, galaxies and nebulae. The spectra obtained can be used to find out details, including temperature, movement and chemical make-up.
The scientist used a spectroscope to take a picture of the spectrum of a galaxy.

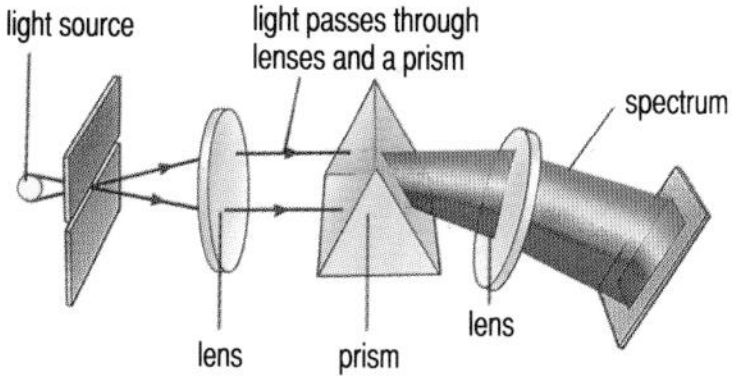

spectrum (plural **spectra**) *noun*
A spectrum is a band of colours. It is made when a beam of **electromagnetic radiation** splits into its different **wavelengths**. Each colour of the spectrum corresponds to a wavelength. Long wavelengths show as red. Short wavelengths show as violet. The most common way of making a spectrum is to pass a beam of light through a **prism**.
A rainbow is a very familiar spectrum.

space shuttle *noun*
The space shuttles are a series of **spacecraft** built by the United States of America. The space shuttles are launched with **rockets**, but they can land like an aircraft on a runway. They can be re-used. Other countries have worked on re-usable spacecraft. The Soviet Union built **Buran**, and the Europeans are planning a shuttle called **Hermes**.
The first space shuttle flight was made by Columbia on 12 April 1981.

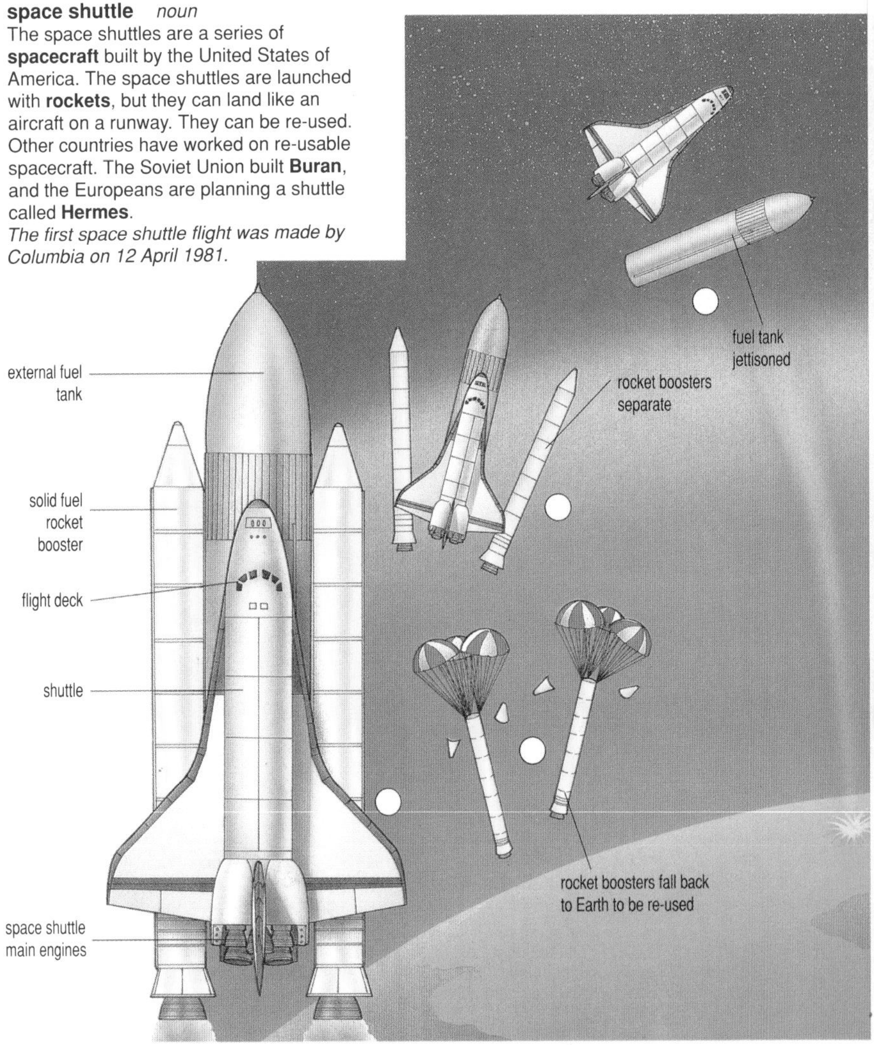

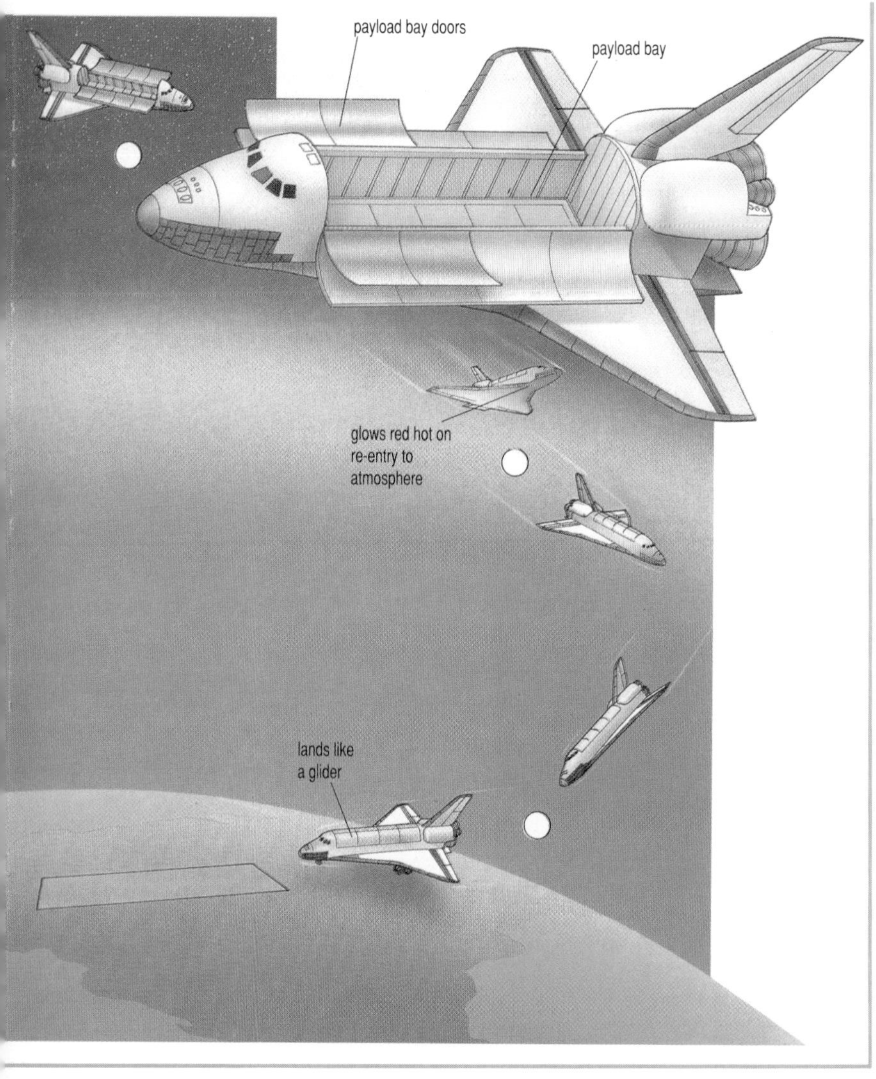
payload bay doors
payload bay
glows red hot on
re-entry to
atmosphere
lands like
a glider

space station *noun*
A space station is a large **spacecraft** in permanent **orbit**. It is designed to allow **crews** to live on it for long periods of time, and for observations and experiments to be carried out. **Docking** ports allow smaller spacecraft to fly up to the space station to supply crews and materials. Space stations use **solar panels** for their energy supply. The first two space stations were **Salyut** and **Skylab**. The **Mir** space station was launched in 1986. The international space station **Freedom** is planned to start work at the end of the 1990s.
Space station Freedom will be built by Japan, Canada, the European Space Agency and the United States of America.

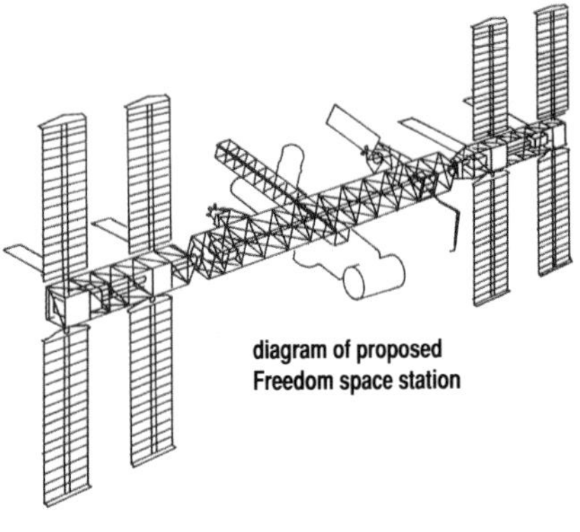

diagram of proposed Freedom space station

Skylab space station

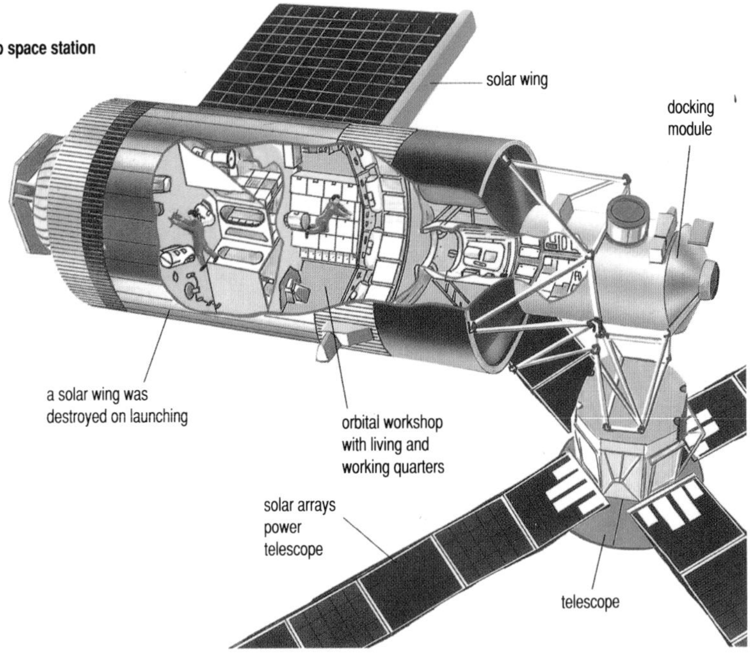

space suit *noun*
A space suit is a garment worn by **astronauts**. The outer covering of the space suit protects the astronaut from harmful **radiation** and very hot or very cold **temperatures**. A space suit covers the whole body. A backpack provides oxygen, electrical power and radio communication.
The space suit includes all the systems that are needed to keep people alive in space.

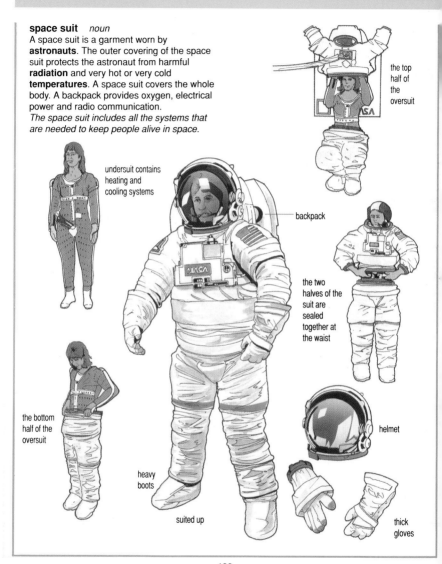

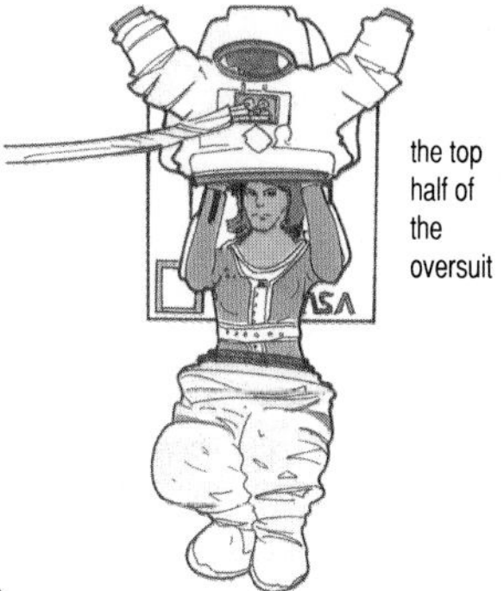

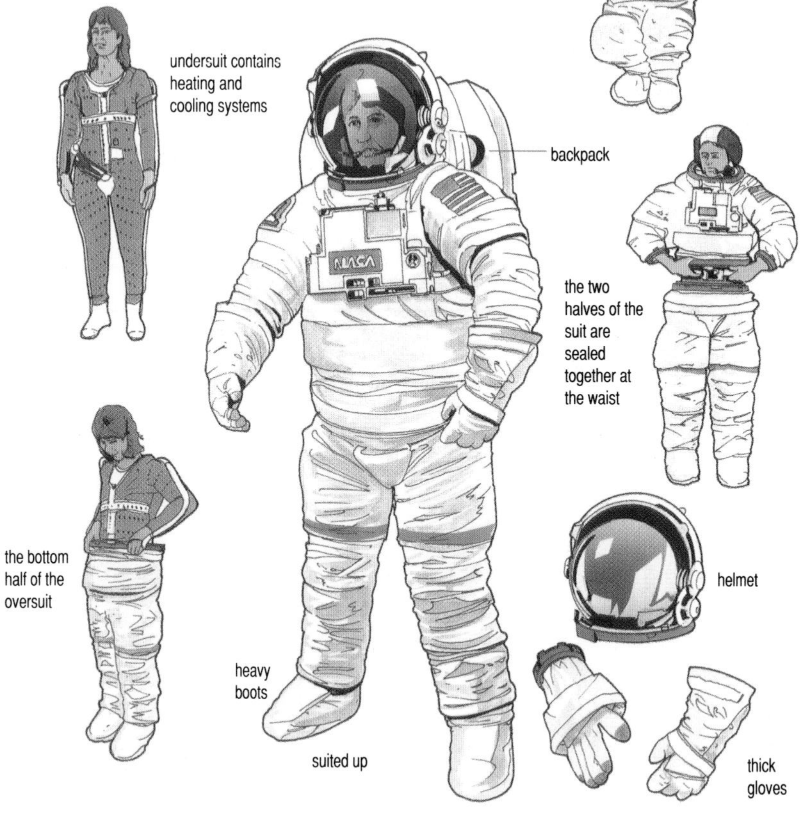

star *noun*
A star is a luminous ball of **gas**. It is very hot, making energy by thermonuclear reaction. A star stays in a stable state by balancing the outward pressure of gas with the inward pull of **gravity**. Scientists think that stars are born in **clusters**, formed from clouds of gas and dust. The star will burn for thousands of millions of years until its fuel is used up. Then it may become a **red giant** and a **white dwarf**, or it may explode as a **supernova**, leaving behind a **neutron star**, or **pulsar**, or a **black hole**.
The nearest star to the Earth is the Sun.

a young star

The central area of a young star is hot enough to start making nuclear energy.

A star of the mass of the Sun burns its gas for about 10 million years.

A star of the Sun's mass will eventually swell up and become a red giant. It has burned all its hydrogen and has a core of helium.

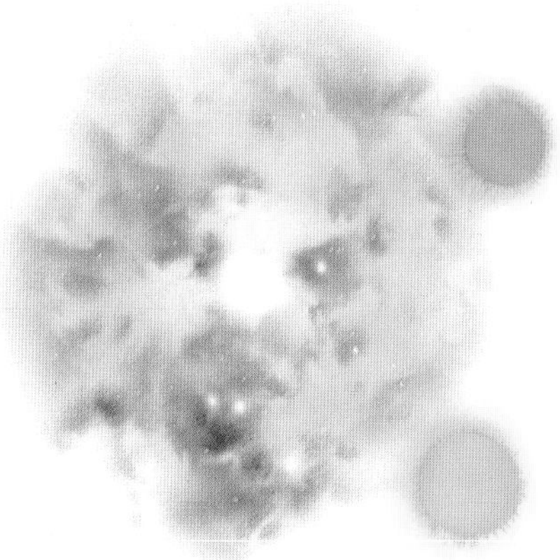

Stars form from the gas and dust of a nebula.

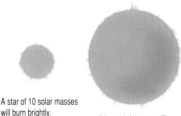

A star of 10 solar masses will burn brightly.

A large, bright star will burn its hydrogen up faster than a star of one solar mass.

A star of 30 or more solar masses may form.

Massive stars have a shorter life than a star with the mass of the Sun. They are extremely bright.

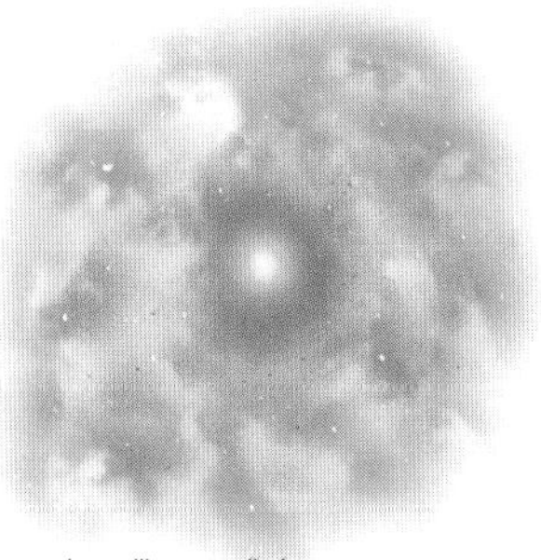

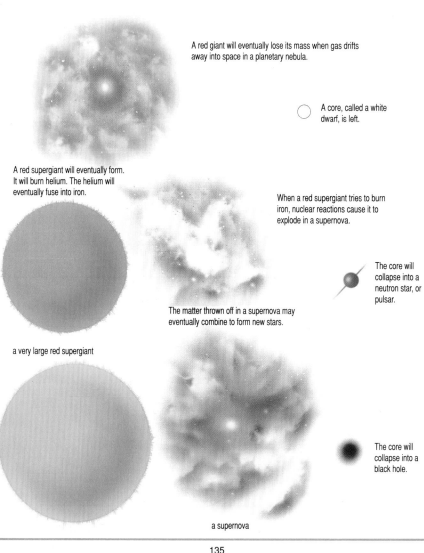

A red giant will eventually lose its mass when gas drifts away into space in a planetary nebula.

A core, called a white dwarf, is left.

A red supergiant will eventually form. It will burn helium. The helium will eventually fuse into iron.

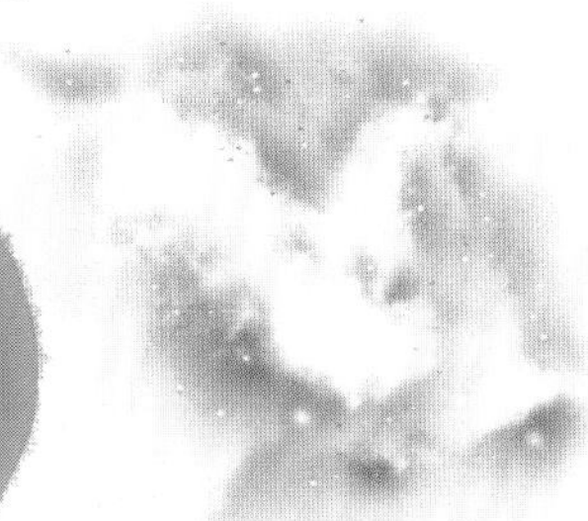

When a red supergiant tries to burn iron, nuclear reactions cause it to explode in a supernova.

The core will collapse into a neutron star, or pulsar.

The matter thrown off in a supernova may eventually combine to form new stars.

a very large red supergiant

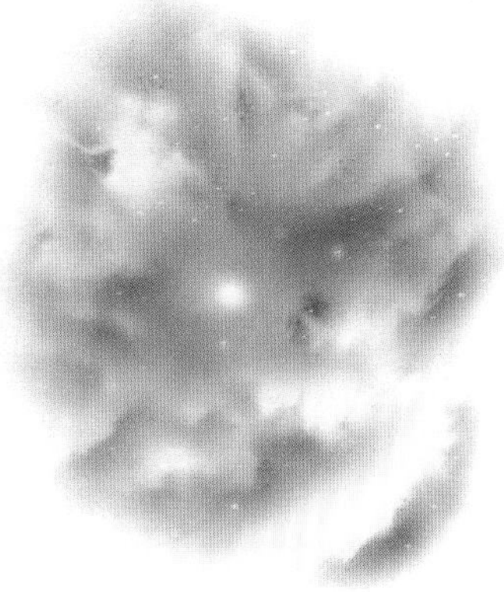

a supernova

The core will collapse into a black hole.

speed of light *noun*
The speed of light is the speed at which **electromagnetic radiation** travels in one second. The speed of light is 299,792 kilometres per second. This is the highest speed known in the **universe**. Some scientists think that it is the highest speed that could ever be reached. In one year, light travels 9,460,800,000,000 kilometres. This distance, called a light year, is used as a measurement for the enormous distances in the universe.
At the speed of light, the Sun's rays take 8.33 minutes to reach the Earth.

sphere *noun*
A sphere is a round, solid shape. All the points on a sphere are the same distance from its centre. The **celestial sphere** is a sphere that has been imagined around the Earth.
A very familiar sphere is a ball.

spiral galaxy *noun*
A spiral galaxy is a **galaxy**. It has arms that bend around it in a spiral shape. Many spiral galaxies have been found. They have been grouped by the **Hubble classification** into spiral galaxies and barred spiral galaxies. In most spiral galaxies, stars that are forming and young stars, are found in the arms. Older stars are found in a bulge at the centre, where the density of stars is greatest.
The Milky Way Galaxy is a spiral galaxy that includes our solar system.

splashdown *noun*
Splashdown describes the moment when astronauts land on Earth. Before the re-usable **space shuttle**, astronauts re-entered the atmosphere of Earth in a **command module**. This was designed to slow down with the help of parachutes, and land gently in the sea. Splashdown describes what happens when a large object falls into water.
The Pacific Ocean was used for splashdown for the Apollo astronauts.

Sputnik *noun*
Sputnik was a series of three satellites. Sputnik was launched by the Soviet Union on 4 October 1957. It was the first artificial satellite to be put into orbit around the Earth. Sputnik was a sphere of metal, 58 centimetres in diameter. It weighed 84 kilograms. Sputnik transmitted information about temperatures for 22 days before its energy gave out. It re-entered the atmosphere and burned up on 4 January 1958. Sputnik reached a height of 933 kilometres, and orbited Earth for 92 days.
Sputnik is the Russian word for 'traveller'.

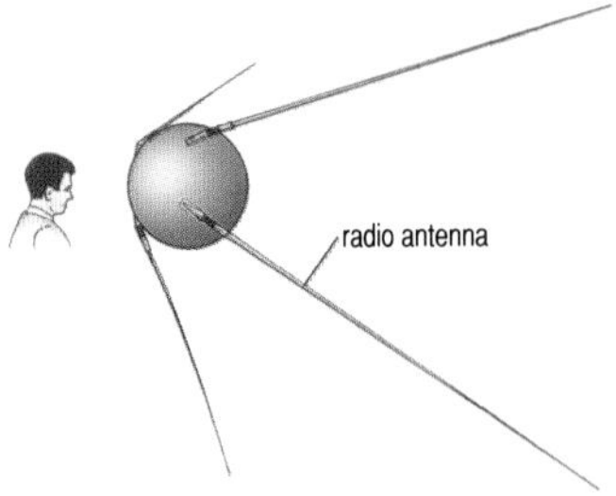

star ► page 134

star atlas *noun*
A star atlas is a collection of maps. These show the positions of **stars** and other objects in the sky.
She used a star atlas to find the constellations of the Zodiac.

star catalogue *noun*
A star catalogue is a list of information about **stars**. The information may include how to find the position of a star, the **magnitude** of a star, and all the stars that can be seen in a region. A star catalogue could also list **binary stars**, or **star clusters**.
The star catalogue listed all the stars brighter than the sixth magnitude.

Sun *noun*

The Sun is a yellow **dwarf star**. It is a ball of hot **hydrogen** and **helium** gas. At the core of the Sun, the hydrogen is changed to helium by **nuclear fusion**. The nuclear fusion produces enormous heat energy. This rises through layers of hydrogen to the surface of the Sun, or **photosphere**. The surface is very active, with **sunspots**, **flares** and **prominences**. The outer part of the Sun is the **corona**. **Electromagnetic radiation** streams from the corona into space.
The Sun turns on its axis once every 27 days.

WARNING.
Never look directly at the Sun.

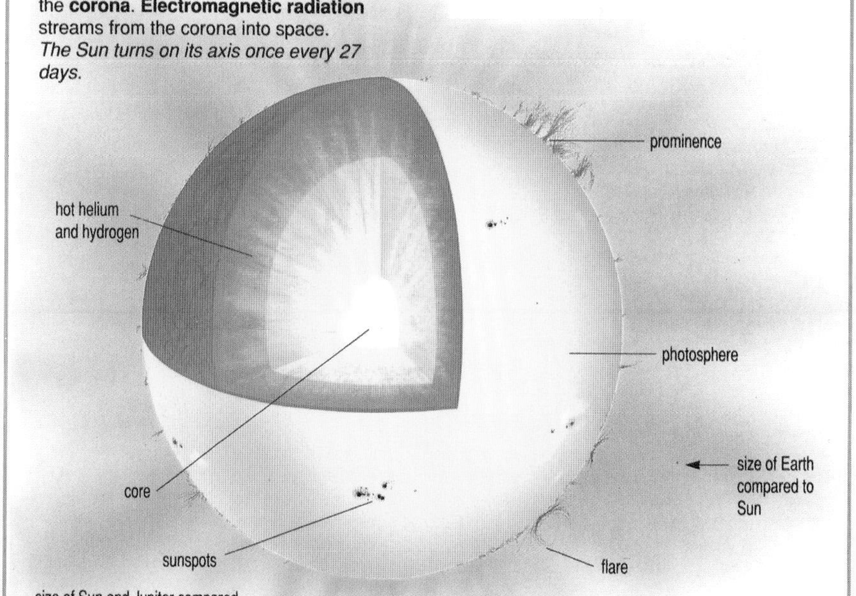

size of Sun and Jupiter compared

Sun facts
Diameter: 1,392,000 kilometres
Distance from Earth: 150,000,000 kilometres
Rotates on axis: once in 27 days
Temperature at core: 15,000,000° degrees kelvin
Temperature at surface: 5,700° kelvin
Apparent magnitude: –27

star cluster *noun*
A star cluster is a group, or an **association**, of **stars**. Scientists think that clusters of stars formed together. There are two kinds of star cluster – globular clusters and open clusters.
There are more than 1,000 open star clusters in the Milky Way Galaxy.

Star Wars *noun*
Star Wars is the popular name for the Strategic Defense Initiative, or SDI. Star Wars aims to protect the United States of America from attack by high-altitude missiles, or **rockets**. Star Wars could include shooting missiles down in space. It could also include destroying the missiles with laser beams or particle beams. There are many problems, including finding the right target, and supplying enough energy for the systems to work.
There are many problems to face before Star Wars can be used.

Steady State theory *noun*
The Steady State theory is an idea about **cosmology**. It is the opposite of the **Big Bang theory**. The Steady State theory put forward the idea that the **universe** had always existed. There had never been a beginning. Scientists thought that new material was forming all the time. This filled in the spaces between the **galaxies** as the galaxies moved outwards.
The discovery of cosmic microwave background radiation upset the Steady State theory.

Suisei *noun*
Suisei was a **space probe** launched by Japan. It was designed to collect information about **Halley's comet**. Suisei flew past the comet in 1986. It was one of the two Japanese space probes to travel past Halley's comet. The other was **Sakigake**.
Suisei is the Japanese word for 'comet'.

Sun ► page 137

sunrise *noun*
Sunrise is the time when the edge, or **limb**, of the **Sun** meets the horizon as the Sun rises in the sky. The **Earth** turns on its axis once every 24 hours. For roughly half that time, part of the Earth has turned out of the light of the Sun. It is passing through night. As Earth goes on rotating, the dark region turns back into the sunlight. This is when sunrise can be seen.
She got up early to see the sunrise.

sunset *noun*
Sunset is the time when the edge, or **limb**, of the **Sun** meets the horizon as the Sun sets in the sky. The Earth turns on its axis once every 24 hours. For roughly half that time, part of the Earth receives the light of the Sun. It is passing through daytime. As the Earth goes on rotating, the light region turns away from the Sun. This is when sunset can be seen.
The light began to fade at sunset.

sunspot *noun*
Sunspots are dark patches on the face of the **Sun** which appear and then disappear over a period of about 11 years. They have temperatures lower than that of the bright-face, or **photosphere**. The centre of a sunspot, or **umbra**, has a temperature of about 4,000 degrees kelvin. The region surrounding the umbra, or **penumbra**, has a temperature of about 5,500 degrees kelvin.
Each sunspot usually lasts about two weeks, as it moves across the face of the Sun.

supercluster *noun*
A supercluster is a large cluster of **galaxies**. Most scientists think that superclusters are the largest objects in the **universe**. They think that galaxies are pulled together by **gravity** to form superclusters. Superclusters are hundreds of millions of light years across.
About 50 superclusters are known.

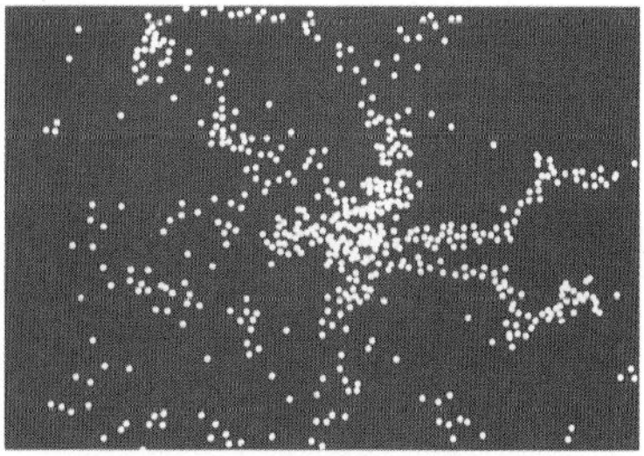

supergiant *noun*
A supergiant is a highly **luminous star**. Supergiants can be 500 times as large as the Sun. Some supergiants, such as **Rigel**, are very hot. Red supergiants, such as **Betelgeuse**, are dying stars. Supergiants may become **supernovae**.
The absolute magnitudes of supergiants range from –4 to –9.

superior planet *noun*
Superior planet describes any of the planets that orbit the **Sun** beyond the **Earth**. **Mars**, **Jupiter**, **Saturn**, **Uranus**, **Neptune** and **Pluto** are all superior planets. The opposite of superior planet is **inferior planet**.
The Voyager space probes were launched to find out about some of the superior planets.

supermassive star *noun*
A supermassive star is a **star** with a very large **mass**. These stars have a mass up to about 100 times that of the Sun.
A supermassive star is not as large as a supergiant.

supernova (plural **supernovae**) *noun*
A supernova is a **star** that explodes. The brightness of the star may increase by as much as 20 **magnitudes**. A supernova happens when a very large, old star runs out of nuclear fuel. The material that remains in the star collapses inwards. This causes the temperature at the centre of the star to rise by millions of degrees. It explodes in a supernova, throwing off into space material which becomes a **supernova remnant**.
In 1987, there was a supernova in the Large Magellanic Cloud galaxy.

supernova remnant *noun*
A supernova remnant is the material thrown into space by a **star** that explodes in a **supernova**. Some supernova remnants can be seen with the **naked eye**. Some give out **radio waves**, or **X-rays**, which have been detected.
The Crab nebula is a supernova remnant.

Surveyor *noun*
Surveyor was the name of a series of seven unmanned **spacecraft**, launched by the United States of America from 1966 to 1968. The Surveyors were sent to the **Moon**. Landing the Surveyors on the Moon gave scientists information on the best way to do this. The information was used later for the **Apollo project**. The Surveyors also took pictures of the surface of the Moon, and carried out experiments on the soil.
Two of the Surveyor spacecraft crash-landed on the Moon.

synchronous orbit ► geosynchronous orbit

synchronous rotation ► captured rotation

syzygy *noun*
Syzygy describes a time during the **orbits** of **Earth** and **Moon** when **Sun**, Earth and Moon are in approximately a straight line.
The Moon is at syzygy when it is new or full.

T

T Tauri star *noun*
A T Tauri star is a very young **star**. In the life of a star, it is at an early stage, and still shrinking. T Tauri stars throw off mass, and the lost mass forms a gassy cloud around the star. Some scientists think that planetary systems might one day form from this material. The star after which the group is named is an irregular **variable star** in the **constellation** Taurus, or the Bull, which lies in the **northern hemisphere**.
There are many T Tauri stars in a dust cloud in the constellation Ophiuchus, or the Serpent Bearer.

tail ► comet

Tarantula nebula *noun*
The Tarantula nebula is a **nebula** in the **southern hemisphere**. It is part of the **Large Magellanic Cloud**, a galaxy which can be found in the **constellation** Dorado, or the Swordfish. The Tarantula nebula is the most brilliant part of the whole cloud. It can be seen with the **naked eye**. The Tarantula nebula is made up of ionized hydrogen. It is the remains of a supernova.
The Tarantula nebula is about 900 light years across.

Taurids *noun*
The Taurids are a **meteor shower** which can be seen from Earth in November. The shower is most active around 8 November. There is a maximum of 10 meteors an hour in the Taurid shower.
The Taurids appear to begin in the constellation Taurus.

Taurus *noun*
Taurus, or the Bull, is a **constellation**. It is one of the constellations of the **Zodiac**. Taurus contains a **red giant** star called Aldebaran. It also contains two star clusters, the **Hyades** and the **Pleiades**. There is also an interesting young star, **T Tauri**. Most interesting of all for astronomers is the **Crab nebula**, also found in Taurus.
There are 14 stars brighter than the fourth magnitude in Taurus.

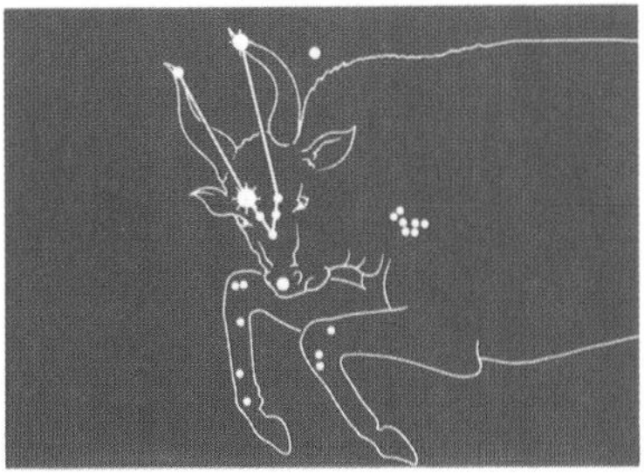

Teal Ruby *noun*
Teal Ruby is a satellite launched by the United States Air Force in 1986. It uses infra-red **sensors** to detect aircraft in flight.
The space shuttle was used to launch Teal Ruby.

tektite *noun*
Tektite is a kind of glass. Tektites are found on the Earth in four main areas. These are Australasia, the Ivory Coast in Africa, Czechoslovakia in Europe, and Texas and Georgia in the United States of America. The glass in tektites seems to have cooled very rapidly. Some scientists think tektites formed when heat from **meteorites** melted rocks at the point where they landed.
Some tektites have been found weighing up to 15 kilograms.

tele- *prefix*
Tele- is a prefix meaning far.
A telescope is an instrument for seeing objects that are far away.

telecommunications *plural noun*
Telecommunications describes the sending and receiving of information by radio transmission. **Radio waves** can be used to send signals, pictures or sounds.
Telecommunications allows scientists to send instructions to spacecraft.

telemetry *noun*
Telemetry is the remote control of **spacecraft**. This is done by sending radio signals to a spacecraft, and receiving radio signals back from it. The kinds of signal that can be sent by telemetry include instructions to the spacecraft, such as a correction to its course. They also include instructions to instruments inside the spacecraft, such as a command to a camera to start taking photographs.
Scientists use computers for telemetry.

telescope ► page 142

Television Infra-Red Orbital Satellite (TIROS) *noun*
The Television Infra-Red Orbital Satellites were two groups of American **weather satellites**. The first group was launched from 1960, and the second from 1970. **Infra-red** sensors could be used at night, and could tell the difference between clouds, sea and land. The later TIROS satellites orbited the Earth over the poles.
The Television Infra-Red Orbital Satellites collected daily weather information from all over Earth.

Telstar *noun*
Telstar was a series of communications **satellites** launched by the United States of America from 1962 to 1965. It was able to send live television pictures across the Atlantic Ocean for the first time. It could also handle telephone calls. This was an enormous advance in **telecommunications**. Telstar orbited the Earth once every three hours. This meant it had to be tracked all the time from **ground stations**. Later four more Telstar satellites were launched. They were all privately owned.
Telstar could handle up to 600 telephone calls at once.

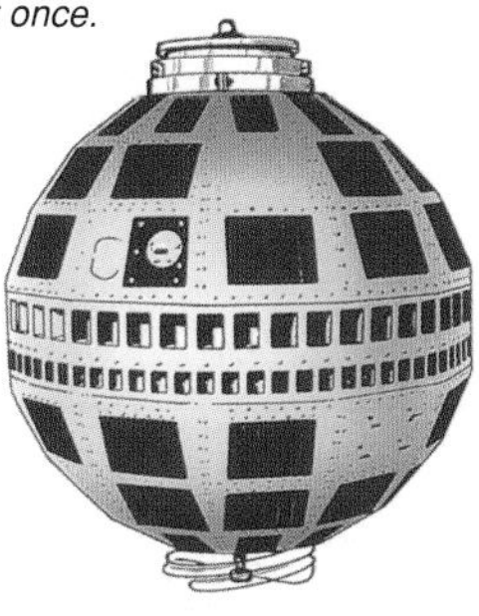

temperature *noun*
A temperature is a measurement. It describes how hot or cold an object is. Temperature is measured in degrees. The main temperature scales are the Fahrenheit scale, the Celsius scale, and the **kelvin scale**.
The surface of the Sun has a temperature of about 6,000 degrees Celsius.

terrestrial planets *noun*
Terrestrial planets is a name given to the four **planets** nearest to the Sun. These are **Mercury**, **Venus**, **Earth** and **Mars**. The terrestrial planets are solid, rocky bodies. Their **orbits** around the Sun are nearly circular.
All the terrestrial planets have been hit by meteorites.

telescope *noun*
A telescope is an instrument that helps people see objects that are far away. A telescope gathers **visible light** or other **radiation**, **focuses** it and magnifies the image. **Refracting telescopes** use **lenses** to bend and focus light. **Reflecting telescopes** use **mirrors** to make an image. **Radio telescopes** collect radio signals. These can be converted into an image.
The world's largest telescope is the 6-metre reflector on Mt Pastukhov in the CIS.

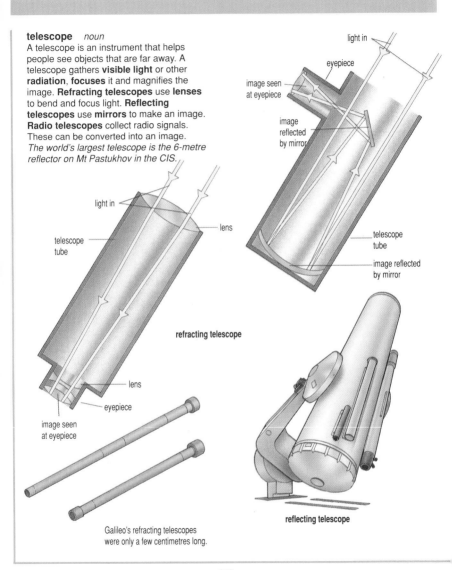

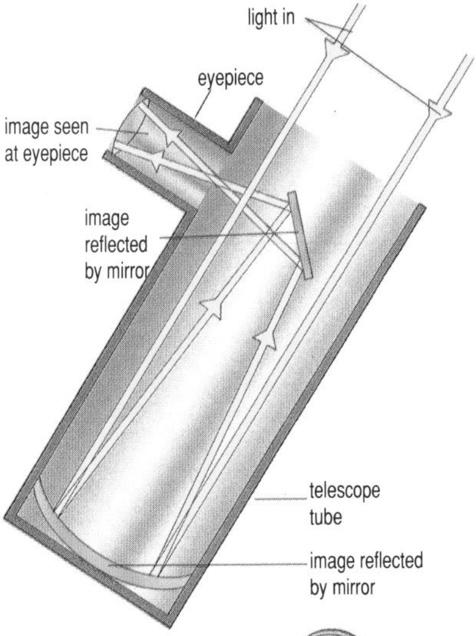

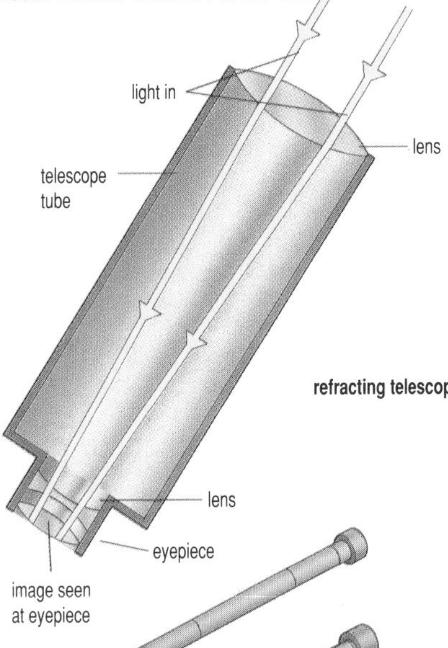

refracting telescope

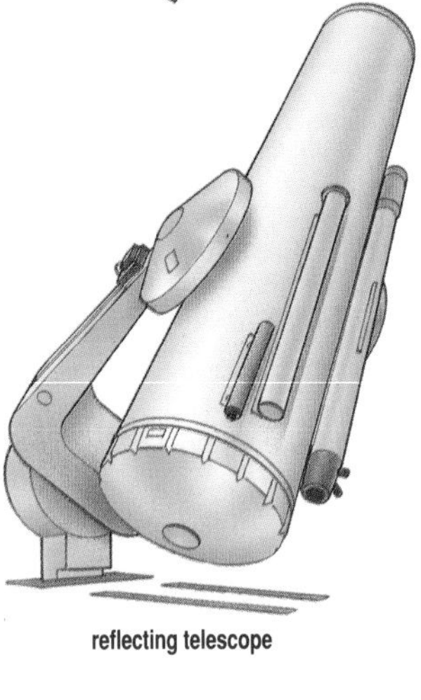

reflecting telescope

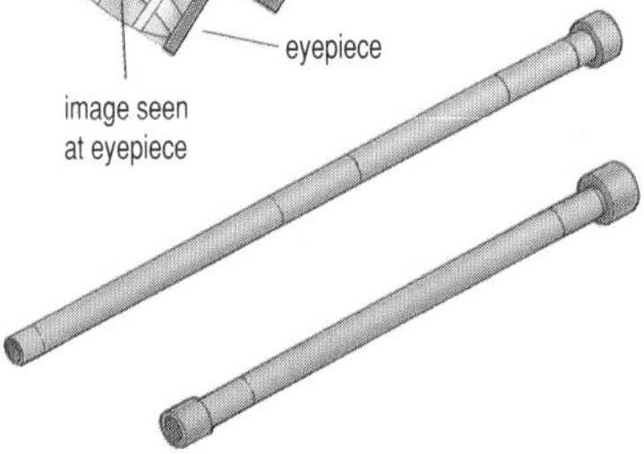

Galileo's refracting telescopes
were only a few centimetres long.

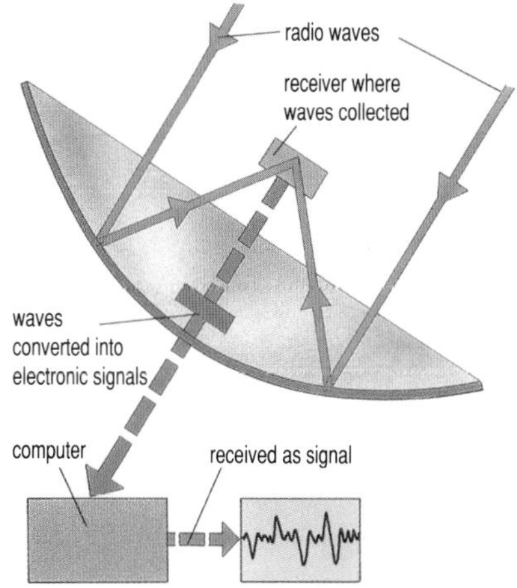
radio waves
receiver where waves collected
waves converted into electronic signals
computer
received as signal

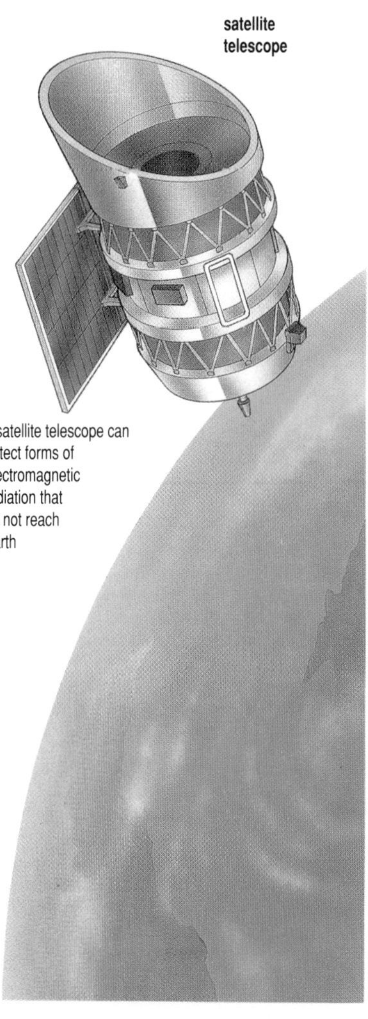
satellite telescope
a satellite telescope can detect forms of electromagnetic radiation that do not reach Earth

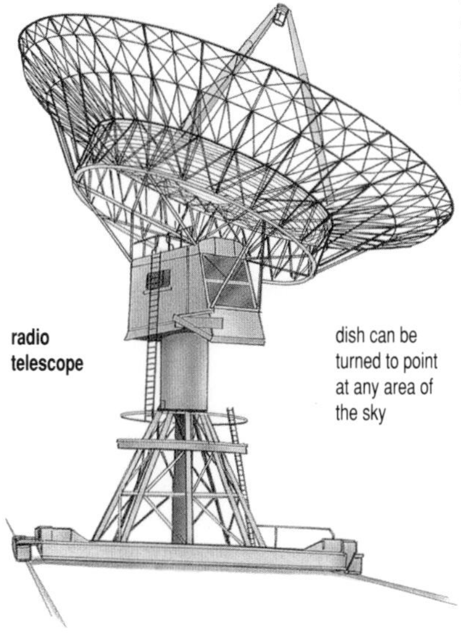
radio telescope
dish can be turned to point at any area of the sky

tethered satellite *noun*
The tethered satellite is a plan. Scientists at NASA want to use the **space shuttle** to tow a **satellite** attached by a line to the shuttle. This would allow a satellite to be used in the Earth's **atmosphere**, at a low **altitude**. The satellite could be released from the shuttle, and taken back into it. An attempt to launch a tethered satellite in 1992 did not succeed. The shuttle crew could not get the copper cable to unwind properly.
A computer on the tethered satellite would be controlled from the shuttle.

Tethys *noun*
Tethys is a **moon**. It is one of the 18 moons of **Saturn**. **Voyager 2** flew by Tethys. Pictures showed many **craters** on the surface, including a large one with a diameter of 400 kilometres. Tethys also has a giant canyon or valley on its surface. Voyager 2 also found that the surface of Tethys was mostly made of ice.
Tethys has a diameter of 1,050 kilometres.

thermonuclear reaction *noun*
Thermonuclear reaction is a process that leads to the release of **nuclear energy**. It takes place at very high **temperatures**. Scientists think that the temperature and the pressure at the **core** of the **Sun** are so great that thermonuclear reactions turn **hydrogen** into **helium**. This gives the Sun its energy.
Thermonuclear reaction takes place at temperatures of about 20–40 million degrees Celsius.

third contact *noun*
Third contact is one of the stages of an **eclipse**. In an eclipse of the **Moon**, third contact is the time when the Moon starts to leave the deep shadow, or **umbra**, cast by **Earth**. In an eclipse of the **Sun**, third contact is the time when the edge of the Moon and the surface of the Sun seem to touch. This happens towards the end of the eclipse.
There is a third contact stage only when an eclipse of the Sun is total or annular.

third quarter *noun*
Third quarter is one of the **phases of the Moon**. It is a time between full Moon and new Moon, when half of the Moon's face can be seen. Third quarter is seen when the Moon is **waning**.
Third quarter can also be called last quarter.

Thor *noun*
Thor was the name of a **rocket**. It was a military rocket, combined with two others in a series of attempts by the United States of America to reach the Moon in 1958. None of these attempts to send a rocket to the Moon succeeded. A later attempt in the series, now called **Pioneer**, did fly past the Moon. Pioneer did not use a Thor rocket.
There were three attempts to reach the Moon using a Thor rocket.

thrust *noun*
Thrust is a force that a **rocket** engine develops as it is fired. Thrust pushes the rocket forward. The Saturn 5 launcher needed a thrust of 3,400 tonnes to get three men and a landing craft to the Moon.
Burning gases pushed out of a rocket produce the thrust.
thruster *noun*

tide *noun*
A tide describes the movement of water or other liquid on the surface of a planet. Tides are caused by the **gravitational** pull of the Sun and the Moon.
There are two high tides on Earth each day.

time *noun*
Time is a kind of measurement. It measures how long events last, and how long the gap is between events. Units of measurement for time have always been taken from astronomical observations. A year is the length of time it takes for the **Earth** to **orbit** the **Sun** once. A day is the time it takes for the **Earth** to rotate once on its axis.
A lunar month is the time it takes for the Moon to orbit the Earth once.

time dilation *noun*
Time dilation is a result of the special theory of **relativity**. Some scientists think that if two people were moving at different speeds, or **velocities**, in relation to each other, and nearly at the **speed of light**, each would think that the other's clock was showing a different time from their own.
The effect of time dilation has been noticed in some particles.

Titan *noun*
Titan is a **moon**. It is one of the 23 moons of **Saturn**. Titan is the second largest moon in the **solar system**, with a diameter of 5,140 kilometres. The **Voyager** space probes flew by Titan, and found that it had a thick **atmosphere**. The atmosphere has an orange colour, and seems to be mostly made of nitrogen.
Titan is the largest moon orbiting Saturn.

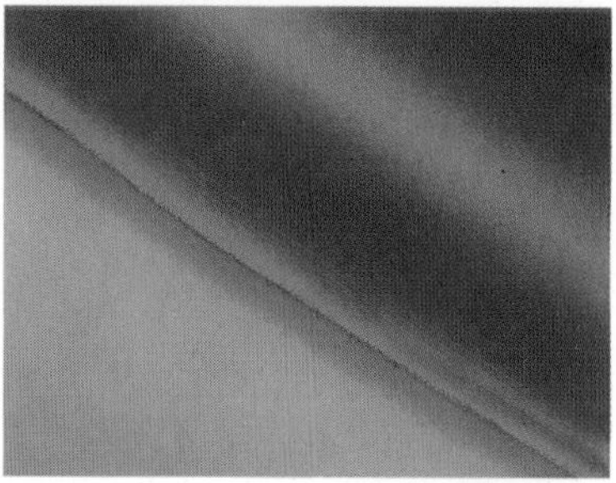

Titan *noun*
Titan was the name given to a group of **rockets** used by the United States of America. Titan rockets were used to launch the **Gemini** orbiting spacecraft. A later, more powerful Titan was used to launch the **Viking** probe to **Mars**, and the two **Voyager** missions to the outer planets.
There are plans for a Titan rocket powerful enough to launch a payload of 75 tonnes.

Titania *noun*
Titania is one of the 15 **moons** of **Uranus**. It is the largest of these moons, with a diameter of 1,590 kilometres. **Voyager** 2 flew by Titania in 1986, and found that the surface was covered with **craters**. The surface is probably made of ice, with a rocky **core** beneath.
Titania is named after a character in one of Shakespeare's plays.

TOPEX *noun*
TOPEX is a project which **NASA** and France have been working on together for many years. TOPEX stands for Topography Experiment. It will use **radar** to measure the height of oceans more accurately than has ever been done before. TOPEX will also chart the currents in the oceans. TOPEX is part of a much bigger project, known as Mission-to-Earth.
The French name for TOPEX is Poseidon.

total eclipse ► eclipse

Tracking and Data Relay Station (TDRS) *noun*
The Tracking and Data Relay Station is a system of four **satellites**. These satellites were launched by **space shuttles** from 1983 to 1989. The Tracking and Data Relay Station can track spacecraft launched by **NASA** and pass on information and commands, using a **telecommunications** system.
The Tracking and Data Relay Station is the first satellite tracking system in space.

tracking station *noun*
A tracking station allows scientists to keep track of **spacecraft**. This can be done with radio **antennae** receiving signals, and with computers which work out, or interpret, the signals. Tracking stations may send the information they have gathered to a central collecting point.
The tracking station followed the path of the weather satellite.

trajectory *noun*
A trajectory is a path made by a body. The body is moving because an outside force is acting on it. **Gravitational** pull will bring bodies back to Earth unless the outside force is strong enough to reach **escape velocity**.
The trajectory of the spacecraft lifted it above Earth's atmosphere, because powerful rockets had been used to launch it.

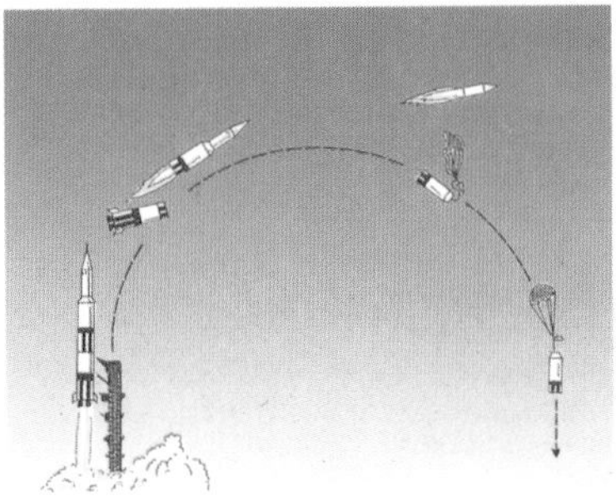

transit *noun*
A transit describes the passage of one body, such as **Venus**, across the face of another body, such as the **Sun**. A transit can also be used to describe the passage of a celestial body across the observer's **meridian**, or line of **longitude**.
The scientists watched the transit of Mars by Phobos.
transitory *adjective*

Transit *noun*
Transit was the name of a series of **satellites** launched by the United States of America from 1960. Transits were navigation satellites, and were owned by the United States Navy. Transits were designed to help submarines fix their position to within two kilometres.
Transits were the world's first navigation satellites.

transmitter *noun*
A transmitter is a machine. It is a machine that can create a **radio wave** and send it out, or broadcast it. The transmitter includes equipment for making the signal, increasing its strength and taking it to an **antenna**. From the antenna the radio signal is sent into space.
A radio signal sent out by a transmitter will be picked up by a receiver.
transmit *verb*

Trifid nebula *noun*
The Trifid nebula is a **nebula** that is found in the **constellation** of Sagittarius, or the Archer. It is an **emission nebula**, made up of glowing gas atoms. The Trifid nebula is split into three by dark patches of dust. It measures about 25 light years across. The Trifid nebula is about 6,000 light years away from Earth.
Stars are forming in the bright gas of the Trifid nebula.

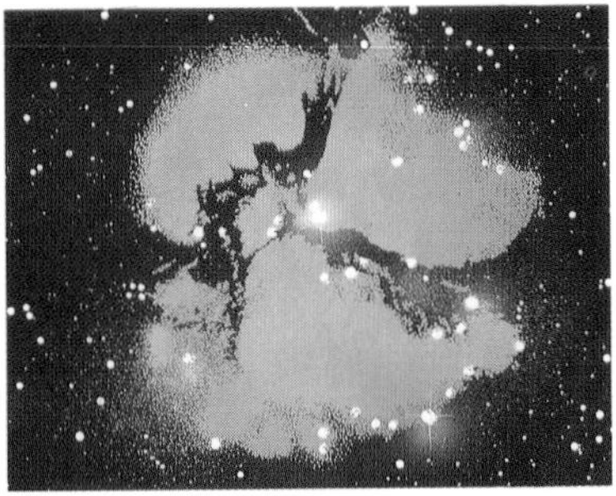

Triton *noun*
Triton is a **moon**. It is one of the eight moons of **Neptune**. Triton is one of the largest moons in the **solar system**. It has a diameter of 2,700 kilometres. **Voyager** 2 flew by Triton, and found that it was very cold. The **temperature** was –235 degrees Celsius. There has been violent volcanic activity on the surface of the planet. The surface has a network of cracks. Triton has a **retrograde motion**. It rotates in the opposite direction to Neptune.
Triton is the coldest object in the solar system.

Trojan asteroids *noun*
The Trojan asteroids are two groups of **asteroids** that share the orbit of Jupiter.
More than 200 asteroids have been found in the Trojan asteroid groups.

Tunguska explosion *noun*
The Tunguska explosion was an event that happened in Siberia, in Russia, on 30 June 1908. A large explosion caused damage over a wide area. Trees were flattened or broken off over a region about 70 kilometres wide. Scientists think that a **comet** or **meteorite** exploded in the **atmosphere**. They have worked out that the explosion must have happened at a height of 8.5 kilometres to cause such damage. No crater was discovered on the ground.
The Tunguska explosion has never really been explained.

twenty-one-centimetre radiation *noun*
Twenty-one-centimetre radiation is a kind of **radio wave**. These radio waves are found all over the universe. They seem to begin in clouds of hydrogen gas. The radio waves group about the twenty-one-centimetre **wavelength**, so they have been given that name. Scientists can use twenty-one-centimetre radiation to find and map patches of hydrogen in the sky.
Twenty-one-centimetre radiation has shown scientists that the temperature of hydrogen in the universe is about –170° Celsius.

twilight *noun*
Twilight is a **time**. It is the time before sunrise and after sunset when the sky is lit by sunlight. As the Earth **rotates** on its axis, a point on its surface will turn towards the Sun. Before the Sun itself can be seen, it lights up the sky in morning twilight. In the evening, the same point on the Earth's surface will turn away from the Sun. the light will change from full daylight, through twilight, to night, when the Sun's light cannot be seen.
Twilight at the equator is very short.

twinkling ► scintillation

Twins ► Gemini

Tycho's star *noun*
Tycho's star is not a **star**. It is a **supernova** in the **constellation** Cassiopeia. At its brightest, it could be seen in daytime. Tycho's star is a source of **X-rays**, and a strong source of **radio waves**. Tycho's star was discovered in 1572.
Tycho's star was found by the Danish astronomer Tycho Brahe.

U

UFO ► unidentified flying object

Uhuru *noun*
Uhuru was the name given to one of the **Explorer** series of **satellites**. Uhuru is a Swahili word, and means 'freedom'. Uhuru was launched from Kenya, and was the first **X-ray astronomy satellite**. The satellite was also able to give information about the strength of the X-rays.
Uhuru was launched on the anniversary of Kenya's independence day, which is 12 December 1970.

ultraviolet astronomy *noun*
Ultraviolet astronomy is the study of **ultraviolet radiation**. Because the Earth's **atmosphere** soaks up most ultraviolet radiation, ultraviolet astronomy takes place from **satellites**, such as the **International Ultraviolet Explorer**. Ultraviolet astronomy is used by scientists studying **galaxies**. The young, hot stars in galaxies are strong sources of this kind of radiation.
Ultraviolet astronomy has found young, hot stars in the Orion nebula.

ultraviolet radiation *noun*
Ultraviolet radiation is a kind of **electromagnetic radiation**. Ultraviolet waves lie between **visible light** and **X-rays**. The Sun is a rich source of ultraviolet radiation. Most rays are stopped from reaching the surface of the Earth, because **ozone** in the atmosphere absorbs most of them. Ultraviolet radiation was first measured using balloons.
Suntan is one effect of ultraviolet radiation.

Ulysses *noun*
Ulysses is the name of a **probe** launched in 1990 by the **European Space Agency**. It is a mission to the **Sun**, planned to pass over the solar south **pole** in 1994, and the solar north pole in 1995. Ulysses will collect information about the way the Sun behaves in these regions. It will also collect information about the **solar wind**.
Ulysses flew past Jupiter before heading for the Sun.

umbra *noun*
1. An umbra is the darkest part of a shadow. It is cast on the Earth by the Moon during an **eclipse** of the Sun. An umbra is also the shadow cast on the Moon by the Earth during an eclipse of the Moon.
A total eclipse of the Sun can only be seen from the umbra.
2. An umbra is the dark centre of a **sunspot**. The umbra is cooler than the surrounding **penumbra**. It is about 4,000 degrees Celsius.
The umbra of a sunspot has a strong magnetic field.

Umbriel *noun*
Umbriel is one of the **moons** of **Uranus**. It is one of the five largest of fifteen moons. **Voyager** 2 showed that Umbriel is much darker than the other moons of Uranus. The surface has many **craters**. One crater is 110 kilometres across and very bright.
Umbriel has a diameter of about 1,170 kilometres.

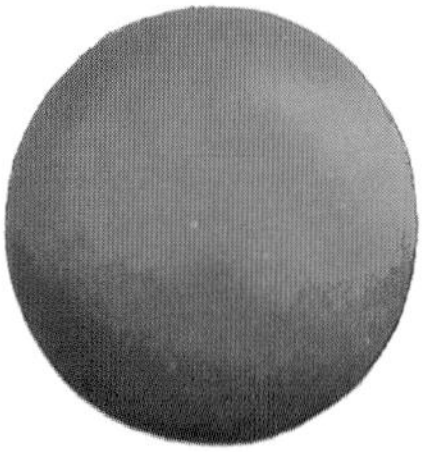

unidentified flying object (UFO) *noun*
An unidentified flying object is something reported in the sky by an **observer** who does not know what it is. Most unidentified flying objects, or UFOs, turn out to be aircraft, weather balloons, clouds or other normal objects. An observer may not have enough information to recognize them. Some unidentified flying objects cannot be explained.
Satellites have often been mistaken for unidentified flying objects.

universal time *noun*
Universal time is a way of measuring **time**. It uses the way the sun seems to move each day. Universal time is used by most people each day to tell the time.
Universal time can also be called Greenwich mean time.

universe *noun*
The universe is the total of all **space**, matter and **radiation**. It includes everything that scientists have discovered, and also includes everything that they have guessed or suggested as a theory. The size of the universe is limited by the distance **light** has been able to travel since the **Big Bang**. The study of the universe is called **cosmology**.
The universe is expanding rapidly.

uplink *noun*
Uplink describes the **transmitting** of information from the ground to a **spacecraft** or communications **satellite**.
The ground station told the satellite through the uplink to switch on the camera.

uranium *noun*
Uranium is a **radioactive element**. It is a very heavy, greyish-white metal that is used in the process of **nuclear fission** to make energy.
Uranium is used as a fuel in nuclear reactors.

Uranus ► page 150

Ursa Major *noun*
Ursa Major, or the Great Bear, is a **constellation** in the **northern hemisphere**. It is very easy to recognize, as it contains a famous group of seven stars known as the Plough. These seven stars are very bright. They can be used to point the way to Polaris and to other constellations. Ursa Major also contains a group of **galaxies** that belong to the local **supercluster**.
Ursa Major is the third largest constellation in the northern sky.

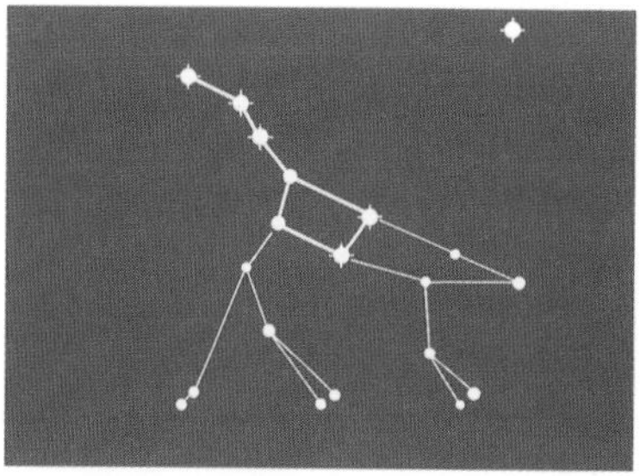

Ursa Minor *noun*
Ursa Minor, or the Little Bear, is a **constellation** in the **northern hemisphere**. One of the stars in the constellation Ursa Minor is Polaris, the **Pole Star**.
Ursa Minor is sometimes called the Little Dipper.

Ursids *noun*
The Ursids are a **meteor shower** which can be seen from Earth in December. The shower is most active around 22 December. There is a maximum of 15 meteors an hour in the Ursid shower.
The Ursids appear to begin in the constellation Ursa Minor.

Uranus *noun*

Uranus is a planet in the **solar system**. It is the seventh planet from the **Sun**. Uranus was discovered in 1781. It is a large ball of gas, four times as big as Earth. The outer layers of gas are hydrogen and helium. Scientists do not know yet what may lie beneath. Some scientists think there is a small, rocky core, surrounded by a mantle of frozen water, ammonia and methane. **Voyager** 2 flew by Uranus in 1986. The axis of Uranus is so tilted that the planet seems to be lying on its side.

The rings of Uranus cannot be seen with a telescope.

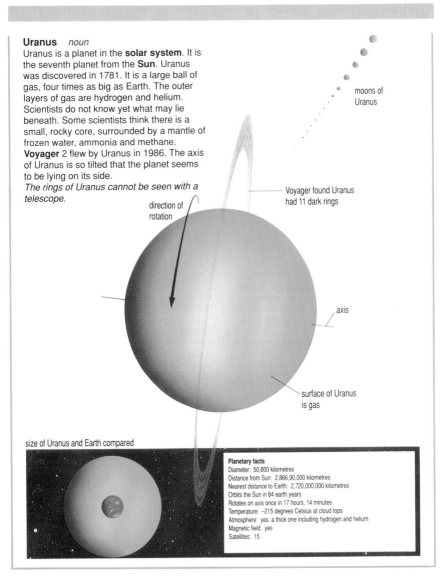

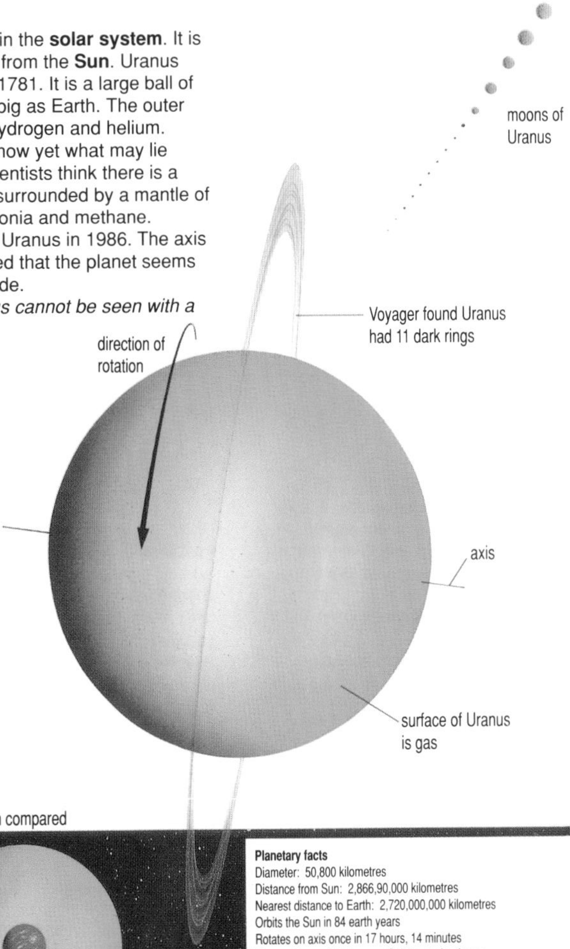

size of Uranus and Earth compared

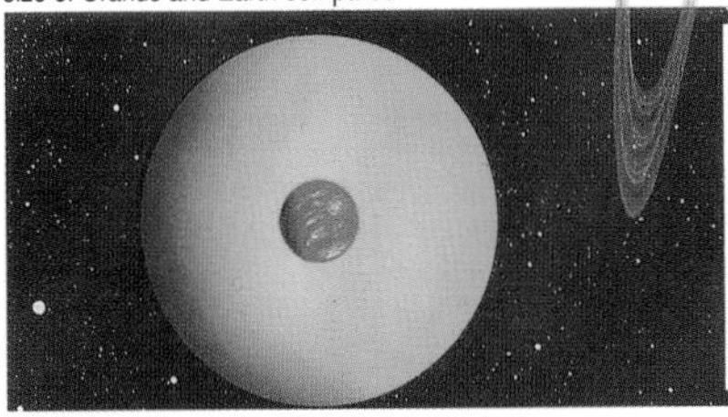

Planetary facts
Diameter: 50,800 kilometres
Distance from Sun: 2,866,90,000 kilometres
Nearest distance to Earth: 2,720,000,000 kilometres
Orbits the Sun in 84 earth years
Rotates on axis once in 17 hours, 14 minutes
Temperature: –215 degrees Celsius at cloud tops
Atmosphere: yes, a thick one including hydrogen and helium
Magnetic field: yes
Satellites: 15

V

V-2 *noun*
The V-2 was a **rocket** developed in Germany in the 1930s. It was fuelled with alcohol and liquid oxygen. The V-2 was 14 metres long and it weighed 12,150 kilograms. After the Second World War, the V-2 scientists helped both the United States of America and the Soviet Union to develop rocket technology, basing their work on the advanced design of the V-2.
The V-2 was first used as a weapon during the Second World War.

Van Allen belts *plural noun*
The Van Allen belts are two barrel-shaped regions in the Earth's **magnetic field**, where electrically-charged particles from space are trapped. The inner belt is found from about 1,000 kilometres to about 5,000 kilometres above the Earth, and the other Van Allen belt is found from about 15,500 kilometres to about 25,000 kilometres above the Earth.
The Van Allen belts were discovered in 1958 by the American satellite Explorer 1.

Vanguard *noun*
Vanguard was the name of a series of **rockets** built by the United States of America in the late 1950s. The Americans hoped that the Vanguard would put a **satellite** into **orbit** during International Geophysical Year, 1957. The first Vanguard launches were failures, but a later Vanguard rocket placed a small satellite in orbit on 17 March 1958. There were two more successful launches before the Vanguard project ended.
Vanguard was a three-stage rocket.

variable star *noun*
A variable star is a **star** the brightness of which changes over a period of time. Variable stars form several groups, including eclipsing **binaries**, **Cepheid variable stars**, **RR Lyrae stars** and **novae**.
The light output of a variable star can be regular or irregular.

Vega *noun*
Vega is a **star** in the **constellation** Lyra. Vega is the fifth brightest star in the sky, and has a blue colour which can be seen with the **naked eye**. Vega is 52 times as bright as the Sun. It is 26 light years away from Earth. Some scientists think Vega is surrounded by a ring of gas and dust. If this is correct, a system of planets may be forming around the star.
The scientific name for Vega is Alpha Lyrae.

Vega *noun*
Vega was the name given to two **probes** launched by the Soviet Union in 1985. The spacecraft were planned to fly by **Venus**, and both dropped probes onto the surface of the planet. These landing craft sent much useful information back to Earth. The Vega spacecraft went on to pass within 9,600 kilometres of **Halley's comet**. They photographed the **nucleus**, and obtained information which proved that the comet was mostly made up of ice.
The name Vega is made up of parts of the Russian words for Venus and Halley.

Vehicle Assembly Building ► Cape Canaveral

Veil nebula *noun*
The Veil nebula is a **nebula** in the **constellation** Cygnus. The Veil nebula forms one part of a circular nebula which is the remains of a **supernova**. It is thought to be 2,500 light years away from Earth. It is also thought to be 30,000 years old.
The Veil nebula will one day fade away completely.

velocity *noun*
Velocity is the speed with which an object moves in one direction. Measurements of velocity include units of length and units of time, for example metres per second. Any moving object has a velocity different from that of any other moving object.
Velocity is used for non-living objects.

Venera *noun*
Venera was the name given to a series of **probes** launched by the Soviet Union. They were aimed at **Venus**. Veneras 5 and 6 landed on Venus in 1967 and sent back information about the **atmosphere**. Veneras 13 and 14 landed on Venus in 1982, and sent colour photographs of the landscape back to Earth.
In 1985, Veneras 15 and 16 landed on the dark side of Venus.

Venus ► page 153

Very Large Array *noun*
The Very Large Array is a **radio telescope**. It has 27 dishes, each 25 metres in diameter. The dishes are connected in such a way that they can give fine details of **radio sources**. They are arranged in a Y-shape. Each of the three arms of the Very Large Array is 21 kilometres long. This gives the power to see details which no optical telescope is large enough to see.
The Very Large Array is at Socorro, New Mexico, in the United States of America.

very long baseline interferometry (VLBI) *noun*
Very long baseline interferometry is a kind of **radio interferometry**. It uses radio **antennae** that are separated from each other by great distances. Each station makes a tape of radio signals, and times the signals very carefully. All the tapes are collected and played through a receiver. The information can then be studied.
Very long baseline interferometry could make a radio telescope the size of Earth.

Vesta *noun*
Vesta is the third largest and the brightest **asteroid**. Vesta is 501 kilometres in diameter. It can sometimes be seen with the **naked eye**. The orbit of Vesta lies between Mars and Jupiter.
Vesta has a highly reflective, rocky surface.

Viking *noun*
Viking was the name given to two **probes** launched by the United States of America in 1975. Both probes were sent to the planet **Mars**. The spacecraft were made up of an orbiter and a landing craft. The orbiters photographed the whole planet and its moons in great detail. They found out that there was ice at the Martian north pole. The landing craft took soil samples, testing them for signs of life.
The Viking landing craft did not find any signs of life in the soil samples that they tested.

Virgin ► **Virgo**

Virgo *noun*
Virgo, the Virgin, is a **constellation** of the **Zodiac**. It is the second largest constellation in the sky. Virgo lies across the **celestial equator**, so it can be seen in both the northern hemisphere and the southern hemisphere. It has one **binary star** of the **first magnitude**.
There is a large cluster of galaxies in Virgo.

Venus *noun*

Venus is a planet in the **solar system**. It is the second nearest planet to the **Sun**. Venus has been looked at by various **spacecraft**. They found that the surface of Venus is covered by a dense **atmosphere** of clouds. These clouds are made up of drops of sulphuric acid and gases, such as carbon dioxide. Venus has a very high atmospheric pressure. Heat from the Sun cannot escape through the thick clouds, and the temperature is very high. This is called the **greenhouse effect**. There are constant thunderstorms. There is no life on Venus.

Venus moves very slowly on its axis.

surface of Venus

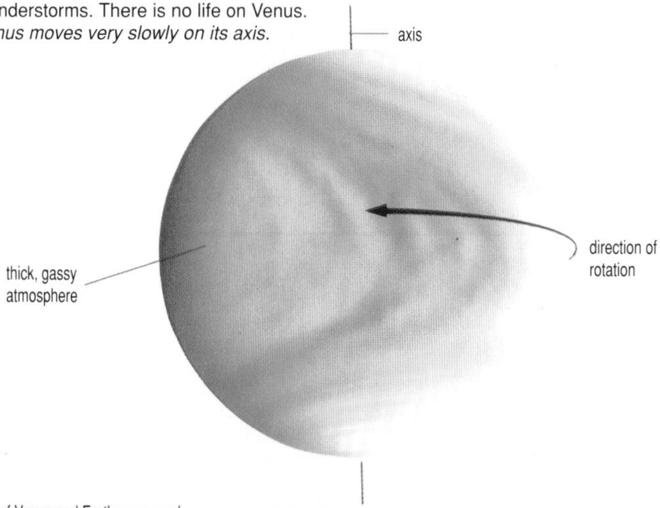

size of Venus and Earth compared

Planetary facts

Diameter: 12,100 kilometres

Distance from Sun: 108,230,000 kilometres

Orbits the Sun in 225 earth days

Nearest distance to Earth: 40,200,000 kilometres

Rotates on axis once in 243 earth days

Surface temperature: 480 degrees Celsius

Voyager *noun*
Voyager was the name given to two **probes** launched by the United States of America in 1977. The Voyager probes were designed to fly to the outer planets. Voyager 1 reached **Jupiter** in 1979, and **Saturn** in 1980. It then headed out of the **solar system**. Voyager 2 visited Jupiter and Saturn, then continued to **Uranus**, which it flew past in 1986, and **Neptune**, which it reached in 1989. It then headed out of the solar system.
Scientists are still receiving information from the radios on Voyager 2.

Voyager 1 flew by Jupiter in March 1979 and Voyager 2 flew by in July 1979. The Voyagers confirmed that there was a ring around Jupiter. They also sent back the first detailed pictures of the four largest moons.

Voyager 1 flew by Saturn in 1980, and Voyager 2 in 1981. They found that Saturn's rings are made up of thousands of narrow ringlets, one kilometre thick. Each ring is made up of pieces of ice.

Voyager 2 flew by Uranus in 1986, after a journey lasting eight and a half years. Voyager 2 discovered two unknown rings around Uranus and 10 new moons. It also found that Uranus had a magnetic field.

Voyager 2 flew by Neptune in 1989. It discovered Neptune's Great Dark Spot. Voyager 2 also detected radio bursts, and found that Neptune has a magnetic field. It also found four rings, and six new moons.

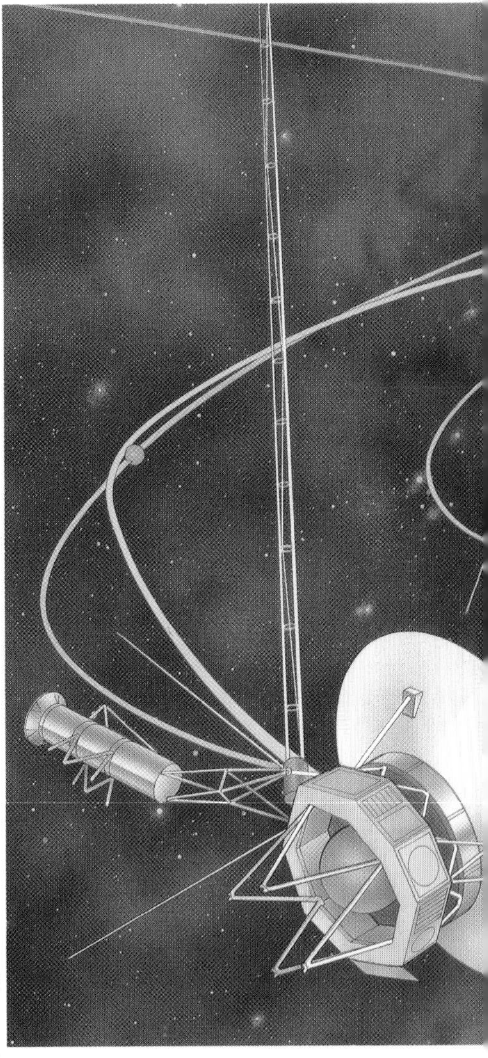

Voyager spacecraft
The Voyager spacecraft each contained 10 **instruments**. Some looked for such things as **magnetic fields**, sources of **radio waves** and charged **particles**. Another set of instruments included television cameras. There was also an **interferometer** to record **infra-red radiation**, a **spectrometer** to record **ultraviolet radiation**, and a bowl-shaped **antenna** to communicate with Earth.

Voyager orbits

Virgo cluster *noun*
The Virgo cluster is a large group of **galaxies**. There are several thousand galaxies in the **cluster**, which is found in the direction of the **constellation Virgo**. The Virgo cluster is between 50 and 60 million light years away from Earth. It is one of the galaxies that make up the **Local Group**.
The Virgo cluster is mostly made up of spiral galaxies.

visible light *noun*
Visible light is the band of light that can be seen by the **naked eye**. Visible light is a form of **electromagnetic radiation**. It is made up of **waves** of energy. The light that is visible to human eyes has about 2,000 waves in every millimetre. Visible light lies between **ultraviolet light**, which has shorter wavelengths, and **infra-red light**, which has longer wavelengths.
Most animals with eyes can see visible light.

volcano *noun*
A volcano is a hole in the ground. Material that is hot and under pressure below the surface of a planet or a moon can be thrown out through the volcano. On some bodies, such as **Venus** or the **Earth**, the material thrown out by a volcano is a mixture of melted rock, called lava, and gas. On bodies such as **Io** or **Triton**, the material thrown out seems to be mostly gases.
Olympus Mons, a volcano on Mars, is 25 kilometres high.

Voskhod *noun*
Voskhod was the name given by the Soviet Union to two **spacecraft** launched in 1964 and 1965. Voskhod 1 carried three **cosmonauts**. It was the first time more than one person had been in space at the same time. There was so little room in the craft, the cosmonauts could not wear **spacesuits**. A cosmonaut from Voskhod 2 was the first man ever to walk in space.
Voskhod is a Russian word meaning 'sunrise'.

Vostok *noun*
Vostok was the name given to a series of six **spacecraft** launched by the Soviet Union. The launches started in 1961. Vostok 1 carried the first man in space, Yuri Gagarin. During the next two years, five more **cosmonauts** went into **orbit** around Earth on Vostock spacecraft. They included the first woman in space, Valentina Tereshkova.
The Vostoks were made in two parts — a descent module, including the cosmonaut's cabin, and an instrument module.

Voyager ► page

W

waning *adjective*
Waning describes one of the **phases of the Moon**. A waning Moon appears to be getting smaller in size, or decreasing. This is because the face of the Moon which reflects sunlight is beginning to turn away from the Earth, so that less of it can be seen. The opposite of waning is **waxing**.
A waning Moon is the phase between a full Moon and a new Moon.
wane *verb*

water *noun*
Water is a liquid with no smell or taste. It is a mixture of hydrogen and oxygen. When it is heated, water forms a gas called water vapour. At temperatures of 0 degrees Celsius and below, water turns into a solid called ice. Life cannot exist without water. **Earth** is the only **planet** with large areas of water. The presence of water on another planet might allow some form of life to exist.
There is no water on the Moon.

Water-bearer ► Aquarius

wave *noun*
A wave describes the movement of some kinds of energy. The energy in a wave **oscillates**, which means it moves backwards and forwards or up and down in a steady pattern. **Ultraviolet** and **infra-red light** are forms of energy that travel in waves. All **electromagnetic radiation** travels in waves. **Frequency** and **wavelength** measure different waves.
A radio telescope collects radio waves for scientists to study.

wavelength *noun*
Wavelength describes the distance between the tops or bottoms of a particular **wave**. This measurement is used to work out what kind of a wave is being studied. Parts of a wave may become stronger and weaker as the wave travels along.
Gamma rays have short wavelengths.

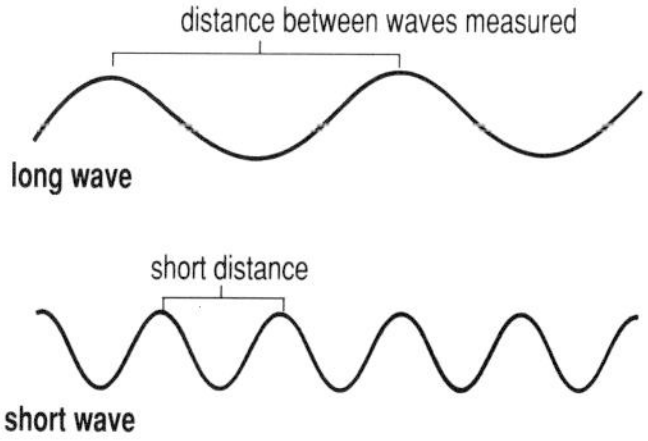

waxing *adjective*
Waxing describes one of the **phases of the Moon**. A waxing Moon appears to be increasing, or getting bigger in size. This is because the face of the Moon which reflects sunlight is turning towards the Earth, so more of it can be seen. The opposite of waxing is **waning**.
A waxing Moon is the phase between a new Moon and a full Moon.
wax *verb*

weather satellite *noun*
Weather satellites are **satellites** that send daily pictures of weather patterns back to Earth. This helps day-to-day weather forecasting to be more accurate. Weather satellites can also warn of hazards, such as tornadoes, hurricanes or icebergs. Most weather satellites are in **geostationary orbits.** Each satellite watches the weather in one part of Earth. Reports from many satellites are put together to make a picture of the weather in a larger area.
Most weather satellites are travelling in orbit about 36,000 kilometres above the Earth.

weight *noun*
Weight describes what happens when **gravity** pulls on the **mass** of an object. The gravitational force of the Earth pulls downwards, attracting everything on Earth or near the Earth, and giving it a weight. The weight of an object can be measured. It would change if a stronger or weaker gravitational force attracted it. The weight of a person on the Moon is much less than on Earth, as the gravity of the Moon is less.
Grams and pounds are two common units of weight.
weigh *verb*

weightlessness *noun*
Weightlessness is something that happens to **astronauts** in **free fall**. They have no **weight** because they are falling towards the Earth at the same rate as the spacecraft. Weightlessness is often called zero gravity, but this is incorrect. Astronauts must train carefully to get used to weightlessness.
It takes about two weeks for the body to get used to most of the effects of weightlessness.

Whirlpool Galaxy *noun*
The Whirlpool Galaxy is a spiral **galaxy** in the **constellation** Canes Venatici. It lies about 13 million light years from Earth. The Whirlpool Galaxy is smaller than the Milky Way Galaxy. It appears face on to Earth, so the spiralling arms are clear. There are **red giants** in the centre of the galaxy.
The Whirlpool Galaxy was the first galaxy to be shown to have a spiral shape.

white dwarf star *noun*
A white dwarf star is an old, dying star. When a star has burned up all its hydrogen, the core that is left cools down and loses its brightness. The atoms that remain collapse inwards, making a very small, dense, hot mass. White dwarfs have very strong **magnetic fields** and forces of **gravity**. After many millions of years, white dwarf stars will become cold, lightless **black dwarfs**.
After about 5,000,000,000 years, the Sun will become a white dwarf star.

white hole *noun*
A white hole is thought by some scientists to be a place where matter appears in the **universe**. No white holes have been found. If a white hole existed, it would be the opposite of a **black hole**.
A white hole is an idea discussed by scientists.

Wilson effect *noun*
The Wilson effect describes a change in the way a **sunspot** appears as it moves across the face of the **Sun.** As the sun rotates, sunspots move towards the edge or **limb**, of the Sun. The Wilson effect describes the **penumbra**, which is wider on the far side of the sunspot. The Wilson effect shows that a sunspot is a hole on the surface of the Sun.
The Wilson effect was discovered by the Scottish astronomer Alexander Wilson.

Wolf-Rayet star *noun*
Wolf-Rayet stars are a rare group of **stars**, with very high surface temperatures. The temperatures can be as high as 50,000 degrees kelvin. Scientists have discovered that Wolf-Rayet stars lose **mass** very rapidly. On a **spectrum**, some Wolf-Rayet stars show that they are giving off, or emitting, carbon. Others show they are emitting nitrogen.
Most Wolf-Rayet stars are binary stars.

X

X-rays noun
X-rays are a form of **electromagnetic radiation**. X-rays are found on the light **spectrum** between gamma rays and ultraviolet light. Most X-rays seem to come from hot regions of space. The first X-rays from the Sun were discovered during rocket flights in the 1950s.
X-rays are powerful enough to kill living things, but are prevented from reaching the Earth by the atmosphere.

X-ray astronomy *noun*
X-ray astronomy is the study of **X-rays**. Because the Earth's atmosphere prevents X-rays from reaching the surface of Earth, all X-ray astronomy must be done by **rockets** and **satellites** in space. X-ray astronomy has found many sources of X-rays, including some **binary star** systems, **supernova** remnants, and areas of hot gas surrounding **galaxies.**
The first satellite used for X-ray astronomy was Uhuru.

X-ray multimirror telescope (XMT) *noun*
The X-ray multimirror telescope is a project of the **European Space Agency**. It will consist of an orbiting **observatory**, and will send back information for at least 10 years.
The X-ray multimirror telescope will give scientists much more information to study.

Y

yagi antenna *noun*
A yagi antenna is a kind of **antenna** used to receive **radio waves**. Groups of yagi antennae are often used in radio astronomy, as part of a radio telescope. A yagi antenna is made up of a number of small rods, arranged in parallel to each other.
The most common yagi antenna that can be seen is a television aerial.

year *noun*
A year is the amount of time it takes for the **Earth** to **orbit** the Sun. A sidereal year measures the Earth's orbit in relation to the stars. It is 365.256 days long. A year is an important measure of time when compiling **calendars**.
Because a year is not an exact number of days, some calendars add an extra day every fourth year.

Z

zenith *noun*
Zenith describes the point on the celestial sphere which is directly above an **observer**.
The opposite of zenith is nadir.

zero gravity ► **weightlessness**

Zodiac noun
The Zodiac is a group of 12 **constellations**. During one year, the Sun and the planets seem to travel past the 12 constellations. Scientists have discovered that the Sun also passes a 13th constellation, Ophiuchus.
The 12 constellations of the Zodiac are Aries, Taurus, Gemini, Cancer, Leo, Virgo, Libra, Scorpius, Sagittarius, Capricornus, Aquarius and Pisces.

zodiacal light *noun*
Zodiacal light is the name given to the faint cone of glowing light that can often be seen at dawn or dusk along the path the Earth takes as it orbits the Sun. It is caused by sunlight reflecting off dust particles.
Zodiacal light is seen on moonless nights, in some parts of the world.

Zond *noun*
Zond was the name of a series of Soviet **space probes** launched between 1963 and 1970. The first two Zonds flew by Mars and Venus, but did not send back any information. Later Zonds flew round the Moon. Western scientists believe that the Soviet Union was planning to use the Zond programme to send a man to the Moon. The programme was cancelled after **Apollo** 8 flew three men round the Moon and returned to Earth.
Zond 5 carried turtles, flies and worms as part of its mission.